Critical Essays on
John Barth

Critical Essays on John Barth

Joseph J. Waldmeir

G. K. Hall & Co. ● Boston, Massachusetts

Library of Congress Cataloging in Publication Data
Main entry under title:

Critical essays on John Barth.

   (Critical essays on American literature)
   Includes index.
   1. Barth, John—Criticism and interpretation—Addresses,
essays, lectures. I. Waldmeir, Joseph J. II. Series.
PS3552.A75Z59   813'.54   80-21427
ISBN 0-8161-8254-X

This publication is printed on permanent/durable, acid-free paper
MANUFACTURED IN THE UNITED STATES OF AMERICA

CRITICAL ESSAYS ON AMERICAN LITERATURE

This series seeks to publish the most important reprinted criticism on writers and topics in American Literature along with, in various volumes, original essays, interviews, bibliographies, letters, manuscript sections, and other materials brought to public attention for the first time. Joseph J. Waldmeir's volume on John Barth is the most substantial collection of criticism ever published on this important contemporary writer. In addition to a brief introduction, the book contains a landmark assessment of Barth criticism by Charles B. Harris along with six other essays which survey the scope of Barth's work and reactions to it. But the heart of the volume is the material relating to individual novels, from *The Floating Opera* to *Chimera*, to reviews and scholarship which probe a fiction rich in both humor and intellectual depth. We are confident that this collection will make a permanent and significant contribution to American literary criticism.

JAMES NAGEL, GENERAL EDITOR

Northeastern University

CONTENTS

INTRODUCTION

The first entry in this anthology is a fine review essay of Barth criticism by Charles B. Harris. It focuses primarily on book-length studies—though there are many references to major periodical essays—on the more comprehensive, the more substantial, the more recent criticism. It is complete, well-written, and highly accurate; and since, at this writing, it is in press at the *Georgia Review* but not yet published, it is also up to date. In fact, it does a great deal of what an introduction such as this one is supposed to do. And I do not propose, nor presume, to re-do what Professor Harris has already done—especially since my effort could be little more than an echo of his.

However, a few words should be said by way of introducing the reader to this anthology, its contents and its organization. First of all, it contains no parts of books at all but rather reviews, review articles, and essays published (or, in one instance, unpublished) in newspapers and periodicals. The idea was to bring together out of the spate of Barth criticism[1] a fairly representative selection of approaches and attitudes, both favorable and unfavorable, toward his work. A related idea was to illustrate the shifts and changes in critical response to Barth's work as that work itself has shifted and changed—Proteus-like, to use a Barthian metaphor—with the passage of time, and the growth, if you will, of his confidence in his art. To these ends, the anthology is organized chronologically, both externally (i.e., after the Survey section, discussions of the novels are presented in the order of publication of each volume), and internally, (i.e., both within the Survey section and within the sections on each novel—in the latter case, beginning where they are available, with reviews of each).

Among the critical responses to Barth's work, plus their shifts and changes, which these selections and this organization illustrate, the following are most noteworthy:

Gradually, charges of immorality, gratuitous sexualism, even salaciousnes as leveled at *The Floating Opera* and *End of the Road* by early reviewers, faded out of consideration. Part of the reason, of course, was the change in reader attitude and expectation with the coming of the explicit sixties and the dulling of the shock value in sexualism. A greater part, however, was the change in critical attitude toward Barth as writer and thinker.

For, along with charges of immorality, indeed coupled with them, had been charges of amorality, of philosophical dilettantism, of rhetorical logic-chopping. But, with the coming of *The Sot-Weed Factor* and its stylistic experimentation, taking Barth away from old-fashioned realism into new-fashioned absurdism, the critics began to give Barth credit for a more conscious, rather than accidental or incidental, philosophical awareness if not position. His amorality became philosophical nihilism and, projected backward upon the first two novels, it made them far clearer and more respectable.

Projected backward also, especially as it developed and was refined in *Giles Goat-Boy* and *Lost in the Funhouse*, was Barth's profound sense of the absurd, his outrageous sense of the ridiculous—so that, for others of the critics, those not so committed to the interpretation of the work as nihilistic, those first two novels were elevated to the level of satire and the later novels treated as sophisticated refinements of early ideas in the satirical mode.

The question of satire versus nihilism (not always in these explicit terms, of course) became a minor issue in Barth criticism for a time. Additionally, one might note, apropos of both poles of the conflict, that Barth has never been accepted as a "serious" writer by the social critical critics, satirist or not. They not only reject him, they often actively dislike him for the obvious reasons that he not only refuses to be a serious social critic but that he seems often actively to reject the taking of a position of serious social criticism.[2]

Indeed, his work has gradually turned in upon itself, has become increasingly self-conscious, reflexive, like a Moebius strip seen in a set of mirrors—until Barth himself has become one of the centers of the neo-New Criticism. But one wonders, recalling Barth's remark in "The Literature of Exhaustion," that if he thought the novel was dead, he'd write a novel about it, if perhaps he is writing not reflexive fiction but fiction about reflexivity, with the joker and the joke being the Structuralist critic, circling endlessly within a semiotic swamp somewhere in Maryland.

I said above that the essays and reviews in this anthology were chosen to be representative of all of these critical responses to Barth's work in all of their shifts and changes and ramifications. It should be added here, and not as an afterthought, that they were also chosen because of their excellence in conception, in content, and in writing. They are some of the best of Barth criticism from *The Floating Opera* through *Chimera*. Because of this, I am confident that this collection fills that "curious lacuna in Barth studies" which Professor Harris refers to early in his essay as he regrets the absence of such a collection. Many thanks are due to John Waldmeir and to Donna Kern for invaluable assistance in preparing this book for publication.

JOSEPH WALDMEIR

Notes

1. The two major bibliographies of Barth criticism—that by Joseph Weixlmann (Garland, 1976) and that by Thomas P Walsh and Cameron Northouse (G. K. Hall, 1977)—cite and annotate both reviews and critical books and articles, and their citations point up the expansion and proliferation of Barth criticism over the years since *The Floating Opera* as well as the length and depth of it as the Barth canon has grown. Even more telling perhaps, both also cite theses and dissertations, and merely counting reveals that twelve Masters theses were devoted to Barth exclusively between 1967 and 1969; that thirty-two Ph.D. dissertations have dealt exclusively with him since the first one in 1968, and that he has been included as part of innumerable thematic theses and dissertations throughout those years as well.

2. It should be noted in passing here that at just about this juncture in Barth criticism, with the publication of *Giles Goat-Boy*, most reviewers, so obviously heavily influenced (or intimidated) by the growing heap of scholarship and criticism, became either timidly tentative or, to cover themselves, turned their reviews into mini-essays on the body of the fiction.

SURVEYS

John Barth and the Critics: An Overview

Charles B. Harris*

The publication of Joseph Weixlmann's *John Barth: A Bibliography* is significant for at least two reasons. First, amidst the current glut of checklists, reference guides, and bibliographies, Weixlmann's volume stands as a model of clarity and comprehensiveness. One reason for this is that Weixlmann is a trained bibliographer (compilers of many recent bibliographies are not), and his expertise pays off. Size alone suggests the superiority of Weixlmann's book over rival bibliographies: it is more than twice the length of Richard Allan Vine's *John Barth: An Annotated Bibliography* (Metuchen, N.J.: Scarecrow Press, 1977), and longer by a third than the Walsh and Northouse reference guide, although that guide covers three authors. But quality not quantity of presentation distinguishes Weixlmann's book. His section on Barth's separate publications, for example, contains clearly reproduced plates of the title page of each of Barth's first editions as well as precise descriptions of all editions complete down to the size of the book, its price, and the number of copies printed. The descriptive catalogue of Barth manuscripts housed in United States libraries, a section unique to most bibliographies, will, one hopes, stimulate use of that all but untapped resource. If less unique, the bibliography of secondary materials is nonetheless distinctive for the virtual completeness of its listings (through 1975) and the accuracy of its

John Barth: A Bibliography, by Joseph Weixlmann. New York & London: Garland, 1976. xi, 214 pp. $23. *John Barth: The Comic Sublimity of Paradox*, by Jac Tharpe. Carbondale & Edwardsville: Southern Illinois University Press, 1974, paperback 1977. xi, 133 pp. $2.95. *The Literature of Exhaustion: Borges, Nabokov, Barth*, by John Stark. Durham, N.C.: Duke Univ. Press, 1974. 196 pp. $7.95. *John Barth: An Introduction*, by David Morrell. University Park & London: Pennsylvania State Univ. Press, 1976, xviii, 194 pp. $10. *Cosmic Satire in the Contemporary Novel*, by John W. Tilton. Lewisburg, Pa.: Bucknell Univ. Press, 1977. 108 pp. $8.50. *Four Postwar American Novelists: Bellow, Mailer, Barth, and Pynchon*, by Frank D. McConnell. Chicago & London: University of Chicago Press, 1977, xxix, 206 pp. $15. *John Barth, Jerzy Kosinski, and Thomas Pynchon: A Reference Guide* by Thomas P. Walsh and Cameron Northouse. Boston: G. K. Hall, 1977. xii, 145 pp. $15.
*Reprinted by permission of author.

3

annotations. Weixlmann concludes his thoroughly researched book with five carefully arranged indexes.

Apart from its intrinsic value, Weixlmann's bibliography possesses as well what might be termed indicative significance. For if one gauge of a writer's status is the amount of critical attention his work has received, the almost three hundred and fifty studies listed by Weixlmann clearly signal Barth's arrival as a major figure among living American writers. Arranged chronologically, the secondary bibliography provides a clear picture of the development of Barth criticism. Brief critical mention began as early as 1959, but the first extended commentary occurred in 1963 when *Critique* devoted a generous portion of its winter issue to Barth studies (a practice that journal has repeated in 1966, 1972, and 1976). Though still useful, the four essays in that issue concentrate primarily on Barth's themes. With the 1967 publication of *The Fabulators* by Robert Scholes, that focus began to shift. British and American writers such as Barth, Scholes maintained, take an especial delight in formal design for its own sake, an observation that almost singlehandedly redirected critical attention away from them toward Barth's formal inventiveness. Jerry H. Bryant's *The Open Decision* (The Free Press), the first general study of recent American fiction to include an extensive section on Barth, appeared in 1970, as did Gerhard Joseph's Minnesota pamphlet, which remained the standard introduction to Barth's life and works until Morrel's book (see below) superseded it in 1976.

Three more general studies of recent American fiction containing chapters on Barth's novels appeared in 1971: Tony Tanner's *City of Words* (Harper and Row), perhaps the best book on contemporary American fiction; Richard Boyd Hauck's *A Cheerful Nihilism* (Indiana), which places Barth in the American tradition of the absurd that Hauck believes began with the Puritans; and my own *Contemporary American Novelists of the Absurd* (College and University Press), also a study of absurdist tendencies in Barth's fiction. That year also saw the publication of Campbell Tatham's seminal essay, "John Barth and the Aesthetics of Artifice," *Contemporary Literature*, 12 (1971), still the best single statement of the Barthian aesthetic. Since 1971 the corpus of Barth criticism has continued to expand in scope and sophistication. Nor is there any sign of its abatement. Weixlmann's bibliography is virtually complete through 1975; under "John Barth," the 1976 *International Bibliography* lists twenty-nine separate entries, more than for any other living American writer.[1]

The major critical statements about Barth fall into three rather obvious categories: articles in professional journals, chapters in books, and book-length studies. Conventionally, reviewers do not evaluate journal articles. But so many of Barth's more astute critics have not yet written books and so many essential studies of Barth's fiction are available only in article form that I feel obliged to depart briefly from that convention.

Book-length collections of previously published articles on recent American writers are common, but no such collection of the best of Barth criticism exists, a curious lacuna in Barth studies that one hopes some enterprising scholar will soon fill. That collection should include at least one essay by Campbell Tatham, possibly Barth's best critic (although his recent experiments in "paracriticism," while still rewarding, can be exasperating). Other critics whose articles have made important contributions to an understanding of Barth's various fictions include Daniel Majdiak (*End of the Road*), Beverly Gray Bienstock, Robert F. Kiernan, and Victor J. Vintanza (*Lost in the Funhouse*), Barbara C. Ewell (*The Sot-Weed Factor*), and Cynthia Davis (*Chimera*).

In the second category, books not already cited that deserve mention include the following: Raymond M. Olderman's *Beyond the Wasteland* (Yale, 1972), which devotes its single chapter on Barth exclusively to *Giles Goat-Boy*; Richard Lehan's *A Dangerous Crossing* (Southern Illinois University, 1973) and Jean E. Kennard's *Number and Nightmare* (Archon, 1975), which trace the influence of French existentialism on Barth's books; and Max F. Schulz's *Black Humor Fiction of the Sixties* (Ohio, 1973), which says little about humor but does adroitly examine the thematic and formal implications of multiplicity in Barth's work. Lengthy interviews with Barth are contained in Joe David Bellamy's *The New Fiction* (Illinois, 1974), Frank Gado's *First Person* (Union College Press, 1973), and L. S. Pembo and Cyrena N. Pondrom's *The Contemporary Writers* (Wisconsin, 1972). Because it represents the only feminist critique of Barth's fiction , Mary Allen's *The Necessary Blankness* (Illinois, 1976) is also of interest. Allen finds Barth "exemplary among all writers of the sixties in his sympathetic view of women's peculiar problems." This, I believe, is an accurate perception. Though hardly a social novelist, Barth has confessed to a preoccupation as a private citizen with the women's liberation movement, which he suggests is one of the themes of *Chimera*, a novel omitted from Allen's study. Insofar as Allen calls attention to this previously overlooked aspect of Barth's fiction, her study is of value. Unfortunately, she occasionally distorts Barth's fiction to fit her thesis. Because she finds women treated as commodities in *The Sot-Weed Factor*, Allen calls Anna Cooke a prostitute, despite the fact that Anna, like Eben, remains at least a technical virgin until late in life. Allen also argues that because Ebenezer idealizes women, he "never treats Joan [Toast] cruelly and remains devoted to her to the story's end," overlooking the fact that Eben takes Joan's money and deserts her shortly after their marriage. Apparently unaware of the several articles that trace Barth's deliberate use of Joseph Campbell's monomyth in *Giles Goat-Boy*, Allen writes that Barth "inadvertently" followed Campbell's pattern. She also misreads the epiphanic third descent of George and Anastasia into WESCAC's belly as a "satire on the idealization of romantic love."

The third category of Barth criticism remains the slightest. Only three books about Barth plus the two bibliographies have been published. Two of these—Joseph's pamphlet and Morrell's book—are introductions, thus necessarily quite general. Jac Tharpe's excellent volume therefore provides the only full-length study of Barth's fiction that assumes a thorough acquaintance with that fiction by the reader.

Before turning more specifically to those books which have occasioned this review, a general evaluative comment about the "state" of Barth criticism seems appropriate. Any such comment, if it is to be frank, will inevitably assume the form of the old good news/bad news vaudeville routine. For while much in the present corpus of Barth criticism is admirable, certain chronic weaknesses persist. The most vexatious of these is the factual error. Now for whatever the cause, entropy or gremlins, factual inaccuracies will creep occasionally into the work of even the most careful of scholars. Fortunately, these errors are normally read out of the manuscript at some point in the editorial process. Such has not been the case with many of the books considered here, however. Indeed, the mistakes cited in Mary Allen's study are typical of much recent writing about Barth and, for that matter, recent American fiction in general. American literature since 1945 is our newest literary period; consequently, many scholars of the period are less than a decade out of graduate school. A surprisingly large number of the books mentioned in this review are, like Allen's study, barely revised doctoral dissertations. But it would be inaccurate, as well as pompous and condescending, to dismiss the errors in these books as the natural lapses of fledgling critics still learning their trade. For even the books of older, more established critics are not immune. In *City of Words*, for example, Tony Tanner has Jake Horner receive advice from *two* black doctors, calls Heller's Milo Minderbinder Minderbender, and reverses the name of Ellison's Tod Clifton to Clifton Tod. Similarly, Max Schulz refers to that Argentine sorcerer Jorges Borges as European, and omits *Catch-22* from his study of novels of the sixties because he thinks it was published in 1955. More recently, Frank D. McConnell, who, though not yet forty, is a full professor at Northwestern University and the author of four books, commits a series of gaffes in *Four Postwar American Novelists*. After assuring the reader that *The Sot-Weed Factor*, "for all its great length, range of action, and immense cast of characters, is a remarkably simple book to summarize," McConnell proceeds to botch his summary, calling Henry Burlingame III the *son* of Sir Henry Burlingame and an Indian squaw (Henry's father is Chicamec, a half-breed Indian chief, and his mother, also a half-breed, is Father Fitzmaurice's daughter), pronouncing Anna Cooke Henry's bride (they never marry though Anna does bear his child), and proclaiming that Joan Toast will cede possession of Malden to Eben only if he marries her (they are already wed; her price is the consummation of that marriage).

One does not wish to carp, nor does one delight in taking to task his fellow critics for oversights not altogether absent from his own writing.[2]

But if critics of recent American literature are to maintain the respect of critics in other areas of literary study, we must abide by the same standards of scholarly care. These standards demand not only scrupulous use of factual detail, but close attention to the existing body of relevant secondary materials. The recent demise of New Criticism has produced a pluralistic babel of competing jargons and paradigms, each claiming heir-apparency. Whatever school or schools survive the skirmish, criticism as an institution will no doubt remain what at its best it has always been: a continuing dialogue among scholars. But for many of the critics here reviewed, that dialogue has been reduced to monologue. With some important exceptions, these critics seem unaware of, or simply uninterested in, the growing body of books and articles about Barth. McConnell's study, for instance, contains neither footnotes nor bibliography, nor does his chapter on Barth reveal any hint that he has read a single critical statement about his subject. His grasp of the primary bibliography fares little better, as demonstrated by his analysis of the 1956 edition of *The Floating Opera* rather than the authorized 1967 edition. (Can McConnell possibly have been ignorant of Barth's drastic revision of that earlier version?) John Stark also uses the unauthorized edition, but most startling is the pronouncement with which he concludes the Barth section of his 1974 study, *The Literature of Exhaustion*. Barth, he writes, "has too few readers perhaps because he has too few critics: the longest analysis of his work aside from this one is Joseph's forty-page pamphlet, and the essays about him are mainly book reviews and therefore almost inevitably ephemeral." Stark then supports this self-serving statement by omitting from his bibliography most of the significant books and articles published on Barth before 1974. One of course remains mindful that what Alfred Appel, Jr., calls "the vagaries and vagrancies of publishing" can result in an extended time lapse between the acceptance of a manuscript and its eventual publication. Yet Stark's study does include *Chimera*, published in 1972, and his bibliography lists at least one article published in 1973, so it is hardly unfair to hold him responsible for overlooking the nine books and numerous articles dealing extensively with Barth that were published by 1973. Even David Morrell, who provides an extensive bibliography of Barth materials through 1975, incorporates no study into the text of his otherwise excellent introduction that was not published before 1970.

Dr. Johnson once advised aspirant sages to acquaint themselves thoroughly with "what has been transacted in former times." "If no use is made of the labours of past ages," he sternly counseled, "the world must remain always in the infancy of knowledge." Johnson was talking about the ancients, but his wisdom applies to contemporary criticism as well. If we do not read one another we are bound to repeat one another. Or our judgments, conceived in a vacuum, will lack the fine edge of ideas honed by the clash of perspectives. In short, if we are to avoid becoming like that nameless minstrel of Barth's "Anomymiad," sending forth our scriblings with little hope or expectation that they will be discovered or read, our scholarly obligation to keep up with the field must be honored.

So much for the bad news. If I have seemed querulous, I have wished only to be constructive. In any event, any quarrel I may have with my fellow critics is, like Frost's with the world, a lover's quarrel. For even the most flawed of these books contains sufficient value to justify its purchase price. That is the good news. Perhaps because Barth's books are so difficult and challenging, they frequently attract readers capable of subtle and sometimes brilliant insights. Taken collectively, the five books to which I now turn, plus Weixlmann's bibliography, constitute a valuable *vade mecum* for travellers through Barth's labyrinthian fictions.

The place to begin a proper study of John Barth is with David Morrell's *John Barth: An Introduction*. A revision of Morrell's 1970 dissertation, this book's importance lies in the wealth of its biographical material; the information it provides about Barth's juvenilia (including *Shirt of Nessus*, Barth's unpublished M.A. thesis), his unpublished works (including the aborted *Dorchester Tales* and his current work-in-progress, *Letters*), the genesis and critical reception of his published novels, and his working habits as a novelist; and the ample quotations it includes from conversations with Barth and letters he, his agents, and his editors have exchanged with Morrell—material unavailable anywhere else. Barth gave Morrell access to this information so that, as he is quoted as saying, "When I'm asked facts about my work and personal questions about myself . . . I can refer them to you." As a compendium of pertinent facts about Barth's life and work, Morrell's book is indispensable. If it is less successful as literary analysis that is probably because Morrell, properly mindful of the introductory nature of his study, deliberately kept his interpretative remarks general, at times merely summarizing the plots of Barth's novels.

The chief weakness of Morrell's study derives from his decision not to revise the entire original manuscript thoroughly. Instead, he simply updated his bibliography and added a final chapter on *Chimera*. Chapter seven particularly suffers from this editorial inattention. An overview of Barth's themes and techniques, it offers little more than a reworking of Scholes's earlier treatment of Barth as fabulator. How much more valuable this chapter could have been had Morrell incorporated into it the various theoretical statements about formal innovation which have followed Scholes's book. But even in its present form, Morrell's introduction is a major addition to Barth scholarship. We owe a debt of gratitude to the Pennsylvania State University Press for making this important and frequently cited dissertation available at long last in book form.

Though equally general, *Four Postwar American Novelists*, for reasons already suggested, is vastly less reliable than Morrell's study. Published by the prestigious University of Chicago Press and written by the author of *The Spoken Seen* (John Hopkins, 1975), a justly esteemed film study, McConnell's book raises high expectations. Unfortunately, those expectations are only partially fulfilled. The "besetting disease" of postmodern man, McConnell writes, is "inauthenticity," his word for that sense of lost selfhood critics of literature and art have discussed for years. Compounding this loss of personality is the loss of the Good City—"the true field of human civilization"—and a consequent mass feeling of failure. Writers such as Bellow, Mailer, Pynchon, and Barth revert from this apocalyptic vision, and "attempt to locate, within the very center of the contemporary wasteland, mythologies of psychic survival and social, political health." The various myths "reconsolodated" by these writers include the humanism of Bellow, the "purely personal, existential stylization" of Mailer, and the "redemption of history" (no less) by Pynchon. Barth stands precariously balanced between the humanism of Bellow and the existentialism of Mailer, insisting on the primacy of tradition while simultaneously searching "strenuously for the radical articulation of the individual mind, the outsider's vision. . . ."

As generalizations, such comments seem solid enough, even familiar. But McConnell seldom demonstrates systematically the validity of his assertions. For example, he tells us that the "archetypcal situation" of Barth's major characters is the sudden and unsettling suspicion that they may be trapped in a fictional plot—a familiar enough truism in Barth studies. "Therefore," McConnell continues, "the plot of Barth's novels is largely the plot of discovering the underlying myths, the archfictions which will allow us to live with the smaller, less satisfying fictions of everyday life and still to believe in ourselves as conscious, creative agents." Now that has the ring of insight. But McConnell leaves this richly suggestive sentiment hovering unsupported in abstract space. Thus it provokes rather than enlightens us. Repeatedly, McConnell assures us that Barth's vision is positive, that his novels explore the key to the treasure of authentic selfhood. Perhaps so. But Barthian treasures lie deep beneath the surface of his fictions, and McConnell seldom plumbs those depths. A remarkably dexterous prose style almost diverts our attention from the shallowness of McConnell's method. Few critics turn a phrase with greater alacrity. But eloquence is no substitute for substance. And little of substance graces McConnell's commentary on Barth.

Yet, in a way I am sure McConnell did not intend, his study may serve a substantive purpose. His insistence, repeated if seldom demonstrated, that Barth is not only affirmative but the "heir to Bellow" (of all writers!) could provoke a reassessment of Barth's fiction by those critics who have seen him as either altogether pessimistic, the cheerful nihilist, or as ceding at the most a limited value to "writing as an anodyne to painful living" (Morrell). Such a reassessment, I believe, is due. But if Barth's vision is affirmative, its values are derived not from the humanistic and existential paradigms of the recent past, but from some as yet not fully articulated paradigm awaiting us, like the mysterious She of "Night Sea

Journey," in a not-too-distant future. The danger of McConnell's book, then, is not that it may irritate the specialists—irritation, like the grain of sand in an oyster's craw, can prove valuable—but that it may mislead the general reader. And when all is said and done, one suspects that for whatever reason, it is the general reader to whom McConnell directed his book in the first place.

John Stark's discussion, on the other hand, is definitely intended for the serious Barthian, offering a more complex reading of Barth's fiction than any book here reviewed except Tharpe's. Beginning with a consideration of Barth's use of Chinese boxes, Stark proceeds to a discussion of the infinite regress as a Barthian strategy for exhausting "reality," then investigates several of Barth's main themes, the most important of which are the theme of art and the theme of the opposite. Like McConnell, Stark alludes to Barth's interest in the theory that reality is linguistically based, but neither critic discusses this important idea in depth. Of particular value is Stark's eight-page analysis of the relationship between Barth's themes and his style. Except for Peter Mercer's fine article, "The Rhetoric of *Giles Goat-Boy*," *Novel*, 4 (1971), this is the only extensive consideration I have seen of Barth's language. Obviously, Stark derives his title from Barth's influential 1967 essay, and he traces the implications of that essay—literature is used up; writers should "invent and exhaust possibilities and thus create for literature an infinite scope"—in the works of Nabokov and Borges as well as Barth. Despite its bibliographical abuses, its oddly disjointed presentation, and a prose style as pedestrian as McConnell's is eloquent, Stark's study provides a number of new perspectives on important elements of Barth's fiction.

"The literature of exhaustion," "fabulation," "black humor," "literary disruption," the novel of "number" or "nightmare" or "the absurd"—critics will have their coinages, and the list of rubrics for the problematic postmodern (yet another rubric!) novel grows daily. John W. Tilton's contribution is "cosmic satire." According to Tilton, the novels examined in his slender study—Burgess's *A Clockwork Orange*, Vonnegut's *Slaughterhouse-Five*, and Barth's *Giles Goat-Boy*—achieve "a 'larger, darker, and more compassionate' satire that transcends even the functions of the satire of attack or exposure: it creates a profound satiric vision, a vision, ultimately tragic in its implications, of man desperately refusing to face what he is and just as desperately—and unsuccessfully—trying to become what he thinks he ought to be." Neither corrective nor utilitarian in function, cosmic satire conveys the "conviction that man will always find fantasy or illusion preferable to reality." By "reality" Tilton refers less to the objective world than to a fully individuated psyche. "Barth's central concern," for example, "is to illuminate mythopoeically the plight of man divided against himself. . . . Barth interprets the plight of man as a universal condition, universal because it arises from a fragmentation of the psyche witnessed in the myths of all ages and countries."

Like so many of the critics already cited, Tilton blithely advances his thesis as though he is breaking fresh ground. But what he calls "cosmic satire" has been thoroughly discussed as Menippean satire by at least two Barthian critics. Echoing Tilton's notion about the relationship between satire and reality, James T. Gresham writes: "Menippean satire . . . differs from conventional satire in its norm, which is not the Good or the Ideal, but the Real. Lucidity—perception of 'reality'—is its goal, and the delusory Ideal is generally viewed as a manifestation of reductive system-building . . ." (*"Giles Goat-Boy:* Satyr, Satire, and Tragedy Twined," *Genre,* 7 [1974]). Similarly, James F. Walter anticipates Tilton's concern with satire and the integrated psyche: ". . . the theme of interior disorder and illness caused by a division between human faculties which naturally complement each other in the act of knowing," Walter writes, "is, of course, a common one in Western literature; a certain vein of that literature, however, which extends to us from the satires of a Syrian Cynic named Menippus, takes this theme as its primary obsession" ("A Psychochronology of Lust in the Menippean Tradition: *Giles Goat-Boy,*" *TCL,* 21[1975]). Now it remains questionable whether Barth writes satire at all (he says he does not), and any application of the term "reality" to the works of so notable an irrealist requires much more qualification than any of these critics provide. Be that as it may, a body of criticism does exist which claims to locate a traditional satire in some of Barth's fiction. Because Tilton neglects to place his speculations explicitly in the context of these earlier studies, his book, though competent enough, adds little that is new to our understanding of postmodernist satire.

Jac Tharpe's terse study is the best of the books on Barth, and one to which the nonspecialist should turn only after having acquired a close acquaintance with Barth's fiction and at least some of the more accessible commentaries. One's initial response to the book is skepticism that Barth's mammoth *oeuvre* can be adequately assessed in so slim a volume (the actual text covers only 117 pages). But an assiduously pared prose style allows Tharpe to develop sufficiently his ambitious thesis. That thesis is that Barth's novels "are all philosophical, and as a group they comprise a history of philosophy." The first pair of novels deals with ethics, a concern Barth never altogether abandons; the next pair with questions of ontology, cosmology, and epistemology; the final pair with ontology and aesthetics. Logic is used throughout as an organizing principle but ultimately "to point out the deficiencies and absurdities . . . of the methodology itself."

Absent from Barth's philosophy is a metaphysics, without which philosophical certainty becomes impossible. As Tharpe tellingly explains: "For epistemology, the question finally is whether we can know anything to be certainly true if we do not know some ultimate truth to use as a standard for checking ideas. For ethics, the question is whether any activity is either required or proscribed in a universe where we cannot know any truth as certain. . . . In Barth's terminology, the question for both epistemology and ethics is not only what the Answer is but whether an Answer even exists. . . ." If it does, Barth never finds it. Interested in all theories, he can subscribe to none.

Yet Barth's skepticism, Tharpe assures us, stops short of nihilism. "Obviously a decent man," Barth "has no wish to send out the message that anything goes." His ethical imperative, however, may involve little more than "muddling compromise"—the cultivation of moderate behavior and "relative order." Craftsmanship—a sense of style in life and art—comes closest to the nature of a value in Barth's cosmos. "Style is man—*homo faber*, the heroic craftsman, who orders a chaotic funhouse." Yet the pureness of art's pleasure, like Kant's Idea of the Beautiful, increases in direct proportion to the degree of "its gratuitous uselessness."

Between a thought-provoking introduction and a brief but brilliant conclusion, Tharpe includes separate chapters on each of Barth's six books. The richness of these discussions resists adequate paraphrase, but among the topics analyzed are Barth's "carnal vision" with its twin poles of sex and death in *The Floating Opera*, cosmopsis and mythotherapy in *The End of the Road*, the theme of innocence and the role of the Ideal Woman in *The Sot-Weed Factor*, cyclology, paradox, and "phylogenic tragedy" in *Giles Goat-Boy*, the discussion of which constitutes about a third of Tharpe's book; the "twin themes" of art and love in *Lost in the Funhouse*, and the hero as artist motif in *Chimera*. Tharpe's comments about the relationship between language and "reality" in Barth's fiction, though scattered, are acute. "Since we cannot find out what reality is," Tharpe writes, "we shall simply create one to serve. Ordinarily, the result of this process was either myth or ideology. In Barth's case, it is to create a world of fiction, not a fictional world." To be sure, Tharpe does not teach us everything we need to know about Barth's fiction. But as the first book-length study of that fiction it is eminently worthy of its subject, and a book no future critic of John Barth can responsibly omit from account.

On balance, the state of Barth criticism, with certain hedges and reservations, may be pronounced as healthy. Much remains to be done, of course. Barth's status has produced a recent backlash of sorts, and these detractors need to be answered. In *Literary Disruptions* (Illinois, 1975), for example, Jerome Klinkowitz dismisses Barth as a "regressive parodist," a writer of "literary suicide notes," and John Gardner, in his peevish *On Moral Fiction* (Basic Books, 1978), actually calls Barth's fiction immoral. Klinkowitz's charge lacks adequate support; Gardner's is merely strident. But even thoughtful critics such as Tony Tanner and Campbell Tatham have registered cautious exception to what they perceive as Barth's preference of the word to the world. I suspect we may be entering an era in which questions about the moral and ethical implications of an artist's vision once again achieve priority. Therefore the careful and unhysterical assessment of Barth's ethical concerns already begun by Tharpe needs to be continued.

Also needed is a systematic exploration of the nature and function of Barth's humor. Bruce Janoff has contributed a series of articles on this important subject,[3] but further analysis seems necessary. Stylistic examinations of Barth's language which supplement the rudimentary studies by Stark and Mercer would also prove beneficial. Tharpe maintains that Barth has no style, only styles that shift among and within his various fictions. But certainly a distinctive fictional *voice* begins to emerge in *The Sot-Weed Factor*. That voice, too, requires description and analysis. Moreover, Barth's interest in the notion that "reality" is linguistically based requires the attention of a critic preferably schooled in the new linguistically oriented critical approaches (though I hope he will spare us the jargon). And the relationship between the framing devices of Barth's later fiction and the traditional frame-tale remains generally unexamined. Naturally the future direction of Barth criticism will be guided by whatever priorities and assumptions prevail among tomorrow's critics. The current unsettled state of criticism in America makes conjectures about those priorities and assumptions even more provisional than usual. But at least two predictions may be made with some assurance: Barth's stature as a major writer will remain secure, and Barth criticism worthy of its brief but already rich heritage will continue to be produced.

Notes

1. Including Ellison (26 entries), Bellow and Pynchon (25 entries apiece), Vonnegut (22 entries), and Mailer (16 entries).

2. Jerome Klinkowitz catches me in an embarrassing bibliographical inaccuracy. See his generally negative review of my *Contemporary American Novelists of the Absurd*, "Not By Theme Alone," *Novel*, 6, No. 3 (1973), 268–272.

3. "Black Humor: Beyond Satire," *The Ohio Review*, 14, No. 1 (1972), 5–20, "Black Humor, Absurdity, and Technique," *Studies in the Twentieth Century*, No. 13 (1974), pp. 39–49; "Black Humor, Existentialism, and Absurdity: A Generic Confusion," *Arizona Quarterly*, 30 (1974), 293–304.

John Barth and the Novel
of Comic Nihilism

Richard W. Noland*

I

When Nietzsche announced the death of God toward the end of the nineteenth century, he also added further stimulus to one of the obsessive themes of contemporary literature—the problem of the loss of value and meaning in human life and the search for new value and meaning to replace the old. And since Nietzsche's conception of the Dionysian was generally misinterpreted as a call for the abandonment of reason and intelligence (the Apollonian),[1] one of the most frequent answers to the problem of value has been an effort to return to the primitive, the anti-intellectual, and the irrational.

But this attempt to replace the Western Apollonian ego with a Dionysian consciousness has never been entirely satisfactory. The return to the irrational in philosophy, literature, and politics has produced an important body of writing—Lawrence, Miller, the surrealists, some of the existentialists, for example—but it has also distorted the nature of man by its radical insistence on an absolute conflict between the Apollonian and the Dionysian. Such a view, moreover, is liable to very dubious and destructive social and political applications—applications which, since the irrationalist's political hero is as likely to be Hitler's as he is Nietzsche's superman, may well lead to totalitarian possibilities rather than to political emancipation.

Other sources of value, therefore, have been sought, some within more traditional modes of thought (the neo-orthodox theology of Barth, Brunner, and Niebuhr, for example), some which attempt to assert conscious and rational possibilities as well as unconscious and irrational ones (such a man as Camus, for example, who is concerned both with the absurdity of existence and with free and moral choice). Still others have simply taken the fact of nihilism as the subject matter of their work without necessarily developing a single philosophical position on which to base a system of values.

*Reprinted by permission of Contemporary Literature, VII (Autumn 1966), 239–57.

Such is the case with John Barth. Barth establishes his affinity with the nihilistic tradition and with the existential novel in his first book, *The Floating Opera* (1956). The world of the existentialist novel, says Ihab Hassan, is largely devoid of "presuppositions" about "values, traditions, or beliefs." Thus, "whatever values man creates, he does so in isolation, and starting from scratch."[2] So Todd Andrews, the narrator and protagonist of *The Floating Opera: "Nothing has intrinsic value*"[3] And if nothing has value, *"There is, then, no 'reason' for living"* (p. 243). Thus the novel begins and ends on the problem which Camus has made central to existential thought—that of suicide. "There is but one truly serious philosophical problem," Camus says, "and that is suicide. Judging whether life is or is not worth living amounts to answering the fundamental question of philosophy."[4]

This is the question which Todd ("Tod is death . . . *Todd* is almost *Tod*—that is, almost death . . ."[p. 9]) must answer. Todd is a lawyer in Cambridge, Maryland (a town on the East Shore). He tells his story as an aging man who thinks back to a day in 1937 when he woke up and decided to commit suicide. This decision, so Todd thinks, is the result of his long effort to master the fact of his imminent death. Since 1919 he has lived with a diagnosis of subacute bacterial endocarditis ("heart trouble, in English" [p. 11]), and his response to this fact has been a series of masks by which he hopes to hide the reality of his illness from himself: "My heart, reader! My heart! You must comprehend quickly, if you are to comprehend at all, that those masks were not assumed to hide my face, but to hide my heart from my mind, and my mind from my heart (p. 238). Three different masks were required from 1919 to 1937: "a rake, a saint, and then a cynic. . . . when one mask no longer served its purpose of disguise, another had perforce to take its place at once" (p. 239). And one by one these masks fail. Todd passes from the hedonism of the rake to the self-restraint and renunciation of the saint to the disenchantment of the cynic—but a cynic who at least believes in the value of cynicism. Even this mask fails finally, and one morning in 1937, after a long night of despair, he suddenly realizes that he must destroy himself:

> Here is what I saw: that all my masks were half-conscious attempts to master the fact with which I had to live; that none had made me master of that fact; that where cynicism had failed, no future mask could succeed. . . . the conclusion that swallowed me in its overwhelming despair was this: *There is no way to master the fact with which I live.* (p. 241)

But we have only Todd's word for it that the fact of his death caused the failure of his masks, and so of meaning. It is equally clear, however, that Todd's masks are at least as much an effort to avoid life as to master death. So much Todd himself makes clear when he fills in what he considers the crucial emotional experiences of his life. These he rationally calculates as five in number: first, from his initiation into love he learns mirth, the sense that all human copulation is essentially ridiculous; second, from his experience in the First World War he learns fear; third, from his father's death he learns frustration; fourth, from his only real love affair he learns surprise; and fifth, from his accumulated experience he learns despair.

Two of these emotional lessons are of particular importance. Todd remains obsessed with his father's suicide after financial losses in the depression. Unable to accept the fact that it was really over money, Todd is baffled by the real motive for this act. Such frustration of understanding, he thinks, can only be a result of an "imperfect communication" (p. 235) between him and his father—the same imperfect communication which afflicts all his personal relations. So he begins his interminable *Inquiry*—a complete written study of his own and his father's lives, which is to include in particular an examination of his father's death in minute detail, a study of the quality of their relationship, and, Kafka-like, a letter of explanation to his father. The task as he conceives it is impossible of completion, yet by 1937 he has filled three peachbaskets and a cardboard box with notes and drafts. Even Todd, it would seem, with his dislike of unconscious motives, could hardly fail to miss the obsessive nature of this effort and the primal human relationship which lies behind it.

But Oedipus requires a triangle, and this is what Todd gets with his only real love affair. This affair is with Jane Mack, wife of his best friend, Harrison Mack. And he learns surprise rather than love, first because Jane suddenly and without warning offers herself to him one day; and second, because he later discovers that she did so because Harrison wanted her to. In fact, both Jane and Harrison want the affair. They want it, they say, out of love for Todd. They want no silly jealousy, no guilt, no recriminations. Richard Schickel considers this episode Barth's commentary on " 'liberal' morality, both political and sexual . . ."[5]; political because of Harrison's left wing sympathies, sexual because of the curious and self-conscious, almost ideological, nature of the affair itself. The Macks, in other words, attempt to order their lives too rationally, too abstractly, as Todd does with his masks. They live by theory, not genuine feeling. They do what any good liberal couple should. Yet the affair succeeds for a number of years—indeed, until 1937, when, on the night before the morning of his decision to commit suicide, Todd is embarrassed by Jane's attention to his clubbed fingers (a clinical sign of bacterial endocarditis, and so a reminder of his mortality) and then finds himself impotent with her. Another mask, the last, crumbles, and he is left with the fifth of his crucial experiences, complete despair.

That Barth is fascinated by this triangular affair in which Todd, Jane, and Harrison engage is shown by its reappearance in the Jacob Horner-Rennie Morgan-Joseph Morgan triangle in *End of the Road* (1958) and by the Ebenezer Cooke-Anna Cooke-Henry Burlingame triangle in *The Sot-Weed Factor* (1960). Each triangle has its own character and special nuances. Yet basically Barth is playing variations on the same situation, a situation which is also explored by Joyce in *Exiles*, and in which, as Stanley Edgar Hyman says, "two male friends attain symbolic union by sharing the body of a woman."[6] There is thus an implicit homosexual theme running through the three novels, which becomes quite explicit in *The Sot-Weed Factor* and of which Barth is quite aware. What this latent theme serves to suggest is the very Platonic (and Freudian) notion that society is bound together by the erotic, by Eros, or that it must be if it is to remain a society. The failure of this basic human group, which is at once representative of the family (the nuclear social unit), of ordinary people seeking contact with each other, and, through the positions taken by each person, of various ideas and ideologies, is more than personal. It is symbolic of a failure of contact of the members of a whole society on the most basic level possible. And since love and friendship are not erotically directed, only abstract systems are left by which people attempt to communicate with each other. But this in turn leads to the constant change and inadequacy of these supposedly rational efforts. Or it leads, as it does with Jacob Horner in *End of the Road*, to a complete paralysis of will.

Todd is not completely paralyzed. But neither is he the man of reason he thinks he is. It is Todd, not Barth, who thinks of himself in this way. To Barth, he is a man in whom reason and emotion run in separate directions. Without emotion, reason can give him no purpose for living. It cannot establish permanent value or affirm life. It can only determine that there are no absolutes.[7] Without reason, emotion turns sour and makes Todd, as Hyman says, a "victim of his Oedipus complex, a latent homosexual, a cold fish, and a malicious sadist" (p. 21).[8] The implication, of course, is that Todd can find value and affirm life only by a unity of reason and emotion. A passionate reason is required for a genuine involvement.

And when Todd finally decides not to commit suicide, it is because for once he responds passionately rather than rationally. Jeannine, Jane's daughter and possibly Todd's, has a convulsion just as Todd is about to kill himself.[9] Todd realizes that he must know how serious it is, that he cares what happens to Jeannine, though there is really no reason for such concern. Barth is no doubt sentimental here, as Hyman observes, when he relates Todd's change of mind to Jeannine. This ending is undoubtedly "too sudden, too easy, too pat a solution to the difficult existential questions he has raised" (Schickel, p. 65). Todd should have killed himself or, even more appropriately, simply gone on as before. But at least the response to Jeannine is consistent in that Todd needs to find value that is not purely rational but an impulsive and spontaneous involvement with life.

Such an involvement, of course, does not satisfy Todd. He must formulate his experience in some way, which he does at once. He decides that if there are no absolute values, there are at least relative values, and that "a value is no less authentic, no less genuine, no less compelling, no less 'real,' for its being relative!" There is an enormous difference, he decides, between saying "Values are *only* relative . . ." and "There *are* relative values!" (p. 271). But he does not say what these relative values are. The real tone of the ending is caught by a much less affirmative statement: "If nothing makes any final difference, that fact makes no final difference either, and there is no more reason to commit suicide, say, than not to, in the last analysis" (p. 270).

II

Jacob Horner, the narrator of *End of the Road*, is a successor to Todd. " 'I deliberately had him [Todd] end up with that brave ethical subjectivism,' " Barth says in a letter quoted by Gregory Bluestone, " 'in order that Jacob Horner might undo that position in #2 and carry all non-mystical value-thinking to the end of the road!' "[10] Herbert Fingarette has observed that an acceptance of the arbitrariness of value combined with the recognition of the necessity to commit oneself to this uncertainty can lead to one of three possible consequences:

> (1) integrity, the willingness to treat one's decisions seriously and to live by them; (2) evasion, the making of decisions without serious concern for or acceptance of the implications of our act; and (3) dogmatism, initial commitment with subsequent refusal to face the recurrence of anxiety and the need for those new acts of commitment which life forces upon us from time to time.[11]

In *End of the Road*, little integrity is evident, but there is much evasion and dogmatism. Jacob Horner is a portrait of Todd Andrews with a complete paralysis of will, which Barth calls cosmopsis. But the paralysis is not always total. There are degrees. At times it may take simply the form of an inability to make a decision, when for all arguments in favor of something (the taking of a teaching job, for example) "a corresponding number of refutations lined up opposite them, one for one, so that the question of my application was held static like the rope marker in a tug-o'-war where the opposing teams are perfectly matched."[12] At other times, Jacob is the passive victim of moods. He may be manic or depressed, or he may have no mood at all. At such times he is, as he says, "without a personality" (p. 31).

But these periods of no mood usually pass or are easily broken by outside interference. They are related to Jacob's doubts as to his identity—"*In a sense, I am Jacob Horner,*" he says in the opening statement of the novel. Only once does he reach a state of complete cosmopsis. In the Pennsylvania Station in Baltimore, where, after abandoning graduate study at Johns Hopkins, he has gone to take a train to any place he can afford, he runs out of motives and remains seated on a bench, like Melville's Bartleby, for the next eleven hours. "There was no reason to do anything," he says.

My eyes . . . were sightless, gazing on eternity, fixed on ultimacy, and when that is the case there is no reason to do anything—even to change the focus of one's eyes . . . It is the malady *cosmopsis*, the cosmic view, that afflicted me. (p. 60).

The spell is broken by the Doctor, an elderly Negro who operates an extra-legal farm for the treatment of immobility and paralysis. He is, says Jacob, "some combination of quack and prophet . . . running a semi-legitimate rest home for senile eccentrics . . ." (p. 69). As "a kind of superpragmatist" (p. 68), the Doctor adapts his treatment to the patient. He has a system of therapy for any kind of person or illness, and he takes Jacob to his farm to treat the cosmopsis. Jacob, he says, must act impulsively. He must also take a job teaching prescriptive, not descriptive, grammar, which leads Jacob to the Wicomico State Teachers College on Maryland's Eastern Shore, the scene of the main action of the book. And he must be instructed in Mythotherapy, which is, the Doctor says, based on two assumptions: " 'that human existence precedes human essence, if either of the two terms really signifies anything; and that a man is free not only to choose his own essence but to change it at will' " (p. 71). The point for Jacob, of course, is that he is to assume a role, any role, to adopt quite arbitrarily a character which will be an alternative to the nonidentity of cosmopsis. " 'This kind of role-assigning is myth-making, and when it's done consciously or unconsciously for the purpose of aggrandizing or protecting your ego . . . it becomes Mythotherapy' " (p. 72).

So Jacob adopts this pragmatic, arbitrary, yet fluid therapy as a way of avoiding cosmopsis. The role he assumes is unimportant, so long as it is a role. He can change when he wishes to. But Joseph Morgan, who teaches history at Wicomico State, cannot. Like the Doctor, he understands the arbitrariness and relativity of all roles and values. But on this awareness he builds his own arbitrary but dogmatic system by which he lives. Unlike Jacob, Joe is always certain of what he does. "Indecision," Jacob says of him, ". . . was apparently foreign to him; he was always sure of his ground; he acted quickly, explained his actions lucidly if questioned, and would have regarded apologies for missteps as superfluous" (p. 29). But his grounds of action are as arbitrary as Jacob's. He knows that his personal code is not logically defensible, that it is subjective, and that he is only right from his own point of view. One operates in this way, as he says, " 'because there's nothing else' " (p. 39).

But what might for a man of the Enlightenment be the basis for a pluralistic and tolerant view of value becomes for Joe a personally absolute system on which he is as unyielding as the most committed ideologue. One of these absolutes is "marital fidelity," "taking your wife seriously" (p. 39). As a result of this view, Joe becomes Pygmalion to his wife, Rennie. He attempts to mold her into his idea of what Joe Morgan's wife should be. And to test her fidelity to their private code he exposes her deliberately to Jacob. Herbert F. Smith sees the ensuing struggle between Jacob and Joe for Rennie as a kind of philosophical paradigm. Joe, he thinks, represents Reason (Being), Jacob Unreason (Not-Being or moral nihilism), and Rennie the *tabula rasa.*[13] In this scheme Joe is God, the creating and ordering force, but "one who does not understand what has happened to his otherwise sufficient rules of causality" (p. 72). This is a bit too allegorical, and it also misses the extent to which both Jacob and Joe represent not-being. Joe's single abstract system is ultimately no more creative than Jacob's more flexible one. Both systems are simply a response to the sense of nothingness. And both systems fail in the final analysis because, like Todd's masks, they are not adequate to a concrete situation in which concern and responsibility are required, not an abstract code of behavior. Thus Jacob and Joe share the responsibility for Rennie's death by criminal abortion (she refuses to have the child when she cannot know whether it is Jacob's or Joe's; this is her way of acting as she thinks Joe Morgan's wife should). She is the "ethical vacuum" (Smith, p. 75) on whom both impose their abstract roles, Jacob inadvertently, Joe actively. What begins as an *"ideological farce"*[14] thus moves, like Waugh's *A Handful of Dust,* grimly and efficiently from comedy to tragedy.

III

The existential novel, says Hassan, is neither "wholly tragic nor truly comic." It cannot achieve the finality and awareness of these forms because there is no finality or awareness in the world which it records. For in this world everything is tentative, relative, or (probably) meaningless. The existential novelist, therefore, must present this world in a form which contains an awareness of relativity, a form which includes both terror and laughter. Such a form, Hassan observes, is typically ironic, which allows "the recognition not only of irreconcilible conflicts but actually of *absurdity."*[15] Barth's novels exhibit precisely this mixture of tragedy and comedy. A past suicide, an attempted suicide, and a contemplated suicide dominate *The Floating Opera,* while a sudden and seemingly unnecessary death climaxes *End of the Road.* Yet the tragedy, or near tragedy, is qualified. Todd decides to live, to be sure, but he does not do so because of a new perception of the meaning and value of life. He decides merely that there is no more reason to die than to live. And neither Jacob nor Joe clearly comprehends a larger meaning to Rennie's death. Jacob, in fact, is at the end of the novel on his way to meet the Doctor, presumably to resume his therapy and to seek other identities.

Barth's comedy is equally ambiguous and ironic. Its characteristic form is parody or burlesque. For one thing, any abstract system or ideology is parodied—that liberal urge, for example, which leads the Macks to offer Todd such a curious kind of love. Existentialism itself is parodied in the Doctor's various systems (he advises Jacob to read Sartre as preparation for therapy), as well as the various systems of psychotherapy. Barth may even burlesque the most ordinary and customary human activity: sex, for example, which Todd finds ludicrous; the seeking of a teaching job (*End of the Road* seems at first to be an American *Lucky Jim*, in which the misadventures of a chronic misfit at a provincial college are recounted); or the pursuit of one's profession, which for Todd is a kind of elaborate game. The entire legal procedure, in fact, is parodied in *The Floating Opera* in a lawsuit worthy of a place in *Bleak House*—a lawsuit which involves seventeen wills left by Harrison Mack's father, President of Mack Pickle Co., each will containing clauses that conflict with clauses in all the other wills. "In any world but ours," Todd observes, "the case of the Mack estate would be fantastic; even in ours, it received considerable publicity from the Maryland press" (p. 93). Such parody points up the absurdity of all man's activities. Even jurisprudence and justice, Todd says, have "no more intrinsic value than, say, oyster-shucking" (p. 81).

In *The Sot-Weed Factor*, this mode of parody and burlesque reaches its fullest development. So much so, in fact, that Earl Rovit has called this novel a "kind of prolonged academic joke . . . somewhat perversely fixed on a puristic conception of the factuality of source materials." What Barth has done, he argues, is to write parody for the sake of parody rather than to seek new meaning or vision or to use the parody as a technique of criticism. *The Sot-Weed Factor* is thus a *cul-de-sac*, like *Finnegan's Wake*, and exhibits "an eccentric faith in the limitations (rather then the possibilities) of the imagination and the creative process."[16]

There is considerable force in this view. And this force is contained in a very simple formulation: Barth has written a very good eighteenth-century novel. What Rovit is questioning, of course, is why a twentieth-century writer should do such a thing, if by it he deliberately cuts himself off from the resources of the language and technique of his own time. It is as if Barth had accepted Todd's belief that one does something not because it is intrinsically valuable but simply to occupy one's time. If one builds a boat, as Todd does, one may as well do as good a job as possible on it. And if one writes an eighteenth-century novel, one may as well write a good eighteenth-century novel. Language, form, and content should be as close to the original as possible, as they were in Thackeray's *Henry Esmond*. Rovit admits that in Henry Burlingame Barth seems concerned with contemporary identity problems, but for him the parody for its own sake dominates everything else in the novel. He is attacking Barth, in other words, for abandoning the serious novelist's task of dealing with his own time.

But this view is only partially true. At the heart of Barth's work says Alan Trachtenberg, "is the problem of existence and identity."[17] And since existence and identity are two of the main themes of the book, *The Sot-Weed Factor* stands quite easily as a successor to *The Floating Opera* and *End of the Road*. Barth, in fact, intended this progression, but, as he says, "What happened was, I had thought I was writing about values and it turned out I was writing about innocence."[18] Not only did he add the theme of innocence, he also added the dimension of history—specifically, of American colonial history. The form of the novel now becomes genuinely significant. For Barth has combined the eighteenth-century picaresque novel and the eighteenth-century philosophical tale (such as *Candide*[19] or *Rasselas*) with the picaresque form which many twentieth-century existential novels have taken.[20] What results is a kind of existential study of American colonial history, and also of the traditional themes and concerns of American literature, notably the theme of innocence.

The innocent in *The Sot-Weed Factor* is Ebenezer Cooke, the central character.[21] Ebenezer is Barth's version of that perennial figure of American fiction, the American Adam, an image, as R. W. B. Lewis says, "of the authentic American as a figure of heroic innocence and vast potentialities, poised at the start of a new history."[22] Lewis sees this theme of innocence as a movement between two extremes, between what he calls the party of Hope, which accepted the idea of innocence without qualification, and the party of Memory, which tended toward a doctrine of original sin which denies innocence. The main tradition of American literature, he thinks, involves a dialectic between these extremes which simultaneously affirms and denies the possibility of innocence, and which reaches its tragic apotheosis in *Moby Dick*, its transcendent affirmation of innocence in *Billy Budd*. Barth examines this dialectic comically rather than tragically.

Ebenezer does not come by his innocence naturally. He acquires, or rather assumes, it. And he does so only after suffering for many years from Jacob Horner's malady, cosmopsis. He is indecisive, equally attracted to all ways of life, and content to drift with "the tide of chance." He is "consistently no special sort of person." And once he reaches complete immobility, when "one day he did not deign even to dress himself or eat, but sat immobile in the window seat in his nightshirt and stared at the activity in the street below, unable to choose a motion at all even when, some hours later, his untutored bladder suggested one."[23]

This chronic inability to achieve an identity is responsible initially for Ebenezer's sexual innocence. Such is his incapacity to assume a definite character that he cannot decide whether to be bold or bashful, the young innocent or the old lecher when confronted with a woman—a woman, for example, like Joan Toast, London prostitute, with whom he falls in love. Unable to play a role, he usually ends up "either turning down the chance or, what was more usually the case, retreating gracelessly and in confusion, if not always embarrassment" (p. 57). But with Joan Toast he finds himself suddenly propelled into a role. He is in love; she is interested only in pursuing her profession. So Ebenezer decides that he will be what he already is, virgin. And he will also be a poet: " 'What am I? What am I? *Virgin*, sir! *Poet*, sir! I am a virgin and a poet; less than mortal and more; not a man, but Mankind!' " (pp. 71–72). And in a hymn to innocence which he writes on the spot and signs "*Ebenezer Cooke, Gent., Poet and Laureate of England*," he reveals more of the source and meaning of this choice than he is ever aware:

> Preserv'd, my Innocence preserveth me
> From Life, from Time, from Death, from History;
> Without it I must breathe Man's mortal Breath:
> Commence a Life—and thus commence my Death! (p. 71)

What Ebenezer unconciously seeks, in other words, is permanence, something above the flux which he sees all around him. He understands what his friend and former tutor, Henry Burlingame, tells him—that " 'we sit here on a blind rock careening through space; we are all of us rushing headlong to the grave' " (p. 36). The search for a soul, Burlingame says, reveals only a " 'black Cosmos whence we sprang and through which we fall . . .' " (p. 364). So " 'One must needs make and sieze his soul, and then cleave fast to 't, or go babbling in the corner. . . . One must *assert, assert, assert*, or go screaming mad' " (p. 365). Both Ebenezer and Burlingame attempt to create and assert their souls. But where Burlingame does so by immersing himself in the shifting and ambiguous historical process, Ebenezer seeks a way above this process. He seeks being itself; Burlingame is content with becoming. While Burlingame searches for the identity of his parentage, he accepts change and morality in a way that Ebenezer does not. Like Joe Morgan, Ebenezer must have an absolute with which to shield himself from what he and Burlingame know as reality: "Blind Nature" (p. 364) and chaos.

The central action of the novel is the fate of Ebenezer's innocence and Burlingame's search for identity. From the outset it is clear that Ebenezer's innocence is dangerous to himself and to others. He is ignorant of himself (which is what the sexual innocence turns out to mean) and of the world at large. He sets out to guard his virginity like Joseph Andrews and to impose his vision on the world like Don Quixote. But he finds only a world for which he is not prepared and which he cannot understand. He sets out from England to manage his father's tobacco plantation in Maryland and to assume his newly appointed post as laureate of Maryland. But a journey that was to be a kind of odyssey turns into a nightmare of confused identities and unknown conspirators (it turns out that it was actually Burlingame, in the role of Lord Baltimore, who commissioned Ebenezer laureate of Maryland). Maryland is not the beautiful land about which Ebenezer writes glowing lines before he has even seen it. It is simply a place where slavery and exploitation of the Indian are commonplaces of life; where the planters are barbarous, rude, and illiterate; and where the law is dishonest and badly abused (" 'This is my court,' " says a judge, " 'and I mean to run it honestly: nobody gets a verdict he hath not paid for!' " [p. 417]). By the time he gets to his father's plantation, it has been turned into an opium den and brothel. The New World, he discovers, is a place where all the evils of the Old World persist: commercial intrigue, dishonest and intriguing governors, hatred and violence between the separate colonies, mob violence, conspiracy and counterconspiracy with the French, the Indians, and the Dutch to seize various colonies—all the Machiavellian politics which Howard Mumford Jones has documented as a part of American life from the very beginning.[24] Ebenezer is thoroughly confused: " ' 'T'is all shifting and confounded!' " (p. 544). And he is thoroughly disenchanted: " 'Here's naught but scoundrels and perverts, hovels and brothels, corruption and poltroonery! What glory, to be singer of such a sewer!' " (p. 483).

So Ebenezer sheds his worldly innocence. He learns what Burlingame has told him all along, that it is dangerous. It causes him to lose his father's plantation. And it destroys Joan Toast, who, attracted by his innocence, winds up a syphilis-ridden opium addict in a Maryland brothel. After such an experience, Ebenezer cannot write the grand epic, the *Marylandiad*, he had once projected. The appropriate form for America is satire. And so he writes "The Sot-Weed Factor," a bitter assault on the horrors of Maryland.

Even as he loses his innocence, however, he affirms its value. If he no longer believes that justice, beauty, and truth "live not in the world, but as transcendent entities, noumenal and pure" (p. 408), he does see value in the innocence which once allowed him so to believe, or to act as if he believed. Such innocence may have been a kind of pride. Yet, he reflects, "the very un-Naturalness, the vanity, the *hubris*, as it were, of heroism in general and martyrdom in particular were their most appealing qualities . . . there was something brave, defiantly human, about the passenger on this dust-mote who perished for some dream of Value" (p. 732). Thus, there is loss as well as gain in Ebenezer's end of innocence, and Ebenezer remains ambivalent about it: " '. . . a voice in me cries, "Down with 't, then!" while another stands in awe before the enterprise; sees in the vain construction all nobleness allowed to fallen men' " (p. 670).

Nor is Maryland any the less ambiguous. Barth may show a colonial America of lawlessness and disorder, but he also draws an America of as yet unharnessed energy.[25] It is not, of course, the ordered and pleasant land of American mythology. And it is not the ordered and gracious Paradise which Lord Baltimore paints to Ebenezer in England. It is a land, as Burlingame says, where " 'the soil is vast and new where the sot-weed hath not drained it and oft will sprout wild seeds of energy in men that had lain fallow here' " (p. 180). The seeds of energy are erotic, and the society portrayed is a lusty and uninhibited place. It is well characterized by Mary Mungummory, the Traveling Whore o' Dorset; by the long exchange of insults between two prostitutes where each epithet is a synonym for prostitute (pp. 466–472); by the seduction of Sir Harry Russecks' daughter, an incident described as if it were fabliau out of Chaucer; and by the unorthodox glimpse into American history provided by the secret journal of Captain John Smith, where a very different version of the Pocahontas episode is given.[26] In *End of the Road*, Jacob Horner wonders "what could be more charming than to believe that the whole vaudeville of the world, the entire dizzy circus of history, was but a fancy mating dance?" This Jacob calls the "Absolute Genital" (p. 75), and in *The Sot-Weed Factor* Barth sees the world in part in its terms. It is absolute because no other value is needed to supplement it. The passion it releases is reason enough for living, unlike the detached rationality of Todd.

And in Burlingame, Barth suggests even further erotic possibilities. A man of many identities, yet of no one identity, Burlingame is congenitally impotent. Yet he embraces an exuberant pansexuality which includes all living things, indeed all of nature. But Barth is no latterday D. H. Lawrence. He does not offer the Absolute Genital as the source of all value, nor does he elevate it to mystical status. The anarchic passion of America may be more innocent than the political, but it too generates its own problems. Sir Harry Russecks does, after all, die. Pirates do rape a whole shipload of women. Unbridled sexuality, in other words, can be brutal and aggressive. And passion may as often be unsanctioned as innocent, as in the incestuous bond which Ebenezer and his twin sister, Anna, finally recognize.[27] Barth has indeed written, as Leslie Fiedler has suggested, a "kind of subversive erotic tale with historic trimmings which Mark Twain tried and failed at in *1601*."[28] But he has also provided material with which to undercut the erotic as an absolute.

Burlingame, furthermore, for all his affirmation of the freedom of pansexuality,[29] finds this freedom a burden. He can accept change and uncertainty, he can live with shifting identities, and he can affirm life—but only up to a point. The freedom of having no history, he finds, " 'throws one on his own resources . . . makes every man an orphan like myself and can as well demoralize as elevate' " (p. 181). Thus he is driven to seek the truth of his birth. He finds it, and he also finds the secret of his family's virility. Freedom of identity and sexuality are lost, as Ebenezer's innocence is lost. Again, both gain and loss are implied: marriage and stable identity are now possible, but the range of possible activities is narrowed. As a comment on America, this change portrays the loss of an impossible freedom, as Ebenezer's education portrays the loss of an impossible and dangerous innocence.

And gain and loss are implied as well by the ending. The elaborate plot is tidied up, of course. But what would in Fielding have been the emergence of a new society in which new knowledge and identity replace outworn innocence and unknown identity fails to appear in *The Sot-Weed Factor*: ". . . it cannot be said that the life of any of our characters was markedly blissful; some, to be sure, were rather more serene, but others took more or less serious turns for the worse, and a few were terminated far before their time" (p. 794). The apparently happy ending is only the prelude to further loss and change. Thus form parodies a universe which at this point in the twentieth century is, to many, inconceivable. The rational, ordered, and moral world of the age of reason is now seen as an unsuccessful attempt to create order, value, and identity out of the same shifting, uncertain, and meaningless chaos that has tormented writers in the twentieth century. So the present is not measured against the past. Rather the past is assimilated to the present. And the perennial themes of American literature—the idea of innocence, the place of the artist in American society, the Indian as evil or noble savage, the wilderness as paradise or anti-paradise, the initiation into society, the problem of identity, and the international theme (here reversed; Ebenezer encounters experience in America, not Europe)—are examined against the background of an absurd universe. The result is a comic view of the American experience, but a comic view qualified by an awareness of absurdity in tragi-comedy.

IV

Barth is surely one of the most interesting American novelists to appear in the last decade. He is original and independent. So, for example, one might expect him to continue to explore the Eastern Shore of Maryland, the location of the main action of all three novels, and turn it into his own Yoknapatawpha County.[30] But Barth will fortunately do as he pleases: his next novel is to be *Giles Goat-Boy*, a "new Old Testament, a comic Old Testament."[31] Originality and independence, however, do not mean perfection. None of the novels is without flaw: *The Floating Opera* is marred by the sentimental and forced happy ending; *End of the Road* by a weakness in characterization (Joe is never much more than a spokesman for his system of conduct; Jacob seems composed of disembodied forces); and *The Sot-Weed Factor* by what Rovit sees as the perverseness of its parody and a continued thinness of character drawing.

This thinness of character (except for Todd) is to be expected. Barth is interested in dramatizing ideas in character, and his most interesting and important achievement to date is the embodiment of philosophical ideas in a form both tragic and comic. He suggests the extent to which psychological need determines ideas and beliefs, but he does not probe deeply. He achieves meaning through incident rather than depth of characterization. He considers each of the ways in which Western man has attempted to fill his life with value after the death of the old gods—love, liberal and radical politics, the quest for power (the Machiavellian politics of early Maryland), primitivism (the noble savage and the return to nature), art, and private systems—only to find all of them inadequate. What would be adequate, if anything, he does not show. And if his intention of carrying " 'all non-mystical value-thinking to the end of the road' " implies a personal belief, it is a belief which has not as yet found expression in his work. Sooner or later, however, Barth will have to answer Rovit's objections more completely: he will have to show whether his parody is a kind of artistic trap, and hence an evasion of genuine engagement; or whether it is a real critical technique which reflects Barth's own moral vision. Barth may use parody as a way of clearing his vision, but he can hardly rest in it if he is to develop at all.

Notes

1. See Walter Kaufmann, *Nietzsche: Philosopher, Psychologist, Anti-Christ* (New York, 1964). Kaufmann argues convincingly that Nietzsche's Dionysus is actually a union of the Apollonian with his earlier conception of the Dionysian. Hence the chaos of the instinctual and the orgiastic is controlled and used by reason. The superman is the man in whom these elements are most highly unified (pp. 130, 145).

2. Ihab Hassan, "The Existential Novel," *The Massachusetts Review*, III (Autumn 1961-Summer 1962), 795–797.

3. John Barth, *The Floating Opera* (New York, 1965), p. 232. All italics in subsequent quotations are Barth's.

4. Albert Camus, *The Myth of Sisyphus*, trans. Justin O'Brien (New York, 1960), p. 3.

5. Richard Schickel, "The Floating Opera," *Critique*, VI (Fall 1963), 58.

6. Stanley Edgar Hyman, "John Barth's First Novel," *The New Leader* (April 12, 1965), 21. As far as I know, Hyman was the first to suggest the theme of Joyce's *Exiles* when, in *The Tangled Bank* (New York, 1962), p. 392, he connected it with a paper by Freud on neurotic mechanisms in jealousy.

7. So Brigid Brophy, in *Mozart the Dramatist* (New York, 1964): "Reason was necessary to illuminate him [man], but it was never the enlightenment's main objective, because it could not supply the motive-power of life or even any reason for living at all. Those had to be provided by the natural instinct towards pleasure" (p. 63).

8. The sadism can be seen, for example, in the way in which he goads Mister Haecker, a seventy-nine year old retired high school principal and fellow resident of Todd's hotel, to attempted suicide.

9. Todd is in the galley of a showboat, *Adam's Original & Unparalled Floating Opera*, with the gas on when Jeannine has her seizure. The novel, of course, takes its title from the name of the showboat, which Todd explains as being symbolic of life itself, in which "our friends float past; we become involved with them; they float on, and we must rely on hearsay or lose track of them completely; they float back again, and we must either renew our friendship . . . or find that they and we don't comprehend each other any more" (pp. 13–14). But it is life as Todd sees it, not everybody—the life of the uninvolved and impartial spectator observing the human comedy.

10. Gregory Bluestone, "John Wain and John Barth: The Angry and the Accurate," *The Massachusetts Review*, I (Fall 1959–Summer 1960), 586.

11. Herbert Fingarette, *The Self in Transformation* (New York and Evanston, 1965), p. 102.

12. John Barth, *End of the Road* (New York, 1960), p. 8. All italics in subsequent quotations are Barth's.

13. Herbert F. Smith, "Barth's Endless Road," *Critique*, VI (Fall 1963), 68–76.

14. David Kerner, "Psychodrama in Eden," *Chicago Review*, XIII (Winter–Spring 1959), 60. Auther's italics.

15. Hassan, "The Existential Novel," 797. Author's italics. For an elaboration of Hassan's views in this short article, see his longer critical study, *Radical Innocence: Studies in the Contemporary American Novel* (Princeton, 1961).

16. Earl Rovit, "The Novel as Parody: John Barth," *Critique*, VI (Fall 1963), 77.

17. Alan Trachtenberg, "Barth and Hawkes: Two Fabulists," *Critique*, VI (Fall 1963), 9. It is worth noting that in a short story, "Ambrose, His Mark," *Esquire*, LIX (Feb. 1963), 97, 122–127, Barth writes a comic tale of the way in which choosing a name is also choosing an identity.

18. "John Barth: An Interview," *Wisconsin Studies in Contemporary Literature*, VI (Winter–Spring 1965), 11.

19. Stanley Edgar Hyman has made the suggestive observation that *The Sot-Weed Factor* is a rewriting of *Candide*, which is "The archetypal American novel, as writers from Cooper to Salinger have demonstrated by rewriting it" ("The American Adam," *The New Leader*, [March 2, 1964], 21).

20. As R. W. B. Lewis has argued in *The Picaresque Saint* (Philadelphia and New York, 1959). Robert Alter, in *Rogue's Progress* (Cambridge, Massachusetts, 1964), thinks that Lewis has stretched his definition of a picaresque hero a bit too far, so that the "picaroon has unexpectedly become a kind of ne'er-do-well Christ" (p. 12). The picaresque hero, he says, must always remain to some extent a rogue. On this view, Ebenezer Cooke in *The Sot-Weed Factor* is not really a picaresque hero, nor is the novel, strictly speaking, picaresque. It merely has elements of the picaresque. Ebenezer himself is not a rogue except inadvertently. Like Don Quixote, Ebenezer is not a rogue rejected by society, but a man who himself rejects society as it exists and, says Alter of Don Quixote, "brings himself to see the world as it is not" (p. 109). It is of interest in connection with the contemporary use of the picaresque form and hero that Alter finds that the picaresque novel flourishes only in periods of social disintegration. Such disintegration, of course, is the testimony of many twentieth-century novels. The picaresque hero, already an outsider, is easily transformed into the alienated existential hero who seeks the grounds of new meaning and value, or who encounters the pain of the loss of old values. This is the characteristic hero of the so-called New American novel, an anti-hero in a picaresque comedy.

21. It is not of great importance in the novel, but it is interesting to note that Ebenezer Cooke was a real person, about whom nothing is known but who published "The Sot-Weed Factor" in 1708. His complete works are available in a volume called *Early Maryland Poetry* (Baltimore: Maryland Historical Society, 1900), which includes "The Sot-Weed Factor," "Sotweed Redivivus, or the Planter's Looking-Glass," and "An Elegy on the Death of the Honourable Nicholas Lowe, Esq:." A fourth poem in the volume, "Muscipula," is by Edward Holdsworth. The title page to "The Sot-Weed Factor" shows the author as "Eben. Cook, Gent."; that to "Sotweed Redivivus" shows him as "E. C. Gent." and the elegy is signed by "E. Cooke. Laureat.," though, as the author of the introduction observes, laureate of what? The author of "The Sot-Weed Factor" is thought to have been an Englishman who did not like America and so wrote a satirical attack on it—thereby becoming an ancestor of such nineteenth-century travelers in America as Mrs. Frances Trollope, Captain Basil Hall, and Charles Dickens. It is suggested in the introduction that the other two poems were written by a different man, one Ebenezer Cooke who lived in St. Mary's City in 1693. Barth, however, has used one man as author of all these poems and has chosen to spell his name "Cooke" rather than "Cook." A sot-weed factor is a tobacco salesman.

22. R. W. B. Lewis, *The American Adam* (Chicago, 1955), p. 1.

23. John Barth, *The Sot-Weed Factor* (New York, 1964), p. 21. All italics in subsequent quotations are Barth's.

24. Howard Mumford Jones, *O Strange New World* (New York, 1964), p. 114–161.

25. As Jones observes in *O Strange New World*, both of these images of America— as a Paradise and Utopia, on the one hand, and an anti-Paradise, on the other—were present in the European mind from the time of the discovery of the New World (pp. 1–70).

26. Here, of course, Barth burlesques the writing of American history and suggests that much of it may be more fancy than fact and that the facts would be subversive of many orthodoxies.

27. It is implied, in fact, that Ebenezer's sexual innocence may be a defense against an unconscious recognition in this incestuous wish. His ideal is as irrational in origin as are the events in the world around him. The pure being that Ebenezer seeks, that state above death and time with which he concludes his hymm to innocence, may well be the paradaisal and timeless world of his and Anna's childhood. In Burlingame's vision of Ebenezer's and Anna's union as a symbol of "the Whole—the tenon in the mortise, the jointure of polarities, the seamless universe . . ." (p. 526), with himself as a kind of cosmic observer of this totality, the triangular theme of the first two novels reaches its climax. But the unity is never attained. Eros remains fragmented. Had *Love and Death in the American Novel* not appeared in 1960, one might suspect an elaborate spoof of Fiedler in Barth's use of this situation. Yet it seems basic to his view of human relations, and will undoubtedly be worked out in future novels.

28. Leslie A. Fiedler, "John Barth: an Eccentric Genius," *The New Leader*, 44 (February 13, 1961), 23. A more recent example of this contrast of present day sexuality to that of a previous period is to be found in Anthony Burgess's fictional account of Shakespeare in *Nothing Like the Sun*, where the uninhibited eroticism of the Elizabethans is contrasted to the brutalized and sadistic sexuality of *A Clockwork Orange*, a fantasy on the near future of England.

29. " '. . . . I am Suitor of Totality, Embracer of Contradictories, Husband to all Creation, the Cosmic Lover!' " (p. 526).

30. Barth has done a brief imaginative sketch of Maryland's Eastern Shore and one of its aging inhabitants in "Landscape: The Eastern Shore," *Kenyon Review*, 22 (1960), 104–110.

31. "John Barth: An Interview," 8.

The Anti-Novels of John Barth

Beverly Gross*

*"To find a form that accomodates
the mess, that is the task of the
artist now."*
SAMUEL BECKETT

It is near impossible to re-read John Barth. I say this as an admirer of his works, and as an ardent re-reader of them; yet the fact remains that a renewed experience of Barth's novel is a new kind of exasperation. One re-reads *Paradise Lost* or *War and Peace*, even *The Castle*, and one becomes further enlightened. Re-read *The Sot-Weed Factor* and you're still befuddled. It's not that Barth's works are so profoundly difficult or dense—in fact, they are not—it's just that one would hope to get a more vivid impression of John Barth paring his fingernails behind it all, and all one gets is the same kind of slippery ooze that confronts the hero at the end of *Giles Goat-Boy*. The slippery ooze, remember, is the last trace of the vanishing Harold Bray, professed Grand Tutor and champion imposter. In fact, if there is a single character who seems most to capture the spirit of the author in Barth's works it is probably this same Harold Bray: omniscient, omnipresent, a man of many masks but no face, a false prophet, perhaps a true genius. But who is to know?

Certain things do become clear on a re-reading, but they have more to do with the corpus of Barth's works rather than with the novels taken individually. It is striking, for instance, to see how much Barth's fiction has been moving toward the fulfillment of an idea—the idea being the repudiation of narrative art. Barth's most recent works, a group of short stories, take on in their form the very paralysis which in one way or another is the central subject of the novels. That is the paradox of Barth's novels: they are about paralysis, they seem even to affirm paralysis, yet they have more narrative energy than they know what to do with. (In this respect, Barth's novels are the very obverse of Saul Bellow's whose heroes, for all their individualism and psychic exuberance, don't do very much, and end up as laconic and passive accepters of a world they know to be silly and dull. Barth's heroes, for all their scepticism and paralysis of will,

*"The Anti-Novels of John Barth" first appeared in the *Chicago Review*, copyright 1968, xx, 3.

are kept a lot busier in the complex network of Barthian plot strands, and a good deal more involved in their frantic entanglements with other people. Bellow's heroes seem to have been created for Barthian plots; while Barth's heroes would be more comfortable left dangling. It is a great temptation to say that Jacob Horner should have been the writer of Herzog's letters, and that Henderson should have been the one to take Ebenezer Cooke's journey to the New World.)

Barth has written four novels. Each is generally longer, wilder, more ambitious, more outrageous than its predecessor, and at the core of each is a greater nihilism. That growing nihilism is also something of a paradox since the heroes of the first two novels—Todd Andrews in *The Floating Opera* and Jacob Horner in *End of the Road*—would seem to have reached the limits of despair. Todd Andrews spends the entire novel contemplating and almost accomplishing his suicide; Jacob Horner is suffering from what his doctor describes as immobility. In contrast, the heroes of the last two novels—Ebenezer Cooke in *The Sot-Weed Factor* and George Giles in *Giles Goat-Boy*—are bumpkins. Naive, optimistic, ingenuous: impossible vehicles for despair, one would think, except that that is what they become. Nihilism is merely a quirk of character in *The Floating Opera* and *End of the Road;* it is not much more than a setting for comedy, a device for irony. But nihilism is what *The Sot-Weed Factor* and *Giles Goat-Boy* come to. It is the moral, meaning, and upshot of experience in these novels, and it is embedded in their very form. *The Sot-Weed Factor*, disguised as an eighteenth-century novel, is really a radical definition of the novel of the twentieth century. *Giles Goat-Boy*, disguised as cosmic allegory, keeps undercutting its own allegorical premises by denying the possibility of meaning, identity, and answers in a world in which these things are always shifting, masked, and unattainable. The deeper nihilism of Barth's last two novels comes from their proclaiming not so much the impossibility of life but the impossibility of narrative.

All this talk about nihilism suggests the greatest paradox of all. Barth is most immediately a humorist. For a novelist like Bellow, the comedy of life is a reflection of the emotional and moral depth of life. The comedy in Barth's novels is the mockery of emotions and moral values: what his characters feel and perceive is only further grist for hilarity. The suicide issue of *The Floating Opera* is an existential put-on; all issues in Barth's novels come down to some sort of game. And so does the emotional life of his characters. They love as they suffer: it is something they check in and out of. Love is simply a comic absurdity, another game. In fact it is the same game in all four novels: a peculiar adulterous relationship in which the husband urges his wife's infidelity with the hero. Harrison Mack has apparently thought up the idea of pleasing his best friend by offering Todd his wife. Joe Morgan learns that his wife Rennie and Jacob Horner had impulsively slept together one night, and then demands that they keep it up so that he and Rennie can study what is wrong with their marriage. John McAvoy, pimp and lover to Joan Toast, threatens the life of Ebenezer Cooke for having refused to surrender his virginity to the whore. And Maurice Stoker, who achieves his highest sexual gratification in arranging various arcane couplings for his wife, is delighted to present her to the goat-boy. In another writer this affection for the *ménage à trois* could be regarded as quite a hang-up. In Barth it is a kind of touchstone. The ordinary moral and psychological implications don't count here at all. What immediately counts is, on the level of plot, the entanglements; on the level of meaning, the nuttiness. But what also counts, beyond immediate laughter, is a lingering sorrow, an underlying disgust, and a metaphor for the impossible strain of human attachment and commitment.

Another way of putting this: although the potentially weighty inevitability gives way to the comic put-on, the comic put-on is itself the source of meaning. Barth works incongruity from two directions. Take *End of the Road*. The novel, Barth's most blackly humorous, turns a good deal of ugly fact into comedy. Jacob Horner is a desperately sick man; the comic incongruity comes from his general cheeriness about his own emotional, moral, and spiritual vacuity. Todd Andrews' thinking in *The Floating Opera* makes us see suicide his way: as a justified, thoroughly rational gesture. Similarly, Jacob's way of looking at things inspires the reaction that his immobility is what life deserves. The three other characters who most matter in *End of the Road* are Joe and Rennie Morgan and the Doctor, an old negro quack who runs a traveling mental home called the Remobilization Farm. The Doctor finds Jacob in a Baltimore railroad station where Jacob has been sitting paralyzed all night. These blank spells are frequent with Jacob; his problem, the Doctor tells him, is his lack of identity. "In a sense I am Jacob Horner" is the narrator's introduction of himself in the novel's first sentence. Jacob cannot believe that he really exists. He willingly submits to the Doctor's proposal of providing him with an artificial existence through "mythotherapy." Jacob is told to immerse himself in rules, statistics, facts, to read the *World Almanac* at empty moments, to take a job teaching prescriptive grammar. He will be all right as long as he avoids problems, decision-making, close relations. The Morgans enter his life and the complications begin.

Fine black comedy. *End of the Road* seems at first to be much like the other comic monuments of the decade. It has the right ingredients: a psychotic therapist, an identity crisis, a wild *ménage à trois*, ironic views of our crippled society and trivial culture—a groovy corroboration for the disaffected. But something happens to this novel: its ending is appalling. *End of the Road* repudiates itself, or rather it repudiates what would seem to be its glib ability to deal with, and therefore dismiss, ugliness, pain, and despair. Rennie's pregnancy is initially part of the incongruous comedy: the problem is that she doesn't know whose baby she is carrying (the same problem confronts Janet Mack in *The Floating Opera,* but it doesn't bother her for long). Rennie decides to have an abortion. More madcap exasperation for Jacob who has to hunt down an abortionist. But Rennie's butchering on the operating table is the shattering fact of *End of the Road.* The ugliness is sudden, undisguised, unironic. The emotional crisis preceding it (whom does Rennie really love: Jacob or Joe? who really exists: the self-possessed Joe or the characterless, contradictory Jacob?) was only the game. Rennie's hemorrhaging corpse cannot be transformed into comedy, nor does Barth try. That is the second stage of undercutting: having reduced everything to comedy, the book suddenly reduces its comedy to loathesomeness. Jacob's charming inability to take anything seriously becomes hideous when, at the end of the novel, he retreats from the responsibility he claims he wants. He leaves for the Remobilization Farm, presumably to continue his therapy, to try out other roles.

Roles are the motif of all Barth's novels. Todd Andrews' life is a succession of identities—rake, saint, cynic—the search for a character appropriate to his ailing heart. Henry Burlingame reappears in different guises throughout *The Sot-Weed Factor:* he is engaged in a complicated political plot and, significantly, searching for some clue to his parentage, i.e., his identity quite literally. George the Goat-Boy, wavering between goat and boy, seeking the proper stance in which to assert his Grand Tutorship, keeps changing his advice to the people around him with each new modification of what he takes to be his gospel. But most of all it is John Barth who emerges as the seeker of self. He is an author in search of a disposition. The novels are not only about roles—they *are* roles. Barth's novels are comic masks for a tragic face. Barth is an inveterate comedian because he depends on the masks, and not only to hide his face but to discover it, and not only his face, but ours.

That doubtlessly is what makes Barth at once so interesting and so irritating. The comedy which seems to be everything is really nothing: it exists to announce its own inadequacy. Barth's last novel, his most infuriating, makes the strongest declaration of that inadequacy. *Giles Goat-Boy* is Barth's best novel and his worst—a paradox which somehow accords with the tentative theme of the book: that passage and failure are really the same thing.

Giles Goat-Boy is almost impossible to describe, summarize, or account for. Above all, it presents a problem of understanding that is its most unsettling feature. The problem of understanding *Giles Goat-Boy* is the problem of understanding Barth, and more precisely, the extent of Barth's seriousness. In this book Barth wears not one mask but several. Philosophically, the book keeps undermining itself and shatters its own testamentary message in a series of editorial comments at the beginning and postscripts at the end. *Giles Goat-Boy* is a peculiar blending of frivolity and profundity. It often seems to be simultaneously both (a duality we have come to expect from Barth); but at various times one aspect so dominates the other that the reader is made to feel twinges of guilt for having treated as fun so penetrating an exposure of the status of twentieth-century life; at other times he is likely to feel embarrassed for having been so stodgily receiving a book which continually explodes into aimless hilarity. Surprise is one thing, but frustration is another, and *Giles Goat-Boy* is less surprising than it is frustrating. There is something profoundly wrong with *Giles Goat-Boy* and the best explanation I can offer is that the book plays its duality too hard and finally works against itself. This seven hundred page novel is perhaps the world's shaggiest dog story: it comes out meaning nothing at all. Nowadays we don't mind that very much in our art when so much of it is set up to proclaim inanity. The disturbing and perhaps defeating thing about this novel is that it is set up to mean something. The novel leads us to expect a revelation, and at the end there is only a wisecrack.

On the narrative level, *Giles Goat-Boy* is also exasperating. It is enormous, unwieldy, often tedious. It has all the attributes of *Tom Jones* except for a successful form. George Giles is a kind of picaresque hero out to meet his fate. He is also, among other things, an Oedipal figure and a Christ. The grandiose resemblances are hardly there for the sake of symbolic depth; they are part of the enormous welter of lampoonery which is what this novel is. The universe is allegorically transfigured into the University, and George as savior is to be the Grand Tutor to all studentkind. He is to lead them away from the path of flunkage to help them pass and eventually graduate. Besides this quasi-religious allegory there is also a political allegory on twentieth-century global history. The University is divided into many opposing campuses. There have already been two inter-campus riots in recent years, and now West Campus is engaged in a Quite Riot, a life and death struggle with East Campus (Nicholai College) for university control. On another level the book is also a *bildungsroman*. We first meet George as a boy, known then as Billy Bocksfuss. He has been raised as a goat. It is only when he develops self-awareness in his early teens that he begins to question his state; he decides that he is neither human nor goatish and settles on considering himself a goat-boy. The early part of the book shows us Billy suppressing the goat in himself, becoming the boy, renaming himself George, and learning about the great University which lies beyond the goat-farm. But this is only the prelude to George's real struggle. George goes off to the campus to proclaim himself as Grand Tutor and to deliver his message to studentdom. To do this he must conquer the gigantic computer which runs things. The relationship between goat-boy and machine is somewhat complicated by George's premise that he is the son of WESCAC (an acronym for Western Campus Computer) and that therefore he is the GILES (an acronym for near-perfect eugenical specimen which had been stored in WESCAC and one day, almost twenty years earlier, implanted in the womb of a young librarian). Three times George goes into the computer's belly in order to get himself certified. With the first two failures George has to re-think his credo and establish a new set of directives to pass on to his followers. In the course of all this he makes quite a mess of people's lives. And what lives they are. The Stokers, the Sears, Peter Greene, Dr. Eierkopf, Leonid Andreich, Chancellor Rexford, Ira Hector—they exist to be further messed up by their Grand Tutor. Barth's characters have become increasingly eccentric with each new novel. In *Giles Goat-Boy* they are not much more than emblems for their hang-ups.

These are just the barest bones of a plot whose ins and outs are near-impossible to recount. Even *Tom Jones* has fewer complications, digressions, surprises, sub-plots, and reversals. And yet *Giles Goat-Boy* follows a fairly simple, dialetical development: George imparts advice to his tutees according to whatever notion he may be holding about Passage. After an unsuccessful foray in WESCAC's belly George meets his people again to see the disastrous results of his advice. He then discovers some antithetical principle, and advises them to rearrange their lives according to this new idea. Then back to WESCAC's belly, another defeat, and a new confrontation with studentdom. And so it goes. It is only by wrecking the works of WESCAC that George gets the certification he requires. And then he discovers he has no message.

Giles Goat-Boy is thus a dialetic without a synthesis, which explains why, on a certain level, the book is so unsatisfying. The dialetical structure makes for a remarkable tediousness and mechanical predictability; the lack of a synthesis makes for frustration. A horrible hoax is what several critics have called *Giles Goat-Boy*, and a horrible hoax is what it is—the book exists to confute expectations. That is its greatest irritation as well as its chief delight, the source of both its meaning and its meaninglessness.

Why there is no synthesis in *Giles Goat-Boy* is because in this book where everyone is looking for the right Answers to insure Passage, the only point is that there are no Answers. If Barth's novels have a message it is that. Each successive novel is an elaboration on that theme. *The Floating Opera* is propelled by Todd's certainty that absolutes do not exist. So there is no reason for living. What keeps him alive after he has bungled his suicide is his sudden realization that there is no reason for dying either. Jacob Horner operates from the same premise. But Jacob's relativism is so extreme that it is paralyzing. There is no reason for anything—even motion. Although Jacob and Todd undergo reversals at the end, it is not their nihilism that is repudiated but their terms of dealing with that nihilism. Todd discovers a justification for living, if not precisely a justification for life. He decides not to kill himself for the same reason that he had earlier decided he would: in both cases he is struck by the realization that there is no answer to the question "Why bother?" *End of the Road* sets up the rivalry, amounting to a dialetical opposition, between Jacob Horner's quiescence and Joe Morgan's energetic positivism; the ending shows them equally responsible for the horror of Rennie's death, and thus equally incapable of dealing with life. Jacob's blank indifference had been vastly amusing through the book. At the end it is tragic. The point, however, is that neither novel has anything positive to propose, and that despite the reversals at the end, neither Jacob nor Todd is really repudiated. Their nihilistic premises abide.

They abide but they answer nothing. Even in the last two novels where the nihilism is something arrived at it is hardly an answer. Nihilism disqualifies the very possibility of believing in answers, even the answer of nihilism itself. Nevertheless there is something upheld and sanctified in *Giles Goat-Boy* and *The Sot-Weed Factor*: the sheer fact and value of experience. Despite the unreality of these books they are both deeply immersed in life, that is, in life as process. It does not matter that the progress of both novels is a movement toward the very same position with which Todd and Jacob begin. The fact remains that experience has fruition for Ebenezer and George. And, further, that the nihilism which had been merely material in Barth's first two novels becomes, in his last two novels, formal.

Nihilistic form—a contradiction in terms, no doubt, but Barth seems to elicit such things. What is nihilistic about the form of *The Sot-Weed Factor* and *Giles Goat-Boy* is that each book becomes an anti-novelistic assault on itself. The books are not anti-novels in the usual sense. The prefix *anti* has two distinct meanings: it can designate either counter-action (as in "anti-matter" or "antithesis") or hostility (as in "anti-biotic" or "anti-aircraft"). The *anti* in "anti-novel" usually conveys the idea of counter-action: such novels are experimental alternatives to what the novel form has conventionally come to mean; the anti-novel widens the expressive possibility of a genre that has been called dead or dying for the last fifty years. Barth's novels may be doing that, but I would like to suggest that with regard to Barth the *anti* could also carry the second meaning of hostility. *The Sot-Weed Factor* and *Giles Goat-Boy* are not just experiments—they are attacks. Attacks on themselves. Attacks on the novel genre. Attacks on the narrative impulse. And attacks on the author who perpetrated them. At the end of these novels one sees that their madly complicated structures have led nowhere; one suspects that the point of each book was to expose the fraudulence of narrative art and one wonders how Barth was able to write them at all. The books contain frequent pronouncements from the narrator against the very enterprise he is engaged in. Concomitant with the ethical nihilism which is thematic to the novels is this aesthetic nihilism in Barth's own voice.

The Sot-Weed Factor presumably came out of Barth's delight in the eighteenth-century novel. In a prefatory essay which he wrote for a new edition of Smollett's *Roderick Random*[1] Barth declared the eighteenth-century novel a refreshing relief from contemporary anti-novels about anti-heroes. *The Sot-Weed Factor*, which appeared shortly after this essay, is modeled upon the eighteenth-century novel, and yet it cannot escape its twentieth-century bearings: it too is an anti-novel about an anti-hero. *The Sot-Weed Factor* is an eighteenth-century novel only in substance; in essence it is an expression of the twentieth-century vision of John Barth. What emerges out of the convoluted action is profoundly at odds with the rationalistic convictions of the Age of Enlightenment. The book is generated by the spirit of dubiety. Henry Burlingame, Ebenezer's tutor, keeps reappearing in Ebenezer's life, most often so well disguised that Ebenezer fails to recognize him. Eben finds that he cannot grapple with the ins and outs of Henry's deviousness. Is he Eben's friend or enemy? Whose side is he on? Is he loyal to Lord Baltimore or John Coode? Is he the protector or violator of Eben's sister Anna? Is it Anna or Eben himself whom Henry loves? The reversals are so sudden and multitudinous that they produce the first real scepticism in Barth's ingenuous hero; the discovery of dubiety constitutes the real education of Ebenezer Cooke.

The second theme is futility. The plot structure of *The Sot-Weed Factor* is merely a succession of problems, obstacles, mysteries, and disasters which are never quite surmounted or cleared up, only cleared away and only through accident or fortuitous coincidence. Enterprise inevitably makes matters worse and compounds Ebenezer's miseries. And although things appear to terminate in a happy ending, that too is another hoax. At the end of the novel Ebenezer, like Tom Jones, is provided with the very things he had been striving for: marriage to the object of his love, an estate in life, the approbation of his elders, and a hard-won maturity. Yet for Ebenezer nothing is really solved. It is not a Sophia whom he wins, but Joan Toast, former whore, pock-marked with syphilitic scars, hopelessly addicted to opium. Ebenezer "earns" Malden through a legal loophole seized upon by the same colonial kangaroo court which had deprived him of his estates several hundred pages before. And his elders, Andrew Cooke and Henry Burlingame, as well as the neighboring folk of Cooke's Point, esteem him only because he is finally able to contend with their treacheries. Tom Jones reaches his manhood by acquiring prudence and discretion. Eben's manhood comes with the loss of his virginity—a deflowering which is both physical and moral and which amounts to the discovery of the emptiness of his ideals. Ebenezer's experience in *The Sot-Weed Factor* brings him to the same knowledge with which Todd Andrews and Jacob Horner begin: the nihilistic conviction that there are no ends in life, that activity is baffling, frustrating, and self-defeating, and that the fruit of experience is simply the wisdom that sanctifies inanition. There is neither victory nor resolution in any of this, only a precarious equilibrium and a defeat which, if one is to remain sane, had better be accepted as success.

Part IV of *The Sot-Weed Factor* is a kind of epilogue in which the author details the subsequent doings and demises of his characters.

Barth's novel concludes, as no eighteenth-century novel could, with the continuing compounding of disasters. In this afterword, we are casually told how the characters did after all finally meet the hideous fates they had managed to avoid until now. The Russecks ladies, twice saved from pirates earlier in the book, take a sea voyage from Piraeus to Cadiz "and were never heard from again." Similarly Eben and Anna, who had more or less successfully managed to repress their incestuous desires, decide to leave America because of the general suspicion there that Ebenezer has fathered Anna's child. The final irony comes many years later when Ebenezer is officially commissioned poet laureate of Maryland, not for his laudatory *Marylandiad*, which he had never completed, but for his defaming Sot-Weed Factort, a bitter exposé of the horrors of life in the New World. The epilogue epitomizes the real nature of *The Sot-Weed Factor*: the tenuous resolution which had been previously established, is shattered, just as life inevitably manages to shatter all tenuous resolutions—a fact which novelists don't like making much a point of since it would tend to put them out of business. John Barth, on the other hand, is a novelist who gives the impression of longing to be put out of business.

Dubiety, futility, and finally, self-mockery. *The Sot-Weed Factor* stands as a parody of narrative art with all its assumptions, traditions, prerogatives, and ends. That is its ultimate anti-novelism. The book is a put-on of the very thing it seems most to be cherishing: the narrative impulse itself. Barth has always shown an overwhelming self-consciousness about that impulse. *The Floating Opera*, narrated by Todd Andrews, is filled with asides about the trickeries, contortions, and even distortions involved in getting a story told: "Good heavens! How does one write a novel? I mean, how can anyone possibly stick to the story, if he's at all sensitive to the significance of things?" In one form or another that self-consciousness is always there; in the last two novels it takes the particular shape of self-mockery. The concluding section of *The Sot-Weed Factor* is entitled "The Author Apologizes to his Readers," and in it Barth does indeed apologize for playing fast and loose with history, reality, and narrative form.

The self-consciousness of a writer like Henry James is directed toward the exquisiteness of his craft; Barth's self-consciousness is more akin to embarrassment. It is as though Barth wonders how he or anyone could take seriously the novelist's professed aim of giving shape to life. Once the fraudulence of narrative art is assumed, exquisite craftsmanship would only compound the felony. Thus the air of defensiveness in Todd's telling of *The Floating Opera*. And thus the preposterousness of *The Sot-Weed Factor* and *Giles Goat-Boy*. Preposterousness is Barth's solution to his dilemma as a writer: it enables him to avoid dishonesty. Barth's last two novels make no claims to be transfigurations of experience; one is an excursion into history, the other into allegory. Barth thereby frees himself from any obligations not only to probability but to possibility. "If you are an artist of a certain type of temperament," Barth has said in an interview, "then what you really want to do is re-invent the world. God wasn't too bad a novelist, except he was a realist."[2] A re-invented world requires a re-invented novel to accommodate it. And vice versa. It is interesting that Barth chose precisely the milieu of Defoe, Richardson, and Fielding as the setting for his novel which re-invented the genre that they had invented in the eighteenth-century—as though by matching their setting Barth could join them at the starting line. The world of *Giles Goat-Boy* is even more of an invention, Barth no longer competing with the creators of the novel but with the Creator of the world.

Giles Goat-Boy is framed at the beginning and the end with elaborate apologies from not only the author but supposedly the publisher and his editors. Under the heading of "Publisher's Disclaimer" is the novel's opening sentence: "The reader must begin this book with an act of faith and end it with an act of charity." There follows the reports of four editors, all of whom have been somewhat deranged from the experience of reading the manuscript. None of them really claims to like the book; one had resigned his position, another had gone berserk. "The broodings of an ineffectual megalomane" is one editor's evaluation, "a crank at best, very possibly a psychopath." The report of the single editor who voted to publish it declares *Giles Goat-Boy* to be "artistically uneven" and "offensive," and continues with this statement about the writing career of John Barth:

> I found his early work lively but a bit naïve and his last novel wild and excessive in every respect. I frankly don't know quite *what* to make of this one. Where other writers seek fidelity to the facts of modern experience and expose to us the emptiness of our lives, he declares it his aim purely to *astonish*; where others strive for truth, he admits his affinity for lies, the more enormous the better.

The editor concludes with a vision of the author's future:

> He himself declares that nothing gets better, everything gets worse: he will merely grow older and crankier, more quirksome and less clever; his small renown will pass, his vitality become more doggedness. . . . I see him at last alone, unhealthy, embittered, desperately unpleasant, perhaps masturbative, perhaps alcoholic or insane, if not a suicide. We all know the pattern.

Barth uses the mask of Editor C for this perverse anticipation of some of the less complimentary reviews of *Giles Goat-Boy*. There is an odd combination here of tongue-in-cheek and heart-on-sleeve: the exaggeration at the end just barely manages to gloss over the self-mockery, self-doubt, and self-accusation at the beginning. The criticisms are highly amusing and at the same time defensive, ironic and at the same time convincing. This prefatory matter to *Giles Goat-Boy* epitomizes the rhetorical amorphousness of Barth's novels—the troubling sense he gives of not being altogether there. It is Barth's most elaborate masquerade. The elusive author hiding behind these editorial masks has his counterpart in the masked and elusive Harold Bray whom we meet in this novel, and in the disguised and elusive Henry Burlingame whom we met in the last. Bray disappears, leaving behind only the noxious green matter of his lovemaking. Burlingame disappears with the Indians, it being significant that he is the only character in *The Sot-Weed Factor* for whom there is no final fate in the epilogue. But theirs are nothing compared to the disappearances of the author whose tonal ambiguities, ironies, and downright trickiness are so compounded that we can never be sure, and he need never be sure, of where he is and what he is up to.

Before the novel proper begins, we encounter a foreword from the author himself. Barth is in his best disguise here—the mask he is wearing is of his own face. Crippled with writer's block, he frets about his inability to get going on his current novel and laments over the shortcomings of his last one. He then tells about the delivery to him of the manuscript of *Giles Goat-Boy*, of which he claims to be only the editor, the real author being either the goat-boy or the computer which sired him. This elaborate prefatory matter challenging the authorship and quality of *Giles Goat-Boy* as well as the worth of anything that Barth has written is a fanciful disclaimer but a symbolic one as well. On a certain level Barth means what he says. At the end of the book there are two additional disclaimers. In Barth's own Postscript he challenges the authenticity of the epilogue-like Posttape in which the goat-boy gloomily attests to the futility of his tutorship. Barth uses certain textual arguments including the difference in type of "those flunked pages" to support his belief that such bitter nihilism could not possibly be the final testament of the Giles. But at the very bottom of the last page is an editorial footnote which merely states that the type of Barth's Postscript is not the same as the type in his cover-letter—an argument which mitigates against Barth's argument that the Posttape was apocryphal, but which also slyly challenges the reality and existence of John Barth himself.

Symbolically that is what all the editorial matter of *Giles Goat-Boy* is about. John Barth does not exist.[3] The nihilistic tendencies of contemporary thought which have in one direction led to existentialism, have led Barth to non-existence; non-existence in the sense that these novels are written by an author without a face, a stance, an identity, a commitment. His books abound with metaphors for that facelessness. The plight of Jacob Horner, his lack of a specific identity, is one such metaphor. The logical culmination to Barth's fixation is the claim that his latest novel may have been written by a computer.

Barth does not exist because he is merely a welter of contradictions: a moral amoralist, a comic tragedian, an absolute relativist, a nihilistic enthusiast. He writes books whose implications have become more and more gloomy as their shape and quality have become more and more exuberant. And as his books have increasingly taken on the aspect of moral fables, their meaning has become increasingly indecipherable. All that remains clear is their basic nihilism.

> Nothing "works," in the sense we commonly hope for; a certain goat-boy has taught me that; everything only gets worse; our victories are never more than moral, and always pyrrhic; in fact we know only more or less ruinous defeats.

This sentence from the cover-letter of *Giles Goat-Boy* could be pretty fairly appended to the other novels as well. The irony of course is that, convinced of such meaningless, Barth goes on giving joyful expressions to it, and, convinced of the fraudulence of his art, Barth goes on producing 800 page novels.

That irony is the subject of "Title,"[4] a recent short story by Barth. Only minimally a story, "Title" uses the framework of a sporadic dialogue between a man and woman to deploy the impasse of relationships, and simultaneously, the impasse of communicating that impasse. The problem of living and loving in a world which is sick of itself is surpassed only by the problem of writing about it. "I'm as sick of this as you are. There's nothing to say. Say nothing."

"Title" is a cross between an aesthetic treatise and self-therapy. It is about three things: the death of narrative, what it is like to be John Barth, and what it is like to be John Barth convinced of the death of narrative. Although the narrator keeps insisting that he is only the narrator and not really Barth himself, such insistence on the mask actually strengthens the reader's sense that the real John Barth has finally stepped forward and is presenting himself more or less straight: a writer sick of his own cleverness, bored with his own self-consciousness, and desperate. "Can't stand any more of this" is the note which is sounded in every paragraph. For the reader of Barth's novels "Title" offers revelations of the unfathomable person behind them: revelations of temperament ("God, but I am surfeited with clever irony") and method ("We must make something out of nothing. . . . Not only turn contradiction into paradox, but *employ* it").

But it offers something more: the faintest key to the essential paradox about John Barth. There are three possibilities, the narrator asserts without much conviction, for rescuing fiction from the listlessness of life. But he quickly dismisses these possibilities and proposes a fourth possibility instead: "Silence. General anesthesia. Self-extinction. Silence." That would seem to be the concluding note of the novels as well. Those novels, which are so noisy, so exuberant, so immersed in the busyness of the human scene, and which ultimately come down to expressions of weariness, defeat, and disgust—what on earth propels those novels? And what on earth propels John Barth to write them?

The dialogue of "Title" is a nagging harrangue in which the second voice—the woman's—is also the voice of the demanding reader as well as the voice of the unappeasable creative self. "Why do I go on with this?" the narrator keeps asking, and in the story's most desperate moment, he finally pieces together an answer:

> The fact is, you're driving me to it, the fact is that people still lead lives, mean and bleak and brief as they are, briefer than you think, and people have characters and motives that we divine more or less inaccurately from their appearance, speech, behavior, and the rest, you aren't listening, go on then, what do you think I'm doing, people still fall in love, and out, yes, in and out, and out and in, and they please each other, and hurt each other, isn't that the truth, and they do these things in more or less conventionally dramatic fashion, unfashionable or not, go on, I'm going, and what goes on between them is still not only the most interesting but the most important thing in the bloody murderous world, pardon the adjectives.

Convinced of the failure of words, convinced of the failure of feeling, convinced of the failure of both actions (in life) and of action (in fiction), Barth is also convinced of the failure of failure—the blankness of being blank, the stupidity of being stupefied. He is not quite affirming life but he is negating lifelessness. He is not quite affirming art but he is negating silence.

The story does not quite manage to end. But it does have a conclusion of sorts:

> Oh God comma I abhor self-consciousness. I despise what we have come to; I loathe our loathesome loathing, our place our time our situation, our loathesome art, this ditto necessary story.

The key word is *necessary*.

Notes

1. Tobias Smollett, *Roderick Random*, New York: Signet Books, 1958.
2. John J. Enck, "John Barth: An Interview," *WSCL*, VI, 3–14.
3. Amusingly, Barth once said the same thing of Susan Sontag.
4. In *Yale Review*, LVII (Winter 1968), 213–21.

John Barth and the Aesthetics
of Artifice

Campbell Tatham*

In 1948, Ortega y Gasset solemnly predicted the coming death of the novel: "if it is not yet irretrievably exhausted, [it] has certainly entered its last phase."[1] Yet in spite of such an authoritative announcement, we have been offered, since 1948, the contributions of Bellow, Malamud, Pynchon, Nabokov, Hawkes, Heller, Vonnegut, and John Barth. The "last phase" of the novel has somehow endured for twenty years, and there seems to be no indication of an approaching demise.

Yet this is not to say that today's literary scene is characterized by a sense of complacency; at least one writer—Barth—is extremely busy challenging traditional concepts of the novel, of the relationship between the artist, the artifact, and (in this case) the reader. In fact, Barth perceives the possibility that literature may be somehow exhausted, but simultaneously insists on the renewed vigor of a "literature of exhaustion."[2] He sees hope for the novelist imbued with a sense of ultimacy: "His artistic victory, if you like, is that he confronts an intellectual dead end and employs it against itself to accomplish new human work."[3] To appreciate the possibilities of such a victory we must attempt a clarification of Barth's basic aesthetic and distinguish it from that of the majority of his contemporaries—whose assumptions and concerns are worth a brief, initial overview.

W.H. Auden has remarked that "in the case of any really serious social evil, it is conceit and absolute folly for poets to imagine that by writing poems about it they are going to change things."[4] Such may or may not be true in the case of poetry; certainly, it is fair to say that most novelists would find it impossible to accept such a claim with respect to their own craft. Today, writers are impressively concerned—with American culture, with the threat of engulfing technology, with universal suffering, with the conditions of meaningful existence in an apparently alien universe. Behind vast numbers of contemporary novels lies the feeling Kurt Vonnegut captures in this conversation from *Mother Night:*

*Reprinted by permission of *Contemporary Literature* XII (Winter 1971), 60–73.

> "You no longer believe that love is the only thing to live for?" she said.
> "No," I said.
> "Then tell me what to live for—anything at all," she said beseechingly. "It
> doesn't have to be love. Anything at all!" She gestured at objects around the
> shabby room, dramatizing exquisitely my own sense of the world's being a junk
> shop. "I'll live for that chair, that picture, that furnace pipe, that couch, that
> crack in the wall! Tell me to live for it, and I will!" she cried.[5]

Whether they answer with the injunction to love, to suffer, to rejoin the community, or whatever, most novelists assume that the demand "tell me what to live for" obliges the artist to respond, is indeed the only issue worth considering seriously. The response may involve faith, despair, frustrated rage; but it is fundamentally idealistic, based on the premise that literary communication is not only possible—but may even be socially meaningful. The true nihilist would not bother to write novels.

Much of this anguished concern is due to the enormous influence of romantically oriented existentialism;[6] the artist feels the need to be engaged; and, what is most important, feels some degree of confidence that his engagement can produce change. "Although literature is one thing and morality a quite different one," Sartre has insisted, "at the heart of the aesthetic imperative we discern the moral imperative."[7] Therefore, he continues, "we must take up a position in *our literature*, because literature is in essence a taking of position."[8] And novelists as far apart (in other respects) as Bellow and Purdy, Malamud and Pynchon, Updike and Friedman, appear to have accepted implicitly Sartre's position that

> the works deriving from such preoccupations can not aim first to please. They
> irritate and disturb. They offer themselves as tasks to be discharged. They urge
> the reader on to quests without conclusions. They present us with experiences
> whose outcomes are uncertain. The fruits of torments and questions, they can
> not be enjoyment for the reader, but rather questions and torments. If our
> results turn out successful, they will not be diversions, but rather obsessions.
> They will give not a world "to see" but to change.[9]

An interesting example of a novel struggling (somewhat nervously) with the moral imperative might be Pynchon's *The Crying of Lot 49*. Only superficially comic, the novel operates within a tension between the desire to explore matters of structure and form and the impulse toward engagement with contemporary social issues. The protagonist attempts, with increasing frustration, to find the significance of an apparently absurd organization with the unlikely name of Tristero; if the outcome of the tormented search is uncertain, Pynchon leaves little doubt as to its moral importance: "For there either was some Tristero beyond the appearance of the legacy America, or there was just America and if there was just America then it seemed the only way she could continue, and manage to be at all relevant to it, was as an alien, unfurrowed, assumed full circle into some paranoia."[10] For such novelists, the work of art seeks relevance—active or alienated, practical or paranoid—to America and contemporary society.

Accordingly, the impulse toward engagement manifests itself in the aesthetic. Irving Howe claims that "modernist literature . . . downgrades the value of esthetic unity in behalf of even a jagged and fragmented expressiveness," and goes on to explain that the

> . . . expectation of formal unity implies an intellectual and emotional, indeed a philosophic composure; it assumes that the artist stands above his material, controlling it and aware of an impending resolution; it assumes that the artist has answers to his questions or that answers can be had. But for the modern writer none of these assumptions holds, or at least none of them can simply be taken for granted. He presents dilemmas; he cannot and soon does not wish to resolve them; he offers his *struggle* with them as the substance of his testimony; and whatever unity his work possesses, often not very much, comes from the emotional rhythm, the thrust toward completion of that struggle. After Kafka, it becomes hard to believe not only in answers, but even in endings.[11]

Insofar as he implies a loss of control (or a loss of interest in control) on the part of the novelist, Howe is undoubtedly mistaken: Bellow, Malamud, Updike, Berger, and the so-called black humorists are technically competent craftsmen. Yet many of these novelists do appear to have difficulty with endings, and they all compose as if struggle with the moral imperative supersedes matters of aesthetics.

John Barth, on the other hand, manifests rather different assumptions and concerns, for he resolutely denies the primacy of engagement with the moral imperative. More seriously than his tone might imply, he has exclaimed: "Muse spare me (at the desk, I mean) from Social-Historical Responsibility, and in the last analysis from every other kind, except Artistic."[12] Asked by an interviewer, "Do you deliberately incorporate social criticism into your novels?" Barth replied, "I can't in fiction get very interested in such things. My argument is with the facts of life, not the conditions of it. . . . I'm not very responsible in the Social Problems way, I guess."[13] It is a question of emphasis: the urgent need to confront social and moral issues is subordinated to certain aesthetic interests. Ultimately, however, talk about art amounts to talk about the world we live in. What Wallace Stevens has to say about poetry applies as well to Barth's novels:

> We have been trying to get at a truth about poetry, to get at one of the principles that compose the theory of poetry. It comes to this, that poetry is a part of the structure of reality. If this has been demonstrated, it pretty much amounts to saying that the structure of poetry and the structure of reality are one, or, in effect, that poetry and reality are one, or should be. This may be less thesis than hypothesis.[14]

Barth is, as he should be, tentative about the connection between art and life; for him, it is at best hypothesis—but a most useful one, providing a theme for nearly all of his artistic output. Barth's novels are commentaries on theories of the novel; insofar as novels are a part of life, Barth's novels are a commentary on a part of life. The result is the movement of artistic self-consciousness to the foreground of the artifact; the result is the production of "imitations-of-novels" which "attempt to represent not life directly but a representation of life."[15]

Thus, in *The Floating Opera*, Barth suggests the aesthetic implications of necessarily self-conscious narrative art. "In most books," Henry Thoreau noticed, "the *I*, or first person, is omitted. . . . We commonly do not remember that it is, after all, always the first person that is speaking. I should not talk so much about myself if there were anybody else I knew as well."[16] That is, there is a sense in which narrative objectivity is impossible; and behind every novel, as Wayne Booth has shown, there is the organizing consciousness of the direct or implied narrator. What we are given is not a transcript of reality, but rather patterns of response initiated and (to varying degrees) controlled by a particular narrator. Experience itself, that which is out there, is unclassified, massive, potentially overwhelming; the basis of art certainly, and life probably, is selection, classification, and organization. Art becomes essentially a matter of point of view.

And whatever else *The Floating Opera* may be about, it is fundamentally concerned with the definition of the point of view involved in the art of artistic creation. The narrator is an extremely self-conscious novelist, one who takes great pains to emphasize his function as storyteller. "Good heavens," Todd Andrews exclaims, "how does one write a novel! I mean, how can anybody stick to the story, if he's at all sensitive to the significance of things?"[17] Todd's problem is, of course, that of any artist; for significance lies not in things-as-such, but in the perception of the observer. Therefore, Todd's narrative challenges the popular notion that a novel provides an illusion of reality, that it speaks of characters or events as *if* they really lived or really happened; the experiences described have meaning only as referents to the consciousness of the narrator. Art, then, inevitably involves artifice; and "a different way to come to terms with the discrepancy between art and the Real Thing," Barth has claimed, "is to *affirm* the artificial element in art (you can't get rid of it anyhow), and to make the artifice part of your point."[18] And Todd early affirms the artifice of his narrative position: "I intend," he blandly announces, "to introduce myself, caution you against certain possible interpretations of my name, explain the significance of this book's title, and do several other gracious things for you, like a host fussing over a guest, to make you as comfortable as possible and to dunk you gently into the meandering stream of my story—useful activities better preserved than scrapped."[19]

Todd's busily intrusive manner is useful insofar as it emphasizes his own control of his material. Essentially, the novel presents realization of the conflict between man's pretensions to rational behavior and the basic animality which manifests itself in his every act. The concern is hardly a new one, yet its treatment poses interesting aesthetic possibilities. To explore the conflict, Todd embodies its various components: thus, we see Todd-as-character representing poised intellectual detachment, encountering the German sergeant, Betty June Gunter, Jane and Harrison Mack—all representing levels of animality. Eventually, Todd-as-character is brought to an awareness of his personal bestiality; and, no longer able to maintain his detachment, contemplates suicide. Yet, on the edge of the nihilistic abyss, the very fact of his novel suggests a tentative solution. For if one says that the universe is totally irrational, then it follows that the individual is himself irrational; but to believe that such a realization is possible or meaningful, is to assume that the individual is capable of rational statements about himself. In other words, the nihilistic position contains a contradiction, for the ability to perceive disorder implies an ordered viewpoint; if nothing were ordered, the novelist would be logically incapable of recognizing his own position. Thus, Todd's clear and impressive ability to manipulate point of view demonstrates in itself a realm in which order and meaning are apparently inherent. By insisting on aesthetic artifice, he is able to construct a bulwark against the acceptance of personal and universal irrationality; art posits meaning, a momentary stay against encroaching confusion. And Barth has recently called attention to the use of "favorite fictional devices" which turn "the artist's mode or form into a metaphor for his concerns."[20] Such a device, he continues, can become "a paradigm of or metaphor for itself; not just the *form* of the story but the *fact* of the story is symbolic."

In *The Sot-Weed Factor*, Barth puts his aesthetic concerns in a slightly different perspective. Unlike his first two novels, this book exhibits a narrative position exaggerated in its detachment: except for the chapter titles, there are virtually no authorial intrusions until the "Apology" which makes up Part IV, the last twelve pages of the book.[21] Yet the basic interest in the relationship between art and reality remains paramount, here related to the concept of the historical novel and history itself. The impersonal point of view serves to emphasize the difference between the novel and the actual historical poem which lies behind it, to call attention to the manipulation of the past by a modern writer.

For there was, of course, an Ebenezer Cooke who produced a poem entitled "The Sot-Weed Factor," published in 1708.[22] Without belaboring the many parallels between the original eighteenth-century poem and the twentieth-century novel,[23] it is sufficient to point out that Barth took extreme care not to violate either the spirit or the actualities of the history of Dorchester County, Maryland, in the closing years of the seventeenth century. Yet the greater the historical verisimilitude (for example, Barth attempts to use no word in the novel which might not have appeared in the poem), the less the novel is like a scholarly study of colonial Maryland or even an historical fiction of the sort turned out so prolifically today. No doubt for the author, as for Eben Cooke, "the sum of history became in his head no more than the stuff of metaphors."[24] But metaphors for what?

It would be unwise (in spite of a remark attributed to Barth by the jacket of the 1964 Universal Library edition of the novel) to read the work as an allegory. I refer once more to a passage used earlier, in which Barth speaks of the use of history in fiction:

> Joyce's Dedalus calls history a nightmare from which he's trying to wake; some other writers have found it more a wet-dream (and their readers, perhaps, a soporific). For me, also, the past is a dream—but I laugh in my sleep. The use of historical and legendary material, especially in a farcical spirit, has a number of technical virtues, among which are esthetic distance and the opportunity for counter-realism. Attacked with a long face, the historical muse is likely to give birth to costume romances, adult Westerns, tiresome allegories, and ponderous mythologizings; but she responds to a light-hearted approach.[25]

Again, the emphasis on "technical virtues"; but this time "counter-realism"—in other words, the more Barth expends himself in providing historicity, even to the point of using eighteenth-century language, the more he is able to suggest levels of meaning denied the Historical Novelist. The reader is, then, continually astonished not by how quaint these characters are, but how modern they seem to be. The "light-hearted approach," delightful in itself, permits Barth to flirt with ironic parallels between past and present, perhaps to fuse the two: "fusion" in a rather curious sense.

Although Barth did not encounter the writings of Jorge Louis Borges until 1963 (indeed, they were not available in translation until 1962) and although the Argentinian fabulator could not have directly influenced the writing of *The Sot-Weed Factor*, both men were working with some of the same premises, and certain parallels are enlightening. Borges speculates on the possibility of one Pierre Menard writing *Don Quixote*: "He did not want to compose another *Don Quixote*—which would be easy—but the *Don Quixote*. It is unnecessary to add that his aim was never to produce a mechanical transcription of the original; he did not propose to copy it. His admirable ambition was to produce pages which would coincide—word for word and line for line—with those of Miguel de Cervantes."[26] The result of this extraordinary task would not be a mere duplication of Cervantes' book; the words would be exactly the same, of course, but the passage of more than three centuries would supply them with new and possibly enriched meanings; the purpose of what Borges calls "the technique . . . of deliberate anachronism and erroneous attributions"[27] would presumably be to show the contemporaneity, the simultaneity of all works of literature. What this involves is clearly an extension of T.S. Eliot's "historical sense": "a perception, not only of the pastness of the past, but of its presence."[28] Barth has written of Borges' fanciful idea and has ascribed to it "considerable intellectual validity."[29] If, Barth adds, one were to compose Beethoven's Sixth Symphony today, and if it were "done with ironic intent by a composer quite aware of where we've been and where we are," the result would be "an ironic comment . . . more directly on the genre and history of the art than on the state of the culture." In this manner, making use of "a lighthearted approach," past and present interlock, are fused, in ways beyond Eliot's wildest imaginings: the product would be something very like *The Sot-Weed Factor*.

What makes this novel "real" is not the language or the accurate yet involved account of seventeenth-century Dorchester politics—indeed, they make the novel seem more fabulous than otherwise; what makes it real is the "stuff" of the "metaphors," the problems and concerns of the characters which survive to haunt us today. Rational pretensions as opposed to animalistic behavior; sexual innocence in confrontation with orgiastic excess; fixed identity in the face of cosmic elusiveness; the temptation to suicide and the need for engagement; these and more make up the novel's thematic webs. Yet these problems and concerns, for all their relevance, are subordinated to the aesthetic implications of the basic form; and the artifice becomes the basic point.

Once again, although the book at many places suggests the pervasiveness of an existential absurd, of a black and fundamentally disordered cosmos (Burlingame describes "man's lot": "He is by mindless lust engendered and by mindless wrench expelled, from the Eden of the womb to the motley, mindless world. . . . Here we sit upon a blind rock, hurtling through a vacuum, racing to the grave"[30])—yet the fact that Barth was able to supply staggering complexity to his plot without losing track of a single strand suggests at least one realm in which man can control his experience. He can order it aesthetically.

In *Giles Goat-Boy*, Barth shifts his lenses and readjusts his focus, but the object under examination is not new to the readers of his other works. Once again, form determines content. The most obvious—and the most complex—convention permeating the novel is the allegorical framework; but the artifact as a whole is not an allegory. Ordinarily, allegorical characters function simultaneously on levels other than the directly literal; behind them works the interplay of ideas, abstractions. Moreover, the action of the plot is important insofar as it refers to the philosophical backdrop; once the reader discovers the key, the level of abstraction involved, the fiction locks neatly (more or less) into place.

The "key" to *Giles Goat-Boy* is simply the link between the universe and the university. This much is ponderously and superficially obvious. Within this all-encompassing metaphor, the novel parallels innumerable aspects of contemporary experience with campus terminology: mankind becomes studentdom; the countries of the western world become West Campus—set in opposition, of course, to East Campus; World War II becomes Campus Riot II; and so on. Beyond the political parallels are allusions to Judaeo-Christian tradition: Jesus Christ as Enos Enoch; Jews as Moishians; the Sermon on the Mount, the Seminar-on-the-Hill. The allegory takes in, with tedious thoroughness, classical traditions as well:

Rome becomes Remus College; Greece, classical Lykeion. What is essentially a linguistic game is carried, then, to grotesque levels: middle-class is
translated into "mid-percentile"; the man-in-the-street, into "the student-
in-the-path."

On this level, everyone notices, the novel functions as a crossword
puzzle, as a *roman à clef*—but the connections are so outrageously contrived (there is even a reference to "Snow White's forestry major") that it
would be ultimately absurd to take the allegorical level seriously. "Clearly," Barth has admitted, "the allegorical and *roman à clef* aspects of *Giles
Goat-Boy* are deliberately laid on in an obvious way, since they're the
least central elements in the fiction—a mere way of speaking."[31]

The "light-hearted approach" that produced the "counter-realism"
of *The Sot-Weed Factor* here thrives as counter allegory. That is, the
more the allegory is insisted on, the less significant it becomes; the reader
smugly makes the connection between university and universe, only to
find that Barth has only peripheral interest in either. The translation of
the allegorical fabric of *Giles Goat-Boy* is a baroque trap for the superficial reader.

An example may help to clarify the implications of this technique.
Early in the narrative, Giles comes upon some students making love in his
pasture. At first, they translate the physical deed into a series of symbolic
abstractions, constructing their own private allegory. The boy over-
whelms his partner with ejaculative poetry, so that the climax becomes
ecstatic "communication."[32] The primary delight emerges in the way this
odd "coupling" is described:

> His voice mounted over her. "*The campus . . . hath not anything more
> fair. . . .*"
>
> "Don't, please," she begged, but laid her head on his shoulder. My [Giles']
> breath came faster; I was as fired with desire as he when he next declared, "You
> mustn't be afraid of it. You've got to let go."
>
> What would she let go of? I hunkered closer and squinted to see. She
> pressed her nose into his high-necked sweater and protested, "You don't know
> what that poem does to me!"
>
> "Suffer it," ordered her mate. . . .

After "her buck pressed home" with a climatic line, the girl experiences a
sort of orgasm: "the female made a little cry and wrenched away. For some
seconds she lay as if stricken, while her mate, hard respiring, drained off
his drink and flung away the can." This leads to the traditional cigarette,
and all the clichés of undergraduate seduction are cleverly inserted:

> He drew her down with him on the blanket. "Are you sorry we said the
> poem?"
>
> No, she said, she didn't suppose she was sorry. "I'm still a little mid-
> percentile about first dates, I guess. When two people start off with something
> like *that*—what does it leave for later?"

On one level, of course, this is a parody of a seduction scene; but on another, it is a minor allegory within the larger framework. Thus, like the artist, this couple substitutes abstraction for reality; reading the poem takes the place of and refers to copulation. Almost.

For the situation becomes more complex when we realize that the boy has no intention of being satisfied with just a poetry recital; he knows full well the difference between the artifact (the poem) and the thing itself. Soon he is pressing home more than the last line of a poem, breaking down the girl's meager and half-hearted defenses with a lecture in "Beism" (roughly equivalent to existentialism): "You've got to *be*, Chickie! *Be! Be!*" Watching them closely, with mounting excitement, Giles comments: "Beyond any question they Were, locked past discourse in their odd embrace." At this point, we are confronted with converging levels of meaning. First of all, there is the basic artifact of the novel itself; this is not a real scene being described. Then there is the allegorical dimension of that total novel, already discussed. Then, too, there is the lesser set of abstractions, the poetry reading which suggests that art can in some way replace reality. Yet following hard upon that possibility is the reorientation of a kind of reality, actual copulation, which nonetheless introduces a new allegorical dimension: being as the linguistic equivalent of intercourse. Finally, there is the further complication of Giles' point of view. While the boy who is persistently seducing the girl in the pasture (and it turns out that he is better at allegorical manipulation, poetic recital, than at handling the passionate reality of the aroused girl) is able to keep straight the distinctions between poems and copulation, between art and reality, George confuses the two. That is, he takes the metaphor (being) as a literal description of the actual act. Then, when "Lady Creamhair" (who turns out to be his mother) expresses a desire to let Giles "be" with her (meaning "stay" with her), he assumes immediately that she is inviting him to make love to her. And the misunderstanding of basic vocabulary leads to a comic but nearly disastrous coupling. Moreover, the moment the consummation takes place, another (mythic) level is added: for Giles takes on overtones of Oedipus, as we later discover. The complexity is enormous and labyrinthian. We are entertained with a baroque mixing of artifice, symbol, reality, and myth. And the ultimate meaning of the sequence has little to do with any single element within it; it does throw light on what Barth calls "a mere way of speaking" on the way in which language involves and determines reality.

Giles' basic problem in the narrative is his failure to distinguish between artificially constructed allegories, mere ways of speaking (his own concept of Grand Tutorhood), and the fluctuating realities which surround him. His task is to wade through various "inversions-of-inversions long enough to work out the right ones for [himself]"(p. 574), only to discover that there is no externally verifiable reality, that what is true depends utterly on one's point of view. What he does find is not meaning, but a way of talking about the impossibility of fixing meaning.

An art directed at this sort of statement is necessarily contrived; for the essence of Barth's aesthetic is the assertion that even as vision is personal, potentially arbitrary, so art cannot hope and should not try to mirror the existence of an objective reality. Art, Barth is saying again and again, assumes and affirms artifice.

To some, this emphasis is bound to be unsatisfying; when Barth insists that "technical circus-tricks are good clean fun,"[33] serious doubts may well arise. Irving Howe, for example, informs us that the standards for judging any novel are implied in these questions: "how much of our life does it illuminate? how ample a moral vision does it suggest?"[34] Or again, Jonathan Baumbach, not referring specifically to Barth, asks, "Can a novel be about anything when there is nothing real at stake?" and then answers: "If *real* life is not the final stuff of the novel, it is at least the first stuff."[35] Barth makes of such assumptions (that there is an experientially verifiable "moral vision" or "real life") the target of his aesthetic, producing artifices which illuminate the processes of thought rather than its end-product.

One might, of course, claim that it is more than a matter of mere aesthetics; one might claim that it is the way things are. Percy Bridgman prefaces his wide-ranging study of modern existence (entitled, appropriately, *The Way Things Are*) by calling attention to "the two-fold problem of understanding—there [is] the problem of understanding the world around us, and there [is] the problem of understanding the processes of understanding, that is, the problem of understanding the nature of the intellectual tools with which we attempt to understand the world around us."[36] Less awkward than Bridgman but agreeing with him, Barth demonstrates the way in which everything depends on point of view—"it is becoming evident," says Bridgman, "that the problem of the 'observer' must eventually deal with the observer as thinking about what he observes."[37] The principles of aesthetics overlap with the principles of existence, with the way things are.

Yet in the final analysis, one would not want to become too serious in a justification of the Barthian aesthetic. In a recent story (entitled, appropriately, "Title"), the writer carries on a dialogue with his own artifact. "The demise of the novel and short story," the writer pleads, "needn't be the end of narrative art. . . . The final possibility is to turn ultimacy, exhaustion, paralyzing self-consciousness and the adjective weight of accumulated history. . . . To turn ultimacy against itself to make something new and valid, the essence whereof would be the impossibility of making something new."[38] "What a nauseating notion," the story contemptuously replies—but the fact of the narrative, involuted as it is, proves the writer right. "Oh God comma I abhor self-consciousness," he lovingly moans, delighting in his own pose. And the self-conscious pose, riddled with mockery and seemingly exhausted (certainly exhausting), manages somehow to turn back upon itself, confront its own intellectual dead end, and accomplish new human work. The result, in the case of John Barth, is an artistic victory of impressive proportions.

Notes

1. *The Dehumanization of Art and Other Writings on Art and Culture* (New York, 1956), p. 56.

2. "The Literature of Exhaustion," *The Atlantic*, CCXX (August 1967), 29–34.

3. *Ibid.*, p. 31.

4. "Auden on Poetry: A Conversation with Stanley Kunitz," *The Atlantic*, CCXVIII (August 1966), 96.

5. *Mother Night* (New York, 1961), p. 160.

6. For example: "The rationalism of Sartre," writes Iris Murdoch, "is not geared on to the techniques of the modern world; it is solipsistic and romantic, isolated from the sphere of real operations." *Sartre: Romantic Rationalist* (New Haven, Conn., 1959), p. 71.

7. *What is Literature?*, trans. Bernard Frechtman (New York, 1966), p. 40.

8. *Ibid.*, p. 192.

9. *Ibid.*, p. 164.

10. Thomas Pynchon, *The Crying of Lot 49* (New York, 1966), p. 137.

11. "The Idea of the Modern," *Literary Modernism*, ed. Irving Howe (New York, 1967), pp. 29–30.

12. *Book Week* (September 26, 1965), quoted in *The Sense of the Sixties*, ed. Edward Quinn and Paul J. Dolan (New York, 1968), p. 440.

13. "John Barth: An Interview," *Wisconsin Studies in Contemporary Literature*, VI (Winter-Spring 1965), 13.

14. *The Necessary Angel* (New York, 1951), pp. 80–81.

15. "The Literature of Exhaustion," p. 33.

16. *Walden*, ed. Sherman Paul (Cambridge, Mass., 1957), p. 1.

17. *The Floating Opera*, rev. ed. (New York, 1967), p. 2.

18. "John Barth: An Interview," p. 6.

19. *The Floating Opera*, p. 2.

20. "The Literature of Exhaustion," p. 32.

21. *The Sot-Weed Factor*, rev. ed. (New York, 1967), pp. 741–756.

22. *American Antiquary Society Proceedings, New Series*, XLIV (October, 1934), 267–308.

23. See Philip E. Diser, "The Historical Ebenezer Cooke," *Critique*, X (1968), 48–59.

24. *The Sot-Weed Factor*, p. 10.

25. "Muse, Spare Me," pp. 443–444.

26. *Ficciones*, ed. Anthony Kerrigan (New York, 1962), pp. 48–49.

27. *Ibid.*, p. 54.

28. *Selected Essays of T. S. Eliot* (New York, 1950), p. 4.

29. "The Literature of Exhaustion," p. 31.

30. *The Sot-Weed Factor*, pp. 344–345.

31. Letter to Campbell Tatham, March 21, 1968.

32. *Giles Goat-Boy* (Garden City, N.Y., 1966), pp. 31–35.

33. "John Barth: An Interview," p. 6.

34. *Politics and the Novel* (Greenwich, Conn., 1967), p. 25.

35. *The Landscape of Nightmare: Studies in the Contemporary American Novel* (New York, 1965), pp. 7, 8.

36. Percy Bridgman, *The Way Things Are* (Cambridge, Mass., 1959), p. 1.

37. *Ibid.*, p. 2.

38. *Yale Review*, LVII (Winter 1968), 217; reprinted in *Lost in the Funhouse* (Garden City, N.Y., 1968), pp. 105–113.

John Barth's Tenuous Affirmation: "The Absurd, Unending Possibility of Love"

Harold Farwell*

Much of the early criticism of John Barth's novels conveys in almost adulatory terms the sense of discovery that many have felt in reading his work. Since the appearance of *Giles Goat-Boy* (1966), criticism has frequently been adverse, and the irreconcilable split among the judges for the 1972 National Book Award in fiction, which led to an unprecedented sharing of honors (Barth for *Chimera* and John Williams for *Augustus*), focused attention dramatically on what appears to be a developing critical polarization in regard to Barth's worth. Much of this seems misdirected energy to me, but especially so the judgments of critics of both persuasions which are predicated on the notion of Barth's nihilism. The best repudiation of that idea seems to be the author's sheer productivity, especially as the silence of Samuel Beckett has become so profound. Still, what needs to be discussed is what Barth is writing *for*, what his writing reaffirms—however cautiously or hesitantly. If we consider one of Barth's most frequent themes, for example, the ambiguity of love, I think that we find not only great consistency in his thinking, but also an increasing tendency to affirm the possibility of love. Barth's tenuous, limited affirmation of love is most clearly defined in the "Menelaiad," but it is an important motif in all the recent short fiction in which he increasingly identifies the dilemmas of lovers with those of artists. Apparently that kind of love which represents a creative attempt to be free from the prison of the self has become for him at least as noble an affirmation as is the artist's comparable attempt to transcend his limitations in his art.

For Barth, however, the possibility of love is never confused with inevitability or necessity. The qualifications with which he has surrounded all discussion of love are almost overwhelming and seem to have provided him with a buttress against the over-simplifications of his own generation. For although Auden has insisted that the distinctive contribution of modern writers has been to explore love in all its complex manifestations and recent publishing history seems determined to prove his truth with a

*Reprinted by permission of The Georgia Review, XXVIII (1974), 290–306.

vengeance, one must insist that the special limitation of our age—if not of its most consummate artists—has been its refusal to accept as valid any view of love less laudatory than, say, something like that found in "Dover Beach." Especially during the period when Barth was writing novels, love was popularly supposed to be personally redemptive, if not a universal spiritual panacea. Even in the most absurd of worlds, the argument ran, love could establish something of value, as in Arnold's poem, some refuge against the otherwise universal chaos.

In contrast, Barth has regarded love from the beginning as the very essence of the absurd. Like many comic artists Barth uses man's sexual imbroglios to reveal his essential silliness, but he goes beyond many writers in his insistence that there is not necessarily any sense in any kind of love, not only that which is basely sexual. Barth never denies that love exists, nor does he deny its power; he just consistently denies that it has any necessary meaning and often unfashionably insists on showing its powers to be anything but redemptive. From Freya Mooney in Barth's unpublished M.A. thesis, "Shirt of Nessus"(1952), through Rennie Morgan, Ebenezer Cooke, and Menelaus, characters are strewn throughout Barth's fiction for whom the experience of love has been both incomprehensible and frightening—at times even disastrous.

Even Barth's apprentice work, the Hopkins thesis which he dismisses as juvenilia, shows his concern for the ambiguity of love, as its title makes clear. In the legend the centaur, Nessus, gives Deianira a poisoned shirt to revenge himself on Hercules, having falsely promised her that it would act as a love charm to win back her husband's love, should that ever seem necessary. When Deianira's jealousy prompts her to send it to Hercules, its effects are deadly, leading to Deianira's suicide and Hercules's attempted suicide, from which he is saved only by the intervention of the gods. Barth uses the myth suggestively, to focus attention on the agonies that a couple can impose on one another in their love. His story hardly needs even that bit of explication, however, since it is concerned with the marriage of a sadist of almost clinically pure dimensions, Willard Mooney, to a masochist named Freya, who discovers herself and fulfills the promise of her name when she trips off into something uncomfortably close to nymphomania. Beyond suggesting the agonies of love, the title's relevance to the action is not always clear, Barth himself having labeled it "provisional." Willard is not the equal of his father, Trappe, who comes closer to Herculean exploits in his barroom brawls and dockyard fights and also mirrors Hercules's insensitivity and impetuosity—if not his capacity for remorse. Trappe is, of course, the lover who destroys Willard's domestic bliss even as he ironically introduces Freya to joy and the affirmation of life, along with incest.

For our purposes, what is most significant about "Shirt of Nessus" is that the triangular relationship is not resolved, the story line abruptly broken precisely at the point that Freya comes to the awareness, like many women in the published novels, that she cannot give up either of her partners, that each man fulfills some deeply felt need in her life. The opening framework of the story (though not returned to at the end—it is properly sub-titled a "novel-in-progress") tells of the discovery of a body believed to be either Trappe's or Willard's. That, of course, hints at what sort of resolution was planned for the triangle. But Barth does not actually return to that framework to resolve his work, and just as he discards the stylistic mimicry of Hemingway soon after the opening Proem for a more "polytonal" style, he also seems to move further and further away from the flatness of melodrama toward more complicated effects in both plot and characterization. While some of his portraits seem to be fairly stylized grotesques, he develops his three principals with increasing intensity and sensitivity. When the main narrative does stop, it appears almost as if Barth could not in honesty to his characters resolve the psychology of their relationships, but also could not make the impossibility of doing so the point of his fiction.

That, in brief, is the breakthrough that comes with his published work, specifically with the discovery of Todd Andrews at the end of *The Floating Opera* (1956; rev. ed. 1967) that "the truth is that nothing makes any difference, including the truth." Although Todd applies his new awareness specifically to the question of his planned suicide, deciding that if there is no "final reason" for living, there is none for dying either, his truth is both a response to and a reflection upon the absurd love triangle in which he has been involved. In fact, Todd's resolution to his private crisis and quest for a new personal awareness are intimate aspects of the love story he chronicles. His special blending of the tale of the triangular love affair and what is fashionably styled an "identity crisis" creates a pattern of associations that Barth will use frequently in later fiction.

Barth's next novel, *The End of the Road* (1958; rev. ed. 1967), is obviously another application of Todd's truth, the plot itself bearing the burden of the testimonial that Todd has made personally. Again the plot begins with the intrusion of the narrator as a third party into a fragile, privately defined relationship—not unlike that which the narrator calls for in "Dover Beach." In this case it is the Morgans' separate peace which is shattered by the intrusion of Jacob Horner, a man almost crippled by his awareness of the absurdity of absolute values. He is incapable of making choices since "no one choice seems satisfactory for very long by comparison with the aggregate desirability of all the rest, though compared to any *one* of the others it would not be found inferior." He is the victim of moods—which he compares to days without weather—in which he ceases to exist, being "without a personality." Whereas Todd's affair led him to reject suicide as absurd, Jake's affair leads him into a death of the spirit or will—even though he too avoids the option of suicide at the end. Still, essentially the same insight that saves Todd, destroys Jake. A case can be made that *The End of the Road* represents a tragic reworking of the implications of Todd's apparently absolute relativism.

What justifies Barth's own suggestion that both novels were meant to be exercises in nihilism is that the characters' attempts to find justification for or meaning in their actions and emotions inevitably lead nowhere. The intrusion of the third party in each story makes perfectly clear how tenuous and absurd are each of the relationships threatened, but the triangle that results brings its own set of absurdities—as the ironies at the end of the second novel in their "raggedness" make clear. Joe and Rennie Morgan's conventionally structured life perhaps deserves to be destroyed by Jake's chaos, but the triangle is hardly an improvement, as Rennie's death, Joe's loss of his job, and Jake's precipitous flight make clear.

As a rejoinder to the notion that the unexamined life is not worth living, Barth once quipped, "King Oedipus and I aren't so sure." What might pass as just another example of Barthian wit seems to me to represent something close to the heart of his thinking. Obviously, some lives won't bear examining—maybe those like the Morgans'. Barth may also be suggesting that all of us may inevitably have to compromise ourselves to survive—a possibility that generally leads to comedy. Even so there is something to be said for surviving, even with flaws. At the end of his book, Todd Andrews says, "in the real absence of absolutes, values less than absolute mightn't be regarded as in no way inferior and even be lived by." It is a tentative and halting affirmation (as the tortured grammar suggests), but it does open the door for what Barth himself calls "a cheerful nihilism." It even opens up the possibility of affirming love, however absurd it might be, as a value "less than absolute" but "in no way inferior" for that.

Such an affirmation comes in Barth's next two books. In Barth's own Marylandiad, Ebenezer Cooke's ideal (and therefore absolute) love for Joan Toast must in the end be sacrificed for a real (and therefore tarnished) marriage. The celebrated complications of the plot of *The Sot-Weed Factor* (1960; rev. ed. 1967), reflect Ebenezer's shifting planes of awareness concerning the various triangles in which he is involved. At the beginning John McEvoy, Eben's rival, clarifies his weakness: " 'Tis not simply love ye know naught of, 'tis the *entire great real world*." To McEvoy and all the other speakers who even momentarily seem to speak for the author, the world (like love) is a "tangled skein." Just how knotty it really is McEvoy soon discovers when he realizes that Eben's love of Joan, however silly it may seem in its elevation of her to "a principle," is quite capable of ruining his own relationship with her since she prefers to risk being "an hallucination" to being regarded as no more than "just a woman." Later, the changes wrought on Joan and the shocked reactions of Ebenezer to them become the indexes of Eben's education into reality and life. At the end when Ebenezer comes to speak of his innocence as his crime and equate it with original sin, his initiation into the real world, his marriage to Joan, and his love for Joan are all consummated in what he now regards as an act of atonement. The entire story merely clarifies a point made by Todd in *The Floating Opera*—that he who becomes a saint on principle hasn't reasoned completely. Eben becomes wiser, almost saintly, only when he stops acting on principle.

Ebenezer's reasoning is completed largely because of his involvement in another, even more complicated triangle with his twin sister and Henry Burlingame. Whatever Henry's feelings may be, it quickly becomes apparent that the tabooed love of the twins for each other is as much a barrier as any external force or circumstances to their finding fulfillment with others. Not until the incestuous quality of their love is fully confessed is either free to love another. The scene in which that occurs is the climax of the plot. Together in the black hold of a ship, a symbolic womb that Anna fears will be the only Garden the chaste lovers will ever know, the twins face imminent death. Eben tries to convince Anna that there must be something of value to which they might cling in hope, but she rejects all his reasoning. The incorrigible idealist insists, "If aught in life has value to us, we must not give o'er its pursuit," but again she responds, " 'Tis not worth the cost." Apparently misunderstanding her despair as *carpe diem* ("this present hour is all our future") or else simply incapable of resisting her any longer, Eben translates her desire to be throttled by him into something else and apparently attempts to consummate their love—only to send her shrieking across the hold. But the attack having been made, Eben must accept the full implications of his fallen humanity. He does so later in accepting humbly the love of Joan Toast. Although Joan soon dies in childbirth and Burlingame deserts Anna, Malden belongs to the twins, and Eben takes as his heir the child that Anna bears Burlingame out of wedlock. Living together in seclusion almost as if they were the only two people on earth, the twins finally share a few years together in peace—and the ending fulfills the one hope that Anna was able to express while in the black bowels of the ship.

If the conclusion of *The Sot-Weed Factor* suggests a strangely respectable sublimation of the incestuous attractions that have underscored so much of the action of the novel, no such proprieties mar the ending of *Giles Goat-Boy* (1966). Giles also has been engaged in an identity quest that involves not merely winning a patrimony, but also discovering it. The climax of that quest comes in Giles's third and final descent into the Belly of WESCAC, and like Eben before him Giles is led through crisis and into a new awareness by his possible twin sister, now Anastasia, an appropriate name for the agent of his resurrection. Whereas Eben's recognition (and conduct) reflected an acceptance of the lack of meaningful values, Giles's is a transcendent reconciliation of opposites, not so much a rejection of values as an encompassing acceptance of all of them based on an almost Oriental awareness of the arbitrariness of any distinctions. It is also quite simply joyous. It is significant, therefore, that the twins make the final descent into the Belly disguised as one, but even more important is the fact that the moment of awareness for them is also a sexual consummation: "In the sweet place that contained me there was no East, no West, but an entire, single, seamless campus . . . all one, and one with me. *Here* lay with *there, tick* clipped *tock, all* serviced *nothing*; I and My Ladyship, all, were one."

Perhaps Giles's highest moment, his achievement of Grand Tutorhood and Commencement, should not be reduced to a moment of love. Afterward, "Anastasia's eyes still shown with love; my own," he explains, "I think with neutral Truth, dispassionate compassion." Furthermore, he admits that he cannot respond to her declaration of love in simple reciprocity. But the import of his comments seems to be that he has moved through love and beyond it. There is no reason to believe that his new state does not encompass love. In addition, though love is inferior to Truth, it is the means of achieving it, which point Giles seems to recognize when he kisses Anastasia in "gratitude for her having been to me Truth's vessel."

Whatever Giles's ultimate Truth is (and we have good reason in the framework of the novel not to take it too seriously), his story celebrates with Wagnerian shamelessness the redemptive potentiality of love. Like Sieglinde's, Anastasia's love is also more convincing than her brother's heroic achievements. Although Anastasia has been involved in more love triangles than all Barth's heroines put together, she has represented to each man only his own idea of love and has, therefore, remained unfulfilled herself, barren. It is perhaps Giles's greatest feat that he alone can finally accept her in her selfhood, can actually "know" her; ironically, he may even have become the agent of her resurrection, that is, her freshening. Whether or not that happens, the entire relationship affirms the oldest traditions of romantic love.

Barth's short fiction collected in *Lost in the Funhouse* (1968) brings into even sharper focus his complex attitudes toward love. Some of these tales are virtuoso pieces in which the craft of writing becomes the story-stuff, as in "Autobiography," which is narrated by a story in the act of composing itself. Most are more traditional, even though they might employ some of the same self-conscious effects, and most are also centrally concerned with the ambiguities of love. One of the most brilliant of these, "Night-Sea Journey," is narrated by a spermatozoon which is swimming toward union with an ovum and reflecting as it approaches the "shore" on its own origins, history, and future with an uncanny capacity to translate contemporary knowledge of biology into its theological and philosophical implications. The whole monologue is an ironic reversal of the traditional apologia since the sperm cell searches unsuccessfully for some explanation for its existence. It soon sounds uncomfortably like a man; its story becomes a microcosmic mirror of the life of mankind; ontogeny articulately recapitules phylogeny.

In the process of searching for his own justification, appropriately, much worldly wisdom is parodied and rebutted—like common sense: " 'You only swim once.' Why bother, then?"; religion: " 'Except ye drown, ye shall not reach the Shore of Life.' Poppycock"; existentialism: "The thoughtful swimmer's choices, then, they say, are two: give over thrashing and go under for good, or embrace the absurdity; . . . . I find neither course acceptable." Most important, however, is the spermatozoon's rejection of the love-ethic: "Oh, to be sure, 'Love!' I translate: we don't know *what* drives and sustains us, only that we are most miserably driven and, imperfectly, sustained. *Love* is how we call our ignorance of what whips us."

Later the sperm is even more somber, recalling the cynic's insistence that the "genuine heroes" were the suicides: "the hero of heroes would be the swimmer who, in the very presence of the Other, refused Her proffered 'immortality' and thus put an end to at least one cycle of catastrophes." The swimmer finally seems to accept such a posture, even though he knows he will be unable to be that hero. His desperate attempt to assert his identity necessitates the rejection of love, union, transfiguration: "*I am he who abjures and rejects the night-sea journey!*" With the "last twitch of my real self" he enjoins the You he may become to "do what I cannot: terminate this aimless, brutal business! . . . Hate love!" The ultimate irony, of course, is that all these cries against "senseless love, senseless death" are voiced just before the narrator gives himself completely to the singing, " 'Love! Love! Love!' " Far from resolving issues, the "author" of these reflections leaves us wondering whether we should follow his advice or his example.

Something like the sperm's expressed desire is also voiced by the narrator of "Petition," the more backward of Siamese twins unfortunately joined spoon-style. His "petition" is an extended explanation of why he would risk surgical death so that "one of us at least may survive, free of the other." The narrator explains that his unhappiness is largely due to his love for Thalia "a pretty contortionist of good family" with whom the twins were coupled lasciviously on the "naughty stages of a dozen nations" and billed *The Eternal Triangle*. At first Thalia, as her name might suggest, had taught the narrator to "make fun of our predicament," but his comic sense decreases as his love for her increases. More precisely, one should say that his love for that aspect of Thalia which mirrors his own spiritual qualities grows. As he becomes increasingly aware of the degree to which he and his brother divide between them "spirit" and "flesh," he comes to recognize the same division in his Thalia—one Thalia within another, like Oriental dolls, but no less distinct than he and his twin. What the petitioner's dilemma reflects is the traditional dilemma of reconciling spiritual love with the demands of the grossly sensual and physical body. "To be one: paradise! To be two: bliss! But to be both and neither is unspeakable." Of course, the more seriously we take the allegorical dimension, the more impossible his solution appears; for better or worse, body and soul are stuck, like the twins, with each other. To the lover who denies that, death would appear to be more than a risk. It is only the extremity of the narrator's literally awkward situation that enables us to laugh at his willingness to embrace Death "like a lover, if I might share the grave with no other company."

The novelty of "Night-Sea Journey" and "Petition" derive primarily from their unusual points of view rather than from their dialectics, but a great deal of the fun in each comes from Barth's manipulation of his arguments. By comparison the first two stories in the collection that deal with Ambrose appear more conventional. A young boy's trials in achieving even the limited identity guaranteed by a name are catalogued in "Ambrose His Mark." His initiation into an incomprehensible adult world of sex and love is the subject of "Water Message" and also of the more technically complicated story that provides the title for the entire volume, "Lost in the Funhouse." This latter story is unlike the other two in that it includes authorial comments on the developing narrative and on the process of composing fictions, a device that reinforces the theme by confusing the reader in the same way that Ambrose has become confused in the maze of the funhouse. Yet in another important way the latter two Ambrose stories are structured alike since each chronicles a Joycean epiphany—with the added Barthian irony that in each case Ambrose discovers that there is really nothing to "know." In "Water Message" Ambrose finds a bottle washed ashore containing a note which promises secrets even more mysterious than those concerned with girls and sex, from the knowledge of which he has just been excluded by the brother's gang. But the water message is blank.

The funhouse, an emblem of the world itself, proves a maze in which Amby, his story, and his reader all become lost. While in the maze of mirrors Amby loses himself in the reflection that he has "deceived himself into supposing he was a person." His identity crisis represents more than the fictional character accepting himself for what he is, it also represents Amby's psychologically consistent reaction to his sexual humiliation with Magda, his being "wiped out" by his brother. With other authors we are expected to look down our post-Freudian noses at those "tiresome" "sensitive" adolescents—like the narrator of Anderson's "I Want to Know Why"—who can't put one and one together sexually, but with Barth we become aware that Amby's losing Magda, like his losing himself, his sense of his own identity, his place in his fiction—all this is the result of one and one not adding up to anything.

The only thing Amby learned from his water message was that the paper had grains of wood in it; from the funhouse he carries away an even more explicitly aesthetic judgment: the funhouse is so tacky that he himself might create a better, "a truly astonishing funhouse." We are obviously witnessing the birth of an artist curiously like Barth himself, who insisted in a 1965 interview that "if you are an artist of a certain temperament, what you really want to do is re-invent the world." What Barth's comic portraits of the artist as a pre-pubescent demonstrated most clearly is that if epistemological dilemmas cannot be resolved, they *can* be finessed.

To Amby the recourse to art may be a retreat from life and love, both of which have turned out to be rather sordid. The narrator of the "Anonymiad" explains his own turning to art in a similar way: "But I don't fool myself: if I never took seriously the world and its tiresome concerns, it's because I was never able to take myself seriously; and the reason for that, I've known for some while, is the fearsomeness of the facts of life. Merope's love, Helen's whoring, Menelaus's noise, Agamemnon's slicing up his daughter for the weatherman—all the large and deadly passions of men and women, wolves, frogs, nightingales; all this business of seizing life, grabbing hold with both hands—it must've scared the daylights out of me from the first. While the other fellows played with their spears, I learned to play the lyre." To this anonymous poet art is not pure escapism, however. It is still an image—even if an artificial one—of the life it reflects, especially in its frailty: "Gods come and go, new worlds and tongues swim into light, old perish," and like them art "too must perish, with all things deciphered and undeciphered: men and women, stars and sky." Its very frailty makes it more like life; it exists "between the night past and the night to come," an ephemeral record not merely of the passing terrors, but also of those noons "beautiful enough to break the heart." The poet who has experienced so many of the world's terrors can still affirm such moments to the end, and along with them, his love. All his art, he suggests, is a "strange love letter" seeking some heart it might reach. The nameless minstrel, unlike the narrator of "Night-Sea Journey," has reached the shore before he writes, has seen the noon, known love, and can insist to his love that "if some night your voice recalls me . . . I'll commit myself to it . . . to attain you or to drown." This in spite of the fact that love has gotten him nowhere—except marooned on an island. Admittedly, I have edited out the flatness of the style when he speaks of his love letter, a parody of postcard banality; also I have ignored other comic devices of his "ironical coda" to insist upon his capacity to affirm love. But however tenuous it may be, existing like that noon between the night-sea journeys past and to come, that capacity is still there, and a part of the anonymous narrator can still exult as he had earlier with Merope's announcement of her love: "Then nothing is impossible!"

The narrator's other, simultaneous reactions to Merope's declaration of love are also important. One part of the anonymous minstrel cynically wonders whether Merope "was nymph doing penance for rebuffing Zeus or just maid with unaccountable defect of good sense," and another part of him, very similar to that part of Barth himself which responds to every verbal formula as if it were a cue, infers, after Descartes: "Therefore I am." The dialectical extremes of these simultaneously held positions are comparable to those expressed by the narrator of "Menelaiad," apparently Menelaus in some form, who also is torn between cynical doubt and an all-encompassing affirmation of possibilities. Like the minstrel he also recognizes that the declaration of love—in this case from Helen—does more than change his life; it makes him whatever he is. With Menelaus that is not just a problem of whether he is the world's luckiest man or its greatest cuckold, though on the horns of that dilemma hangs much of his tale. What he is has been further obscured (perhaps beyond clarification) by his confrontations with the Delphic Oracle and Proteus.

The encounter at Delphi shapes the dramatic structure of the tale since the Oracle is at a loss to reveal her questioner's identity at the crisis, the literal turning point of the work. In the innermost of some eight tales that the narrator has set within one another, Menelaus tells of his trip to the Oracle in the hope of determining truthfully why Helen chose him as her husband in the first place. Either unable to comprehend or unwilling to believe her explanation that it was simply "Love," he has all but destroyed their marriage with his doubts. To his question as to why Helen chose him from among all her suiters, the Oracle responds: " ' " ' " ' "*No other can as well espouse her.*" ' " ' " ' " Though it does not exactly conflict with Helen's answer, the response does leave something to ambiguity—as well an oracle should—specifically, the meaning of "espouse." Does it mean he will prove the best of husbands or just the only man fool enough to put up with her? Menelaus's own confused attempt to define his role only leads to a crisis of identity: " ' " ' " ' "Espouse? Espouse her? As lover? Advocate? Husband? Can't you speak more plainly? Who am I?" ' " ' " ' " The Oracle responds with the same blank message Ambrose received—only this time we are seven stories deep in quotation marks: " ' " ' " ' " " ' " ' " ' "

The effect has been a little like peeling off the layers of an onion only to find that there is no heart at the center—except that from Barth we come away without tears. The prospect of finding nothing at the mysterious center of one's quest that haunted Melville in images like that of the empty pyramid, for Barth becomes the central joke in terms of which the universe is structured. "The Menelaiad" is comedy precisely because Menelaus survives a joke of these proportions and abandons his quest for absolute answers. After having "heard" the Oracle, " ' " ' " 'Posthaste he returned to Lacedemon, done with questions. He'd reembrace his terrifying chooser [Helen], clasp her past speech, never let go, frig understanding." ' " ' " But if the Oracle's silence has constituted Menelaus's comic peripetaia and brought to an end his obsessive introspection, the news he hastens to is what makes him the fit subject of an "epic" song. For in his absence Paris has abducted his wife. Menelaus's willingness to accept the world as he finds it will now be challenged. His speech continues with particular irony: " ' " ' " ' . . . it would be bride-night, endless; their tale would rebegin. "Menelaus here!" His shout shook the wifeless hall.' " ' " ' " Here, precisely at the point where Menelaus's tale must indeed begin again, Barth's tale begins to stop—that is, to move back through the various episodes that have been interrupted for the telling of each additional tale, to return to its own beginning, which was, significantly, the sentence, "Menelaus here, more or less."

That additional qualifier, the "more or less," is best explained by Menelaus's encounter with Proteus, during which Barth adds one more ingenious shape to the forms that Proteus assumes: "When I understood that Proteus somewhere on the beach became Menelaus holding the Old Man of the Sea, Menelaus ceased. Then I understood further how Proteus thus also was as such no more, being as possibly Menelaus's attempt to hold him, the tale of that vain attempt, the voice that tells it." Slippery as that line of reasoning may be, it does explain the "more or less," and also provides a justification for the Chinese-box structure of the tale, the stories within stories technically eight layers thick, but theoretically infinite.

Menelaus's uncertainties about himself are the key to his actions as well as his methods of story telling. That is no more true in respect to his loss of Helen than it is of their reconciliation. Few people have seen comic possibilities in that reunion. Apparently, not even the Greeks were troubled by the discrepancies between the portrait we get of Helen in the *Iliad* and that at the beginning of the *Odyssey*, when upon Telemachus's visit to Sparta, Helen is quietly settled down with Menelaus, in the process of marrying off her children, the perfect image of a well-to-do, middle-aged matron—though still ravishingly beautiful. Even Stesichorus's revised version of Helen's story was not an attempt to improve on the dramatic inconsistencies of the original version, if we can believe the story about why it was composed. His attempt to white-wash Helen by suggesting that she never did go to Troy but was taken by the gods to Egypt, while a cloud in her shape was given to Paris, is supposedly the poet's recantation of an earlier poem in which he followed Homer and for which he too was struck blind by Helen—now turned goddess. If anything, the version of the reconciliation of Menelaus and Helen advanced by Stesichorus seems even harder to believe.

That may be just what tempts Barth to use it. His version of the reunion is as follows: After having struggled with Proteus and won (maybe), Menelaus is finally sailing home and prepares to dispatch Helen, only to be stopped by her demand to know what Proteus said. When that story is finally told, we learn that Proteus has advised the same sort of course that Menelaus had himself taken after he saw the Oracle in Delphi: Proteus tells Menelaus to sacrifice twin heifers, Curiosity and Common Sense to Aphrodite, adding, " ' " 'beg Love's pardon for your want of faith. Helen chose you without reason because she loves you without cause; embrace her without question and watch the weather change.' " ' " Given that advice and the fact that Menelaus has had Helen at sword's point once before in her bedroom at Troy, whereupon asking her "why" he got the same answer he had given her twenty years earlier when he married her: "Love!"—given all that, one can understand how Menelaus might say to Helen, sprawled on the poop, dagger at her throat: " ' "I believe all. I understand nothing. I love you." ' " In a world in which nothing makes sense, love makes as much sense as anything.

At this point Barth has Helen introduce Stesichorus for one more turn of the screw. " ' "Love!" ' " she snarls back at Menelaus. " ' "Loving may waste us into Echoes," ' "—properly describing what is happening to our narrator's voice at this point—" ' "but it's being loved that kills . . . Do you love me to punish me for loving you?" ' " Marveling that he hasn't heard " ' "such deep Greek since Delphi," ' " Menelaus still refuses to ask (or answer) questions just as Proteus enjoined him. Furious, Helen the Bitch determines to put his love to the test by offering him the Stesichorus version of her story, insisting on her chastity and chastising him for his "decade vagrance" while she languished in Pharos. Since the Helen Menelaus brought from Troy had managed to ward off his advances for seven long years, he has no reason to disbelieve this new version of her story, though he does, with magnificent reticence, express his doubts. The real dilemma is that neither he nor we have any basis for accepting or rejecting either version. Menelaus may be either the greatest fool and biggest cuckold in Greece or its luckiest, most ennobled hero. Yet, to Helen's insistence that he " ' "espouse her without more carp!" ' " he does react . . . finally! In doing so he begins to fulfill Proteus's final prophecy, that he will be taken by the gods into Elysium to be his wife's " ' " 'undying advertisement, her espouser in the gods' slow time . . . forasmuch as and only that you are beloved of Helen, they count you immortal as themselves.' " ' " Like the sperm-narrator of "Night-Sea Journey," Menelaus achieves whatever immortality there is through his affirmation of love. What explains the reconciliation, insofar as anything does, also explains the separation, the war, and the marriage in the beginning—the ambiguity of love.

Apparently, the two equally acceptable yet contradictory versions of the Helen story are causally related to Menelaus's private identity crisis, symbolically realized in his encounter with Proteus. Like the dreams which Menelaus has had that have completely confused him concerning the reality of time, these elements, at any rate, are all part of a design that destroys whatever preconceived notions about life and love Menelaus may have had. So, too, Barth's complicated formal design of layers of stories is also broken sporadically with momentary leaps from one level of story to another (most frequently in the constant interruptions of Peisistratus), disturbing, if not destroying any preconceived notions we might entertain about his form. Such complexities in technical management of the story are the perfect complement to the ambiguities of plot and point of view, all of which in combination force the reader to sympathize with Menelaus in his confusion and to accept as a valid image of the world itself the absurdities of lovers. Barth's point, in contrast to Arnold's is not that love is something we can create or preserve in opposition to a world gone mad, but that it is in its essence the image of that world and its absurdity. The strangest irony of all is that Barth, like the singer of Menelaus's song, seems to insist, "I'm not dismayed." For even while Menelaus decrescends right out of his own song at the end, passing from man to tale to voice that tells it, that same voice realizes that the process can just as meaningfully be regarded as inverted, as an ascending progression, with Menelaus transcending himself when he "turns tale"; that even when that tale itself expires, he will survive, as prophesied, "in Proteus's terrifying last disguise, Beauty's spouse's odd Elysium: the absurd, unending possibility of love."

What makes Menelaus the proper hero of an "epic" seems to be his commitment, tenuous as it is, to that possiblity of love. His story represents, therefore, something of a turning point in Barth's fiction. The same affirmation characterizes not only the "Anonymiad," which follows it in *Lost in the Funhouse*, but also the three "epics" which constitute *Chimera*. In the "Bellerophoniad" Barth speaks explicitly of the "ironically qualified fulfillment" of both Menelaus and Perseus in their search for immortality *especially* in the transformation of each into his own voice or life-story. That key word, *especially*, makes it probable that fulfillment might take other forms, too. In each case it is inextricably involved with (if not simply resolved by) the affirmation of the possibility of love.

Barth's emerging position is offered more openly in the closing section of the "Dunyazadiad." Here the narrator approves of Shah Zaman's plea that Dunyazade love him *as if* it might work, implying that pretense, even fiction, is appropriate in a world in which nothing lasts forever, in which not even the conventions of fiction pretend that lovers can live happily ever after. The Arabic tale traditionally concludes that things go well only until the inevitable appearance of "The Destroyer of Delights." Barth's heroes in these recent novellas are those who accept the inevitability of such destruction, who commit themselves to love, not as an absolute value but as a value more precious for its very fragility. To claim the world has "neither joy, nor love, nor light" seems as silly as to trust too completely in the faithfulness of lovers. Instead, as Todd Andrews first insisted, values (like love) less than absolute can be lived by. Barth's recent fiction seems to be expanding on Todd's wisdom, his own position affirming the possibility of love—absurd though that may be. "To be joyous in the full acceptance" of the inevitability of loss, Barth concludes the "Dunyazadiad," "is to possess a treasure."

THE INDIVIDUAL NOVELS

The Floating Opera

Books of the Times

Orville Prescott*

On the morning of June 23, 1937 (or maybe it was June 24, he couldn't remember exactly), Todd Andrews, the best lawyer on the Eastern Shore of Maryland and the most determinedly eccentric citizen of the tidewater city of Cambridge, decided to commit suicide. Todd was 37 years old, a bachelor and a resident of the Dorset Hotel. Each morning Todd paid his rent for the night before by check, $1.50, and then registered for another night. It wasn't that his endocarditis or his damaged prostate gland made Todd doubtful that he would live out the day, although he was doubtful. It was his pleasure in doing everything differently. Seventeen years later, in 1954, Todd sat down to write an account of that memorable day and why he did not kill himself after all. He had seven peach baskets full of notes on the subject. The book he produced, "The Floating Opera," a first novel by John Barth, is now published.

John Barth comes from Cambridge, Md., himself. He is young, erudite and clever. Every now and then in "The Floating Opera" he is funny. His ability to contrive a really preposterous situation is impressive. His gift of gab is impressive, too.

Nevertheless, "The Floating Opera" isn't anywhere near funny enough to make up for its grievous faults. Most of this odd novel is dull. Most of its humor is labored and flat. Some of its heavy-handed attempts to shock seem cheap in a juvenile and nasty way rather than sophisticated or realistic, as they probably were intended.

Todd Andrews describing his own life from childhood through his great suicide failure twists and turns through so many flashbacks, pauses to consider so many irrelevancies and spouts so much pretentious verbiage that "The Floating Opera" seems permanently grounded on a mud bank. When Todd describes his "magnificent" mistress, the wife of his best friend, and the menage a trois, the three of them kept up for years, he only arouses virulent disbelief and does not make up for it by comedy. It takes a Noel Coward to make the most of such a situation.

When Todd describes his professional shenanigans in several prolonged and wonderfully complicated lawsuits he displays his own attitude

*Reprinted by permission of *The New York Times*, Sept. 3, 1956.

toward the practice of law, but he fails completely to amuse. Todd thought of the law as a game he enjoyed playing. He was not concerned about legal ethics or even very seriously about his clients.

And the reason Todd took nothing seriously and believed in nothing was that he was an amateur existentialist although, of course he had never heard of existentialism. "I insist upon my basic and ultimate irresponsibility," said Todd. Nothing has any intrinsic value, he argued, neither material things like money or success, nor abstractions like love or truth. The reasons that people have for attributing value to things are always ultimately arbitrary. "Men and women are only animals" and "everything we do on earth is absolutely ridiculous."

Todd's ideas on the uselessness and meaninglessness of life are developed at great length in "The Floating Opera" with consequent tedium. It was his negative philosophy that made Todd decide to commit suicide. And that decision is as ridiculous as everything else in this strange book, for Todd's enjoyment of life was enormous. It is impossible to believe that anyone who took such relish in his own sense of humors in Maryland rye and in lovemaking would consider suicide for a moment.

It is difficult to know just how seriously Mr. Barth expects his readers to take the ideas in a story that, after all, is basically a frenzied farce. But they are developed at such length that I suspect that Mr. Barth sets much store by them. This conclusion is reinforced by the fact that the true climax of "The Floating Opera" is philosophical. Todd Andrews discovers everything is not ridiculous, that his love for a little child is real and important. All values, Todd still thinks, may be relative. But nevertheless, "There are relative values. These, at least, we have, and if they are all we have then in no way whatsoever are they inferior."

Such a denouement is hardly earth-shaking. It is reasonable and intelligent as far as it goes. Whether it was a good idea to emphasize philosophizing so prominently in a novel as filled with ludicrous antics and jubilant sexuality as "The Floating Opera" is doubtful. It is almost as if two authors at work on two books had decided to collaborate. One author writes crude farce occasionally brightened by wit. The other broods on the meaning of existence with solemn goodwill. The result is odd indeed.

John Barth:
The Floating Opera

Patrick Haney*

Freedom, Robbe-Grillet says, is freedom to invent. One is reminded of Robbe-Grillet in rereading *The Floating Opera*, John Barth's first novel, reissued now with its ending revised. Todd Andrews, the book's narrator, having lived most of his life with the knowledge that at any moment his heart may conk out on him, decides to commit suicide. Straight narrative of the events of the day which was supposed to culminate in the fatal act, interrupted by flashback and digression, leads us to the book's conclusion—not suicide, but the narrator's recognition of five last things: Nothing has intrinsic value; The reasons for which people attribute value to things are ultimately irrational; There is, therefore, no ultimate "reason" for valuing anything; Living is action; There's no final reason for action; There's no final reason for living (or for suicide). In its original (published) version the book had Andrews concluding that although there may be no absolute values, there are relative ones, and that "if they are all we have, then *in no way whatsoever* are they inferior." That ending was either equivocal in the context, tongue in cheek, or corny—in whichever case, rather nasty. The present ending is tougher and more honest, and in keeping with the book as a whole. It leaves the narrator free—to invent, if he will.

Andrews says he will go on living his life pretty much as he has always lived it, and possibly this is as negative as most readers could wish. On the other hand, Andrews has certainly come to see things more clearly. Above all, he has come to realize that his successive identities in the past of rake, saint, and cynic have been dishonest, the means of hiding his "enigmatic heart" from himself. He is also living on his own at the end of the book, free at last from his father. And he has come to regard the Macks, Harrison and Jane, with whom he has engaged in a long-drawn-out sexual triangle, as human beings instead of objects of comic interest. And, finally , he has written a book called *The Floating Opera*. I am not inclined to see all this as ultimately negative, but then, to me, the five conclusions Andrews comes to are just plain sensible.

*Reprinted by permission of *The Denver Quarterly*, II (Summer 1967), 170–71.

The foregoing will have indicated that Barth is dealing in this first novel with the same things, in general, that concern Donleavy in *Meet My Maker*. Perhaps *The Floating Opera*, too, seemed fresher from this standpoint eleven years ago. The point is that it still seems pretty fresh, even though Barth's approach to his theme is essentially an academic one. Like another first novel, *Wise Blood*, whose theme also resembles Barth's, *The Floating Opera* appears to have been written with a good deal of gusto and to call for gusto on the part of the reader. Certainly, I think, it can be read with gusto. Only towards the end does Barth's invention (I realize I'm not using the word exactly in Robbe-Grillet's sense) flag a little. We are anxious to get through the showboat chapter, although it's obviously germane and all that, and interesting in itself. In addition, once they have moved from the realm of flat characters to the realm of rounder ones, the Macks are disappointing—it almost seems a rule that nice people in our serious fiction have to sound like characters out of a *Family Circle* story.

As elsewhere in Barth's work we are reminded of Sterne when we read *The Floating Opera*, not only by specific things (comical farting, tedious digression, direct address to the reader amounting to a challenge, the continual starting and stopping), but by general format, as well—the unabashed weaving of inventive web, outlandish, often annoying, around a rather dry philosophical idea. To return to my point of origin, *The Floating Opera* is like *The Voyeur*, too, in this respect. Also like *An American Dream*. Academic Barth and non-academic Mailer. What other "famous" American writers at present make you wonder what their next books will be like, even though, quite possibly, you know what they will be about?

John Barth's First Novel

Stanley Edgar Hyman*

John Barth's *The Sot-Weed Factor* was first published in 1960, but I did not catch up with it until last year, when it appeared in paperback. I found it the funniest of all the New American Novels, and I concluded my appreciation of Barth in these pages (March 2, 1964): "Although I cannot imagine what he could write after this book, I look forward to it eagerly." I still cannot imagine what Barth will write next, and I still await it eagerly, but meanwhile his first novel, *The Floating Opera*, originally published in 1956, has now come out in paperback (Avon Books, 272 pp., $.75). It is a most interesting and impressive work.

The Floating Opera is narrated by Todd Andrews, a bachelor lawyer in Cambridge, Maryland, on the Eastern Shore. His narration is leisurely (often too leisurely), opinionated, quirky, full of artful flashbacks and delayed disclosures—so that bald chronological synopsis does the story an injustice. Todd's life has been relatively eventful. He was born in 1900 and is 54 at the time of writing; his mother died when he was seven. Todd was seduced by a worldly young schoolgirl named Betty June Gunter on his 17th birthday, and soon afterward he enlisted in the Army and fought overseas. He was educated at Johns Hopkins and the University of Maryland Law School. Todd's father, also a lawyer and his predecessor as senior partner of the firm, was ruined in 1929, and hanged himself a few months later. Between 1933 and 1937, Todd had a mistress, Janie Mack, the wife of his best friend, Harrison Mack, Jr.; by 1937 he had become largely impotent with her. Since then he has occupied himself with sailing, hunting, and less demanding sports.

Todd describes himself as tall, thin, and handsome, except for ugly clubbed fingers. These are caused by a defective heart, first diagnosed when he was 19. His other ailment is a chronic prostate infection, now under control. Todd describes his life as a series of disguises determined by his misfortunes. He was an ordinary boy until the discovery of the heart condition; then he masked as "a rake" until the discovery of the prostate infection; after that he posed as "a saint" until his father's suicide; since then he has shown himself to the world as "a cynic."

*Reprinted with permission from *The New Leader*, April 12, 1965. Copyright The American Labor Conference on International Affairs, Inc.

Todd's daily routine, at the time we encounter him, is as regular and reassuring as the mailman's. Since his father's death he has lived in Room 307 of the Dorset Hotel, across the street from the courthouse and a block from his office. Todd wakes at six, takes a shot of rye from a quart he keeps on the windowsill, and goes down the hall to have coffee with some elderly neighbors in the hotel. Then he goes downstairs and pays his bill at the desk (he takes his room by the day, to acknowledge his weak heart). At seven Todd goes for a walk, breakfasting on some hard biscuits in his pocket. After his walk, without taking off his good clothes, he works for an hour on a boat he is building, then proceeds to the office. Todd may lunch or dine with a client. After dinner, if it is Tuesday or Friday, Janie appears in his room. Otherwise Todd spends the evening alone, working on what he calls the *Inquiry*, an elaborate research into his father's life and the reasons for his suicide.

Although generally self-satisfied, Todd does not regard himself as particularly passionate. "In my life I have experienced emotion intensely on only five occasions," Todd tells us. These occasions were his initiation by Betty June, his seduction by Janie and final failure with her, and two traumatic experiences of death: he captured a German prisoner during the War, hugged him and kissed him, then bayoneted him; he discovered his father's corpse and cut it down.

Barth's feat has been to make this shallow and conventional Maryland gentleman, so unlike the autobiographical heroes of first novels, not only interesting to us but important. The novel's story consists of one day in June, 1937, on which Todd Andrews changed his mind about committing suicide. The night before he had been miserably impotent with Janie, had known despair, and had recovered his good spirits by the decision to end his life. Then Todd simultaneously ended the *Inquiry* into his father's suicide by writing down his discovery that absolute values do not exist, so that "There is, then, no 'reason' for living."

In the course of the day, during which Janie breaks with him and he makes a half-hearted suicide attempt, he discovers the importance of relative values, corrects his final proposition with the addition that there is no reason for dying prematurely, either, and determines to live. The final chapter title offers this as a "happy ending," and Todd assures us that his life since then has been adequately gratifying, although "there have been no women in my bed since that morning."

Beneath this cheery narrative surface, Barth offers a very different view of Todd Andrews. He is a victim of his Oedipus complex, a latent homosexual, a cold fish, and a malicious sadist. He begins the day with a kindly note to Janie proposing that she exhibit herself to an 83-year-old retired oyster dredger at the hotel; before the day is over he has driven another elderly neighbor to suicide. A cherished part of Todd's cynicism is his vision of human copulation as animal and consequently ludicrous. The day he lost his virginity, Todd enraged Betty June and drove her away in a fury when he caught sight of the two of them in the mirror, "animals in the act of mating," and broke into uncontrollable laughter. When Janie ends their affair, Todd spitefully pictures her and Harrison "permanently locked together" like copulating crabs. A naked matron at a drunken party is a "dugong hoisted from the deep." The "happy ending," in short, is a life free of the embarrassing animality of the female body.

All this makes the book sound far more earnest than it is. Barth sees through Todd Andrews, as it were, with a light eye. The Floating Opera of the title is a showboat that arrives at Cambridge on the day of the story, and becomes the scene of some of the action. It symbolizes, we are flatly told, the law, Todd's mind, life itself, and this book; all are Floating Operas, stages for putting on a show. (Barth uses Todd to explain his symbols, apologize for them, mock them as "Hollywoodish," and, in the course of this, to expand and develop them usefully.) The only way to learn anything, Todd tells us, is "to learn it stingingly, to the heart, through involvement." He himself does not have much heart for involvement, but it is just this ultimate involvement that a floating opera does not require. The minstrels do an old-fashioned walk-around, and the show is over.

The Floating Opera exhibits, in bud, much that was to flower in *The Sot-Weed Factor*. There are periodic roman candles and pinwheels of rhetoric, and the narrative style is an elaborate mock-dialogue with the reader. We are treated to such *Tristram Shandy* devices as breaking the page into repetitive double columns (one for each eye) and ending two chapters with the same formula (on the grounds that the first occasion was premature). The pages that reproduce the Floating Opera handbill typographically and describe the performance in detail give us a foretaste of Barth's Nabokovian talent for elaborate, spurious documentation.

Three wild comic episodes stand out in *The Floating Opera*. One is the legal case of the estate of Harrison Mack, Sr., the Dill Pickle King. It involves 17 wills, each leaving the estate, which includes three million dollars as well as 129 pickle jars in which Mack preserved his excreta, in a different spiteful combination. (Todd eventually wins the money for Harrison and Janie by his discovery that the widow had misapplied, on her zinnia beds, the less desirable part of the bequest.) The second is Todd's reencounter with Betty June in a Baltimore brothel seven years after he laughed at her: she resourcefully tries to dismember him with a broken bottle. The third is Todd's courtship by the richest man in Cambridge, Col. Morton of Morton's Marvelous Tomatoes, which turns into another sort of courtship by the Colonel's lady, a marvelous tomato indeed.

One strand of the book has great satiric bite. It is the manner in which Harrison and Janie Mack talk about Janie's affair with Todd: an affair which, as an emancipated couple, they have contrived jointly. "I did it—we did it—because we like you," Harrison tells Todd after Janie has popped into his bed. "We certainly had no right to expect him not to make love to other women," Harrison later admonishes Janie. "Neither one of us has any regrets that I made love to you," Janie informs Todd when they break off.

Once the cringing stops, we recognize what once I named "the Albertine Strategy," an affair with a man variously disguised as an affair with a woman. (This is that variation of it, obsessive in the work of James Joyce, in which two male friends attain symbolic union by sharing the body of a woman.) The Albertine Strategy is far more overt in *The Sot-Weed Factor*, where Henry Burlingame cheerily confesses that he lusts equally for Ebenezer and his sister. The covert, symbolic homosexuality of *The Floating Opera* (biting in the Macks, farcical in the Mortons, melodramatic in the episode of the German prisoner) becomes the mad polymorphous pansexuality of *The Sot-Weed Factor*.

The principal sign of immaturity in *The Floating Opera* is sentimentality. Some of Todd's memories of his father suggest soap opera, and there is a mistaken effort to relate Todd's change of mind about killing himself to a concern with the Mack's little daughter Jeannine (who may in fact be Todd's daughter). Otherwise the book is quite an achievement for a man of 26. Barth has since gone far beyond it. I can hardly conceive a limit to his eventual attainment.

The Floating Opera Restored

Enoch P. Jordan*

When John Barth's first novel was reissued in 1967, the *Publisher's Weekly* reviewer noted that its conclusion had been changed, but since then the fact that the novel has been revised has largely gone unnoticed,[1] yet the revisions are far more important than the critical silence indicates. Barth points to the nature of the changes in his "Prefatory Note to the Revised Edition":

> One [publisher] finally agreed to launch the *Opera*, but on condition that the builder make certain major changes in its construction, notably about the stern. . . . In this edition the original and correct ending to the story has been restored, as have a number of other, minor passages. . . . I'm pleased that it will sink or float now in its original design.[2]

The original and correct conclusion is radically different from the first edition's, and its denial of the sentimental optimism demanded by the original publisher creates a thematic unity missing in the 1956 edition. The other changes also have significant effects: by omitting one chapter and reordering plot episodes, Barth tightens the novel's structure and satisfies our expectations regarding fictional structure.

Barth's original design begins to re-emerge in Chapter XI, "An instructive, if sophisticated, observation." The chapter is set in the present time of the novel, June 21st or 22nd, 1937. Todd Andrews, the protagonist, is walking down a Cambridge street on his way to an appointment with Dr. Marvin Rose, made in spite of his resolve to commit suicide before the end of the day.

> At the curb in front of a large funeral parlor a sleek black hearse was parked. . . As I approached, a fat black pussycat, scarred with experience and heavy with imminent kittens, trotted wearily out of a hydrangea bush beside the undertaker's porch into the sun, and for no discernible reason curled plumply in the middle of the sidewalk and closed her eyes. Just then the door opened, and the pallbearers came out bringing the casket. Their path was diverted, but not greatly, by the pregnant cat. Some of the pallbearers smiled, and an employee of the funeral home nudged the cat aside with his toe. She got up, stretched, yawned, and padded off to find some less traveled thoroughfare to sleep in; the loading door of the hearse was swung open, and the casket loaded gently inside.

*Reprinted by permission of *Critique*, XVIII, No. 2 (Winter 1976), 5–16.

I smiled and walked on. Nature, coincidence, can often be a heavy-handed symbolizer. (116–7)

At the curb in front of a large funeral parlor a black hearse was parked. . . As I approached, an aged Chesapeake Bay retriever bitch loped from a hydrangea bush out onto the undertaker's porch, followed closely by a prancing, sniffing young mongrel setter. I saw the Chesapeake Bay dog stop to shake herself in front of the door; the setter clambered upon her at once, his long tongue lolling. Just then the door opened and the pallbearers came out with a casket. Their path was blocked by the dogs. Some of the bearers smiled guiltily; an employee caught the setter on his haunches with an unfunereal kick. The bitch trundled off the porch, her lover still half on her, and took up a position in the middle of the sidewalk, near the hearse. The pair then resumed their amours in the glaring sun, to the embarrassment of the company, who pretended not to notice them while the hearse's door was opened and the casket gently loaded aboard.

I smiled and walked on. Nature, coincidence, can be a heavy-handed symbolizer. (R109)

Todd goes on to call the scene a "clumsy 'life-in-the-face-of-death' scenario" and expande the general observation which concludes the quoted passage by supplying a dozen more brief examples of nature's "abundant ingenuousness" (R110).

The cat and dogs serve as recognizable symbols of life, but with the cat as a life-figure the episode's comic edge is blunted and its verbal, visual, and philosophical shock value are almost nonexistent. The placid, maternal cat who partially diverts the pallbearers' path is "nudged aside" and pads sleepily out of the picture; life is serene, gentle, and pregnant, and even the representatives of death are kind. The copulating dogs blocking the pallbearers' path are given "an unfunereal kick" and scramble off the porch to resume their activities on the sidewalk near the hearse; here life is carnal, self-absorbed, and tasteless. The contrasts of the scene become sharper and more savagely comic.

The cat may have replaced the dogs at the insistence of an editor worried about good taste, but Todd's reaction to the copulating dogs foreshadows later events and supports convictions he expresses elsewhere in the novel. Todd calls the dogs "truly funny," which prepares us, with the end of Chapter XII (in the revised edition), for the narration of an event Todd considers one of the two "unforgettable demonstrations of [his] animality" (R61) in Chapter XIII, "A mirror up to life."

In Chapter XII Todd, still on his way to his appointment with Dr. Rose, sits down on a park bench where his eighty-three-year-old friend, Captain Osborn Jones, and the other old men of Cambridge sit in the sun and "ingest with their eyes everything that passes," like "a chorus of ancient oysters" (R112). Their conversation meanders about the funeral being held at the moment, but it serves only as a starting point for personal reminiscences. The chapter is amusing because Barth has captured the mood of the old men "digesting people with a snort and a comment" in realistic dialogue punctuated by rheumatic wheezes, snufflings, and cackles of "mirth and expectoration" (119). It is also of some importance in developing Captain Osborn's character but, in the first edition, creates an awkward interruption in Todd's reflective narrative. It forces the narrator to use a transition to the next chapter which he admits "loses itself, like a surrealist collonade, in an infinite regress of archness" (123). He comments at some length on the trap he has gotten himself into but finds no better bridge to "A mirror up to life" than the apologetically offered coincidence of looking into a reflecting tile wall after he leaves the old men.

In the revised edition, however, the old men's conversation is drawn from the funeral to the dogs, whose amours bring them in front of the bench. Captain Osborn assists the setter, using a foot to help him mount the Chesapeake Bay bitch, and the other old men snicker and encourage the setter to help himself while he can. Todd leaves, "thinking of animals *in coito*" (R116); Barth has managed to keep the irony of the "life-in-the-face-of-death" scenario in front of us through another chapter and has added to its development. He has also provided a natural bridge to "A mirror up to life," a chapter detailing Todd's first sexual encounter.

In Chapter XIII, not only does the virginal adolescent lose his innocence but makes such a determined enemy of his partner that seven years later she assaults him with a broken bottle, an attack described in Chapter XIV. Her hatred is caused by Todd's reaction to their love-making, prepared for by his comment about the dogs at the end of "An instructive, if sophisticated, observation." After he has "bleated like a goat, and roared like a lion" (R123), Todd happens to glance at the mirror on the bedside bureau:

> an unusually large mirror, that gave our images full-length and life-size—and there we were; Betty June's face buried in the pillow, her scrawny little buttocks thrust skywards: me gangly as a whippet and braying like an ass. I exploded with laughter! . . . even as I write this now, thirty-seven years later, I can't expunge that mirror from my mind; I think of it and must smile. To see a pair of crabs, of dogs, of people—even lovely, graceful Jane—I can't finish, reader, can't hold my pen fast to the line: I am convulsed. (R123–4)

Todd's description of himself as a whippet and his later reference to "a pair of dogs" (present in both editions) link the episode to Chapter XI; his reaction to the dogs prepares us for his response to seeing himself and Betty June *in coito*.

The revised edition's Chapter XI, then, presents a more striking scene than the first edition's and also allows Barth to create a more unified series of chapters by introducing the image of copulation. It provides material for a smooth transition from Chapter XII to Chapter XIII and partially foreshadows the content of the latter.

An even more significant difference between the texts is the complete omission of Chapter XXIII of the 1956 edition. The chapter, "Another premise to swallow," is an explication of the preceding chapter, "A tour of the Opera," explaining in some detail the relationship of the three-and-one-half-year-old Jeannine's "Why?" to Todd's value system. In order to understand what effect the omission has on the novel, we must look carefully at both Chapter XXII and the omitted chapter.

In Chapter XXII of both editions Todd tells us that Jeannine's habit when excited was to slip into "the 'Why?' routine," in which she responds to all information with that one question. Todd's patience with Jeannine is entirely in character; he displays here the same tolerance evident in his treatment of the nearly senile members of the Dorchester Explorer's Club and in earlier scenes with Jeannine. The catechism, however, does more than simply add to our appreciation of his humanity; his responses are reinforcements of the philosophical position he has expressed in talking to Mr. Haecker, the Explorer's Club member most dissatisfied with old age and frightened of death. In Chapter XVIII Mr. Haecker and Todd talk about old age and death. Mr. Haecker is trying to convince himself that old age is "the glorious finale of life—the last for which the first was made" (176), and that he is content to be old and dying. Todd recognizes the older man's loneliness and fear of death but is irritated by his pompous attempts at self-deception; being asked for an honest opinion, he tells Mr. Haecker that he is trying to fool himself. Haecker responds with some anger but admits that the alternatives are to "pretend to be content, like a man, or go around wailing and weeping like a child" (180). Todd suggests a third alternative, suicide. In reply to Mr. Haecker's desperate assertion that life has an absolute and intrinsic value, Todd asserts, "Nothing has any intrinsic value" (182). He elaborates in Chapter XIX, "A premise to swallow," supplying specific illustrations and detailing the logical process by which he concludes that "nothing is intrinsically valuable; the value of everything is attributed to it, assigned to it, from outside, by people" (R171).

Todd's responses to Jeannine reinforce his position. She, Todd tells us, is not really interested in her own questions or in his answers but is merely trying to keep him talking. Nevertheless, he responds to her as if she were actually trying to elicit information. The object of her curiosity (and the reason for her excitement) is *Adam's Original and Unparalleled Floating Opera*, and she begins by asking "What's it for?" Todd tries to explain the purpose of the showboat logically. He tells her that "people go on it and listen to music and watch the actors dance and act funny" (215). When she asks why, he tries to explain each of the clauses in his first response, but the effort inevitably tangles him in questions of human motivation and value ascription to which logic cannot supply answers: "Why do they like to be happy?" "That's the end of the line." "Why do they like being alive?" "End of the line again" (215). The function of their question and answer session is clear if we keep in mind the analogy between showboat and life introduced in the first chapter of the novel. If, as the narrator suggests, life is a showboat floating by, then Jeannine's re-iterated "Why?" is an echo of the question Todd had been asking about life, and to which he had found an answer only that morning.

Chapter XXIII of the 1956 edition is an extended comment by the narrator of the philosophical implications of the catechism in Chapter XXII, and its "premise" is in fact a corollary of the premise of Chapter XXVIII. The chapter begins with a more complete set of answers to Jean-nine's questions, but the answers still fall short of solving the problems they suggest:

> Consider: A man attends the *Floating Opera*. Why? Excellent reason: a change from the old routine, a chance to laugh. Why is it better to laugh than not to? Easy: because a laughing man is happy, and it's better to be happy than sad. Why? Well, without happiness, or the hope of it, a man might as well be dead, and surely it's better to be alive than dead. Why? (221)

The final "Why?"—like the "end of the line" in the preceding chapter—is an admission that logic cannot be applied to human values, particularly to the question of suicide, without some previous, rationally indefensible assumptions (such as, if one wants to stay alive, then . . .).

The finally unanswerable question is a reminder, as the narrator here tells us directly, that *"the reasons that people have for attributing value to things are always ultimately arbitrary"* (222). A few paragraphs later Todd tells us again that "There is no ultimate reason for calling anything important or valuable; no ultimate reason for preferring one thing to another" (222), and in the penultimate sentence of the three-page chapter he repeats the idea: "There is . . . no ultimate reason for preferring one thing to another" (223). The repetitions within the short chapter, although obvious, are not in themselves particularly irritating because the philosophical concepts are considered from a relatively abstract perspec-tive; nevertheless, the chapter repeats information presented in a dif-ferent form earlier in the novel. If we look only at the preceding chapter, we find that the philosophical conclusions stated overtly in Chapter XXIII are presented in dramatic rather than discursive form. Whether the chapter was added to the 1956 edition at the suggestion of an editor con-cerned with clarity or was part of the original manuscript, Barth ap-parently decided that the restatement of Todd's conclusions about value was unnecessary.

Omitting the chapter produces yet another effect. The next-to-last sentence (quoted above) provides a direct foreshadowing of Todd's final answer to Hamlet's question, supplying the reader with a conclusion about the question of suicide that Todd himself has yet to reach. At the end of Chapter XXVIII of the revised edition Todd reproduces the note he wrote at home after his abortive suicide attempt aboard the *Floating Opera*: "There's no final reason for living (or for suicide)" (R250)—the logical extension of the position expressed at the end of Chapter XXIII of the 1956 edition. While the after-the-fact narrator may appropriately be aware of the conclusion before the actor in the novel, removing the premature statement of the resolution of Todd's dilemma provides greater suspense by denying the reader access to Todd's final rationalization.

Although each of the variants discussed above has an impact on our perception of the novel, the most extensive and important revisions occur in the last few chapters. The original edition's final three chapters become four, with the action reorganized and the events and their causes radically changed. The scope and nature of these changes can be seen most clearly if the action of the final chapters of the two editions is compared.

Chapter XXVII of the 1956 edition—"Will you smile at my rowboat?"—begins with Todd commenting that a newly formed philosophical position, like a new rowboat, should be allowed "to sit for a day or two at the dock, to let the seams swell tight" (251), but that such a curing period is not always available. The next page and one-half are devoted to a discussion of the relative importance of conscious and unconscious motivations in ethical and philosophical considerations. When Todd has stated his conclusion that neither kind of motive completely accounts for action, he brings Captain Osborn on stage. The Captain invites himself to accompany Todd to the performance on board the *Floating Opera* and presents Todd with a bottle of Southern Comfort, which they begin to share. Todd decides to invite Mr. Haecker to join them and goes up to the old man's room to talk with him. He finds Mr. Haecker stretched out on his bed, unconscious from a deliberate overdose of barbiturates. Todd hurries down to the hotel desk to summon aid and returns with Captain Osborn, the desk clerk, and the bottle of whisky. The ambulance arrives and the attendants take Mr. Haecker away. Todd summarizes Mr. Haecker's subsequent career, which ends in a successful suicide attempt some three years later, and he and Captain Osborn leave for the performance. As they go, Todd remarks that his rowboat is now afloat.

Chapter XXVIII, "The Floating Opera," opens with a description of the showboat and the audience. Captain Adam, the owner and master of ceremonies, introduces Clara Mulloy, who is scheduled to sing but has laryngitis. In place of Clara he offers the audience some culture: T. Wallace Whittaker, "the eminent tragedian" (260), recites three Shakespearean soliloquies to a progressively more bored and hostile audience; by the time he is well launched into Hamlet's soliloquy on suicide the patrons are shouting for the minstrels and throwing pennies. When Whittaker has finished, the minstrels begin their show, to everyone's delight, and run through their complete repertory, much of which is reported to us. Captain Adam introduces the last act, Burley Joe Wells doing imitations; Joe imitates a steam calliope, a buzz saw, and begins to imitate the race of the steamboats *Natchez* and *Robert E. Lee*.

When Burley Joe Wells has the audience entranced, Todd slips out of his seat, goes outside and directly to the galley, turns on the gas burners and the oven without lighting them and sits down. He explains his choice of method by saying that he was attracted by the "opportunity to wait out the minutes between my act and its consequences in utter calm" (270). Todd describes his fading sensations, and then, suddenly, a crewman enters the galley, turns off the gas, and runs into the dining room to escape the fumes. Todd finds himself paralyzed, although he is thoroughly captivated by his rational powers and realizes that there is "no reason to do anything" (270).

Then Todd hears Jane Mack's voice, and its urgency spurs him into action.[3] He runs into the dining room, from which the crewman has disappeared, and finds Jane, Harrison, and Dr. Rose examining Jeannine, who has had a seizure. Todd feels fright, concern, and even some envy of Harrison (apparently as a result of his immediate involvement with Jeannine), and follows the Macks out onto the deck when they leave with Jeannine. He calls after them. "I hope she'll be all right!" (273), wonders how he can tell them not to trust Marvin Rose's competence, and wants "very badly indeed" to go with them. He tells Jane that he will call later on but will not go with them because he does not know how to act in such situations. At this point Todd considers jumping into the Choptank River but feels that the moment for suicide has passed:

> Some qualitative change had occurred, instantly, down in the dining room. The fact is I had no reason to be concerned over little Jeannine, and yet my concern for that child was so intense, and had been so immediately forthcoming, that (I understood now) the first desperate sound of Jane's voice had snapped me out of a paralysis *which there was no reason to terminate.* No reason at all. (274)

Todd returns to the theater, takes his seat, and watches the end of Burley Joe's act, an imitation of a steamboat explosion. It comes to a thunderous end, frightening the audience so badly that some women faint and many scream. The minstrel troupe then goes into an old-fashioned breakdown, and the curtain comes down.

In Chapter XXIX, "A parenthesis, a happy ending, a *Floating Opera*," Todd helps Captain Osborn out of his seat and back to the hotel, and then retreats to his room. He sits and thinks for a while, and then adds a parenthetical phrase to the notes he had made before going to the showboat. The fifth proposition now becomes *"There is, then, no 'reason' for living (or for suicide)"* (278). He finds the negativity of the proposition distasteful but is suddenly excited by the realization that if relative values are all we have, then *"in no way whatsoever* are they inferior" (279). He decides that his insight provides a way for him to live with his weak heart and says that, since the problem of living with the knowledge of coming death is everyone's problem, his solution should work for everyone. With newfound hope Todd goes downstairs to telephone the Macks, "ignoring with a smile the absurd thunderstorm that just then broke over Cambridge" (280).

Although many of the incidents and descriptions presented in the 1956 edition are retained in the revised edition, the order of presentation and a number of crucial passages have been changed. Because Chapter XXIII of the 1956 edition is omitted in the revised edition, Chapter XXVII of the earlier edition is now Chapter XXVI, retitled "The first step" and reduced from five pages to one page. It, too, begins with the statement that new philosophical positions should be allowed to cure for a few days before they are acted upon but that such a waiting period is not always possible. The discussion of motivation has been excised, along with the discovery of Mr. Haecker's suicide attempt. Captain Osborn merely invites himself to the performance, and as they leave for the showboat Todd concludes the chapter by remarking that his rowboat is now afloat.

Chapter XXVII, "The Floating Opera," shows only minor stylistic revisions until Burley Joe Wells is performing and Todd leaves the theater (R242). He goes outside and makes his way below decks, as in Chapter XXVIII of the 1956 edition; instead of going to the galley, he enters the dining room, where he lights the three kerosene lamps that are bracketed to the walls and opens the valve which supplies acetylene to the footlights (for use in towns that do not have electrical connections at their docks, as Cambridge does). Then he goes into the galley, lights one burner of the stove, and turns on the other three burners and the oven without lighting them. He returns to the dining room, removes the chimneys from the lamps, turns up their wicks, and then goes topside and re-enters the theater. As he watches Burley Joe continue his imitation of the race of the *Natchez* and *Robert E. Lee,* he contemplates, "calmly," the idea that Jane and Jeannine will soon be "charred remains" (R243). Burley Joe switches into his imitation of the "great steamboat explosion" without introduction, and Todd continues to wait for the real explosion. The imitation reaches its climax: women scream and faint; the minstrels go into their breakdown, and the curtain falls.

Chapter XXVIII, "A parenthesis," begins with Todd helping Captain Osborn from his seat and leading him toward the gangplank. He notes that he was unconcerned about the reasons for his scheme's failure, which he views without emotion. Todd says that when he asked himself "Why not step into the river?" a new voice answered "On the other hand, why bother?" (R246-7). He has, he feels, turned a corner and unexpectedly given himself new prospects to consider. He and Captain Osborn meet Jane, Harrison and Jeannine at the foot of the gangplank and converse "pleasantly, but without warmth." Todd notes that he has spoken to Harrison only three times since that evening, to Jane only once, and to Jeannine not at all. Todd and the Captain return to the hotel, where the Captain presents him with a bottle of Southern Comfort. As in Chapter XXVII of the 1956 edition, Todd goes up to Mr. Haecker's room to invite him to share the bottle with them, finds him unconscious, calls for help, and awaits the ambulance with Captain Osborn, the desk clerk, and the bottle. The discovery episode has been revised somewhat, but its text is essentially that of the earlier edition. After saying good-night to Captain Osborn, Todd retires to his room to think and adds the parenthesis to his fifth proposition.

In Chapter XXIX, *"The Floating Opera,"* Todd notes that his change of mind amounted to "a simple matter of carrying out [his] premises completely to their conclusions," and that "it was of the essence of my conclusion that no emotion was necessarily involved in it" (R251). Even Hamlet's question, in the face of the fact that nothing makes any difference, is meaningless. He considers the possibility that, in the absence of absolute values, "values less than absolute mightn't be regarded as in no way inferior and even be lived by," but decides that "that's another inquiry, and another story" (R252). He realizes that his "solution" to the problem of living with a weak heart is to live by such relative values but indicates that the solution is good only "for the time being; at least for me" (R252). He undresses, goes to bed, and sleeps well "despite the absurd thunderstorm that soon afterwards broke all around" (R252). Mr. Haecker's suicide attempt and Todd's one-sentence summary of the old man's later life keep some of the potential consequences of Todd's rational approach to value before us, but they serve primarily to tie up loose ends. Placing them in the denouement, after the showboat episode, satisfies formal expectations and keeps the reader's attention focused more closely on Todd's actions and thoughts. The alteration, thus, tightens the structure of the novel and sharpens the focus of the narration but has little impact on thematic concerns.

Thematically more important are the revisions that involve Todd's actions and motivations. His suicide attempt makes the depth of his despair and his fidelity to his conclusions evident. Its fortuitous interruption by the crewman and the galvanizing effect of Jane's voice are doubtless pleasing to readers who have empathized with Todd and respect his attempt to make sense out of his existence. His plan to blow up the *Floating Opera*, however, broadens the implications of his dilemma. Action's dependence on whim in the absense of absolute standards is suggested by Todd's method for deciding whether to send his legal partner a note containing information that would make Harrison three million dollars richer or to allow the information to die with him; he tosses a coin, having decided to leave all to chance, but refuses to abide by the chance decision and sends the note. The dependence on whim or chance becomes more frightening when the decision affects not only the principal but 699 other people, as it does when Todd discovers no answer to the casual question, "Why not blow up the *Floating Opera*?" (R246). In the revised edition his questions and answers involve the whole of his society; a reader cannot ignore them or pass them off as matters relevant only to a few individuals.

Even a reader who has been willing to accept Todd's premises and conclusions without qualification is forced to re-evaluate his responses to Todd's philosophy.

The darker tone of the revised edition's suicide plan continues even when Todd abandons it. The 1956 edition clearly implies that some kind of human concern, some attachment to individuals formed outside the logically explicable areas of conduct, provides a remedy for the paralysis brought about by reason operating in the absence of absolute values. Todd's concern for Jeannine overrides his rational philosophical abstractions; he feels and, therefore, acts. Such an implication is reinforced by the concluding paragraph of the novel, in which Todd goes downstairs to telephone the Macks. In the revised edition, however, Todd's unemotional response to his suicide's failure and his indifference to Jane, Harrison, and Jeannine are emphasized. His failure in suicide is not the result of sudden concern for Jeannine but is a realization that he has not carried his logic to its conclusions. If there are *no* absolutes, "Then the truth is that nothing makes any difference, including that truth. Hamlet's question is, absolutely, meaningless" (R251). Todd continues to exist as a result of inertia. He notes that, faced with an infinite number of alternatives and having no reason to favor one over another, he will probably "go on behaving much as [he] had thitherto, as a rabbit shot on the run keeps running in the same direction until death overtakes him" (R251). Both the analogical vehicle and its content eliminate the decidedly optimistic implications of the first edition's conclusion. Todd is still confronting the abyss and realizes that he may yet take his own life or those of his fellow townspeople. He considers the possibility that relative values may be sufficient, but his ability to depend upon such values is tentatively stated instead of delivered as a final pronouncement. Barth leaves him going to bed "in enormous, soothing solitude" (R252), his potentially chaotic nihilism untempered by sentimentalism.

The 1956 edition of *The Floating Opera* is a good novel, presenting us with a memorable character whose struggle to find adequate values to live by seems to be an extension of the dilemma faced by all modern men. The revised edition is a better novel. The restoration of the original ending and the other incidents creates a more unified whole; moving the discovery of Mr. Haecker's suicide to the penultimate chapter satisfies our normal expectations about fictional structure; and the copulating dogs of the revised Chapter XI provide a firm link to Chapter XII, simultaneously foreshadowing the events of Chapter XIII and developing Todd Andrews' attitude toward sexuality and, by implication, toward sensual experience as a basis for value. The revised edition's suicide plan makes concrete the implications of Todd's nihilism; the method by which his suicide is thwarted and his reactions to the plan's failure and to the Macks deny the facile optimism that Barth's editors demanded.

Notes

1. The exceptions are Richard Boyd Hauck, "Barthiad or Barthiphoniad?—The Authorial Voice in John Barth's Fiction," an unpublished paper presented at Seminar 52, Modern Language Association meeting in New York, 28 December 1972, pp. 5–6; and David B. Morrell, "John Barth: An Introduction," diss. (Pennsylvania State Univ., 1970), p. 20. Neither has commented extensively on the revisions.

2. John Barth, *The Floating Opera*, Revised Edition (Garden City: Doubleday, 1967), v. Subsequent references to this edition are indicated by R. Other references are to the first edition (New York: Appleton Century Crofts, 1956).

3. Jane, the wife of Todd's best friend, Harrison Mack, is also Todd's mistress until the day on which the novel takes place. Jeannine Mack may be Todd's daughter.

End of the Road

Psychodrama in Eden

David Kerner*

In *Time* for July 21, 1958, the lead book review, two columns long, was of a young writer's second novel—John Barth's *The End of the Road*, which was praised as "that rarity of U.S. letters—a true novel of ideas"; but the book was ignored almost everywhere else. It is an original, entertaining, and timely novel, and it is even rarer than *Time* said, for its genre has yet to be named; reviewers may have been unable to see something we have no name for. The area Barth is working in, here as in his first novel, *The Floating Opera* (1956), was described by Lionel Trilling ten years ago in the essay *Art and Fortune*: "Nowadays everyone is involved in ideas—or, to be more accurate, in ideology. . . . Social class and the conflicts it produces may not be any longer a compelling subject to the novelist, but the organization of society into ideological groups presents a subject scarcely less absorbing. Ideological society has, it seems to me, nearly as full a range of passion and nearly as complex a system of manners as a society based on social class. Its promise of comedy and tragedy is enormous." Ten years later, the press, ignoring Barth, attends to John O'Hara's overfamiliar concentration on the badges of social class. Flaubert pioneered in the novel of ideology as novel of manners—first with Homais in *Madame Bovary*—but after a century we still have only the term *novel of ideas*. *The End of the Road* is of a special type, that may be called *ideological farce*. Current examples are few—Nigel Dennis's *Cards of Identity* is one.

The End of the Road describes a battle between two college teachers, a nihilist who teaches English and an existentialist who teaches history: they disagree on the meaning of human nature, and when debate does not resolve the dispute, they turn from words to action.

The existentialist, Joe Morgan, takes the view that, in an ultimately meaningless universe, the one meaningful existence is man's: man has mind—the individual human life can be coherent. But Morgan rejects the ready-made, ill-fitting cultural roles that delude men into feeling the sensations of identity and reality. He "walks on the grass": let the paths be laid where men walk, not vice versa. He thinks he has peeled all acciden-

*Reprinted by permission of *Chicago Review*, XIII (Winter/Spring 1959), 59–67.

tal values from himself, that he has reached the foundation rock of his essential self. Morgan's view, so far, is fairly standard modern ideology. As heirs of the Enlightenment, we believe in original innocence—not original sin; we are committed to the idea of a society that will permit each person to become himself: we believe in an ultimate culture, an ultimate self—these are our heaven and our soul. But Morgan separates himself from other selves, as though there were no human nature but only billions of utterly different, unrelated natures. He says there are only subjective values—"psychological givens": "In my ethics, the most a man can ever do is be right from his point of view." When his wife apologizes to guests for their lack of furniture, Morgan socks her on the jaw; when she comes to, he explains to her that she knows she doesn't want more furniture, so why should she feel apologetic because she's not like those who do want furniture? She apologizes for apologizing, and he socks her again. Morgan's most important subjective value—his god—is his conception of his absolute consciousness, his private coherence: "If there's one thing I'd kill you for," he says to the nihilist, "it's for screwing up the issues so that we have to act before we've thought."

The nihilist, Jake Horner (who is the narrator), sees no meaning in either the universe or man. Like Morgan, Horner doesn't merely *have* this view—he *is* this view. On his 28th birthday he finds himself immobilized on a bench in a railroad station. "There was no reason to do anything. My eyes . . . were sightless, gazing on eternity, fixed on ultimacy. . . . It is the malady *cosmopsis*, the cosmic view. . . . Shortsighted animals all around me hurried in and out of doors leading down to the tracks. . . ." In contrast to Morgan, Horner denies the existence of a fundamental human identity—"Nobody's authentic": every choice of *action* is a piece of *acting*—the assumption of a role, a mask, an arbitrary pretense of identity; under the mask is no "true self"—nobody. Horner *is* this Nobody. Sometimes he rocks on his heels, intoning "Pepsi Cola hits the spot" tunelessly, to make sure he is there, as one tests a microphone by blowing into it. His first words, opening the book, are, "In a sense, I am Jacob Horner"—that is, in the physiological sense. Watching Barth put together this personification of Human Nature Unmasked, we see that Horner has no persistent feelings or values, no personal continuity—he is intermittently capable of watery curiosity, watery guilt-feelings, and consistently capable of sexual desire, animal-self-preservation, male vanity, eating, etc. Human Nature Unmasked turns out to be an intelligent alley cat. For example: Horner picks up an old-maid school teacher of forty and, at the first kiss (in her hotel room), starts unzipping her bathing suit; this efficiency humiliates her—he's treating her like an orange—but (being part of Barth's menagerie) she submits; his business done, Horner walks out and, although they live in the same small town, forgets her existence—until one day, a month later, when he races to her school, in mid-afternoon, catches her as she's leaving, and croaks, "Let's go—it's urgent!" Horner represents a protean, chameleon human nature that will never identify itself with any single civilization; he is a universe of theatrical atoms always ready to explode into new combinations. He threatens anything that claims identity, permanence, meaning, or value. He is the ultimate antagonist.

So the characters' dispute about human nature pits Self against Non-Self, Identity against Protoplasm, The Real against Vacuum. The contest of body and soul, shadow and substance, chaos and order, devil and God suggest a medieval allegory; and Barth provides the battleground that God and devil need—the cosmos to affirm and deny: this is Morgan's wife, Rennie. Morgan married her because she had begged him to re-create her in his image. "She had peered deeply into herself," says Horner, "and found *nothing.*" Before marriage, she herself says, she had been "a big blob of sleep. . . . I threw out every opinion I owned, because I couldn't defend them. I think I completely erased myself . . . so I could start over." But Morgan is not satisfied. After five years of marriage, longing for a final test of his creation's fidelity, Morgan meets Horner and tells Rennie he has "conjured up the Devil out of his own strength, just like God might do." God and devil will struggle for possession of the human personality. It is clear enough that the allegory is taking place in the Garden of Eden: the outcome of this conflict will decide the meaning of human nature, the history of the race. Morgan badgers Snake Horner to come to dinner and to go alone with Rennie on long horseback rides. When the point of crisis is reached at which "a word might knock the cosmos out of kilter," Morgan can even be seen as contriving to give Rennie an ungodlike image of himself, in order to shatter her faith—as God makes it easy for Satan to work on Job. Again Satan wins: Rennie, the human test-case, is protoplasm, like Horner; the cosmos is a vacuum.

As a novel, much of *The End of the Road* has an unnerving power, due primarily to the spectacle of intellectual lunacy. When a man who denies objective values can play God, when a man who believes in ab-solute individual freedom is a tyrant with his wife—then philosophic talk becomes parody, ideological speculation must be seen as doodling of psychiatric more than thematic relevance; faced by this mocking sketch of psychotics using ideology to rationalize their mental sickness, how many of us, contributing to the sea of such talk, can help feeling uneasy? A good part of the book's power is due also to the coherence of the allegory and the depth of Barth's feeling for ideology.

But Barth doesn't choose to take the book's psychoses and ideologies seriously—he clowns. Barth is a graft of Thorne Smith on Dostoevsky.

The book is one lunatic's first-person report, which omits the past of all the characters, accepts the bizarrest behavior without much question, and ignores the human and social setting of the action. This two-dimensionalism is necessitated by the farce; only in a void could these characters and their predicament seem half-way credible. But why need they seem credible? The trouble is that there is too much actuality for the farce: there is enough pretense of credibility—of traditional fiction—to make the reader want more; Oscar Wilde, in *The Importance of Being Earnest*, mixes ideology and farce, but nothing misleads the spectator to expect verisimilitude.

The novel of ideology professes to examine the ideas as they exist—in action. Reinhold Neibuhr once said that there are three standard questions to ask about any idea: (1) what is it? (2) what is its emotional appeal to the holder, aside from its alleged rational justification? (3) what are its consequences? Barth can't answer these questions seriously about existentialism, nihilism, and pragmatism, because he has made his characters both insane and two-dimensional. Dostoevsky sometimes uses extreme, insane characters—for example, Kirillov; and Kirillov, accordingly, had to stay a minor character—his aberration deals too bizarrely, uncharacteristically, with atheism as it existed in Russia in 1875. Ivan Karamazov tells us much more about atheism because he is a whole, though sick, human being. To expose the nature of an ideology, the novelist must show its effect on relatively whole human beings, just as a biochemist traces the effect of a virus through the biological systems of a normal organism. Joe Morgan can teach us nothing about existentialism—the validity of individual "psychological gives" as opposed to general social truths—because he has a subnormal understanding of himself and others; he is too much the psychotic, too little the existentialist. In contrast, Raskolnikov is normal, although split—*raskol* means *schism*. His relationship with his mother and sister is in the book to show the healthy part of his emotional life (and to show its source; and the ideology of the superman is exposed as intolerable to a normal Western human being—intolerable, but attractive, in a society hostile to rational social reform, where practical impotence leads the intelligentsia to delusions of grandeur.

As for Jake Horner's nihilism, insofar as Barth intends it to be the product of thought, the book is pretentious; but insofar as Barth shows that nihilism may only rationalize an inability to feel, we do have one kind of thing the novel of ideology does. Barth may seem to be taking a swing at pragmatism too: the friendly review in *Time* captioned his photograph *Has pragmatism had it? Time* deserves credit for recognizing Barth's originality and vitality, but was the magazine's interest in Barth as much ideological as literary? *Time* is too willing to see nihilism as the legitimate heir of pragmatism, to make Joe Morgan out to be the Liberal playing God, to find the moral: The Pride of Reason Shall Be Chastened. But Barth's intelligence is naturalistic, without the bogeyman-gallery of egghead "tinkerers with God's law" (the status quo) in *Time*'s front-office cosmology.

Barth is only twenty-eight, but at any age a novelist would have to be a Cervantes to blend novel, ideology, allegory, psychodrama, and farce.

Still, the times call for such attempts, as Trilling said ten years ago, and Barth shows his excellence in his intention. *The End of the Road* notifies us of one kind of novel waiting in Plato's heaven for a writer to shadow it forth. Meanwhile, we have Barth's farce, an intellectual's sideshow, and an important one, one that is often charming and stunning. To the Pepsi-Cola song and The Philosopher Socking His Wife could be added many other set-pieces that might, in Horner's style, be capitalized: A Parody of Socrates Giving the Worse as the Better Reason, Interview of a Prospective English Teacher, The Mad Pragmatist's Therapies of Valuelessness (including Informational Therapy, Sexual Therapy, Devotional Therapy, Theotherapy, Atheotherapy, and Mythotherapy). The Mad Pragmatists, who has remobilized Horner, prescribes at their first session: "Take long walks, but always to a previously determined destination, and when you get there, walk right home again, briskly. . . . Above all, act impulsively: don't let yourself get stuck between alternatives, or you're lost. . . . If the alternatives are side by side, choose the one on the left; if they're consecutive in time, choose the earlier. If neither of these applies, choose the alternative whose name begins with the earlier letter of the alphabet. These are the principles of Sinistrality, Antecedence, and Alphabetical Priority. . . . Good-by."

Barth and the Representation of Life

Daniel Majdiak*

Suppose you're a writer by vocation—a "print-oriented bastard" as the McLuhanites call us—and you feel, for example, that the novel . . . has by this hour of the world just about shot its bolt. . . . If you were the author of this . . . [statement] you'd have written something like *The Sot-Weed Factor* or *Giles Goat-Boy*; novels which imitate the form of the Novel, by an author who imitates the role of Author. . . . "History repeats itself as farce"—meaning, of course, in the form or mode of farce, not that history is farcial. The imitation . . . is something new and *may be* quite serious and passionate despite its farcial aspects. This is the important distinction between a proper novel and a deliberate imitation of a novel, or a novel imitative of other sorts of documents. The first attempts . . . to imitate actions more or less directly, and its conventional devices—cause and effect, linear anecdote, characterization, authorial selection, arrangement, and interpretation—can and have long since been objected to as obsolete notions, or metaphors for obsolete notions. . . . There are replies to these objections . . . but . . . they're obviated by imitations-of-novels, which attempt to represent not life directly, but a representation of life.[1]

Critics have amply demonstrated the relevance of the ideas Barth outlines here to the two works he mentions,[2] but no one has looked at his earlier works from his perspective. There are commentaries which point out their "freshness," "invention" and the quality of experiment in them, but the emphasis falls mainly on ideas while technique is described only in the most general terms.[3] In fact, Barth's theory of the fictitious describes both his themes and his technique and is no less important to an understanding of *The Floating Opera* and *The End of the Road* than to *The Sot-Weed Factor* and *Giles Goat-Boy*. I purpose to examine *The End of the Road*, Barth's first wholly successful work, in the terms he suggests because, as I hope to show, his really fine achievement in it can be elucidated only in this way. In addition, I believe this analysis will give us a clearer picture of his ideas and their pertinence to his innovations in fiction. I will begin, then, with the relation of the theme of *The End of the Road* to Barth's "representation of life."

*Reprinted by permission of *Criticism*, XII (Winter 1970), 51–67.

I

With the exception of Sterne, no great writer of English fiction before the twentieth century questioned the concept of personal identity. That character can be fixed, explored in depth, understood, is an assumption shared by all novelists and it has been argued that this is *the* theme of the novel.[4] Even when the novel focuses on society, the argument goes, the resultant analysis tends to define the individual's identity within it. This conception of the novel's subject may be too limited, but it is to the point here because it is what Barth concentrates on in his imitation. He praises writers like Sterne and Borges because they challenge the epistemology of realism and "remind us of the fictitious aspect of our own existence."[5] In Sterne this challenge takes the form of parody and it does in Barth's works too, but the uses to which it is put are completely his own. He does not use the term parody in his commentary but it is implicit in his suggestion that his fiction imitates history in the mode of farce (literally in *The Sot-Weed Factor*) and it is explicit in the opening words of *The End of the Road*: "In a sense I am Jacob Horner."[6]

In Horner's first statement the theme of identity is immediately put in doubt. The qualification of the opening phrase suggests that the "I" is one of many. At the moment of speaking he may be who he says, but at another moment he may be someone else, though he keeps the same name. This is the result of role-playing, behavior predicated on the conception of life as drama, the representation of life that is the subject of *The End of the Road*. Before Horner is four pages into "his" narrative he offers us two different metaphors for his life. The first is not a metaphor in the ordinary sense, but an abstract commentary that can be applied to a life metaphorically: " . . . a recognition of the fact that when one is faced with . . . a multitude of desirable choices, no one choice seems satisfactory for very long by comparison with the aggregate desirability of all the rest, though compared to any one of the others it would not be found inferior" (6). A few paragraphs later he describes himself as one ". . . held static like the rope marker in a tug-o'-war where the opposing teams are perfectly matched" (8). The difference between these statements is in the pictures of human action present; in the first the continually frustrated man who wants to have all of the options, while in the second it is the man who cannot opt at all. But they can both be of "Horner," depending on the role he's playing, so it does not ". . . really matter if it is not just the same story; . . . the same life lends itself to any number of stories—parallel, concentric, mutually habitant, or what you will" (8).

Horner learned this theory from the doctor who treats him for his illness, the paralytic disease Cosmopsis. During the course of this disease one becomes more and more disenchanted with human values until one finds oneself ". . . gazing on eternity, fixed on intimacy . . ., [seeing that] there is no reason to do anything" (60). The man who specializes in the treatment of this disease is "some combination of quack and prophet—Father Divine, Sister Kenney, and Bernarr MacFadden combined . . . with elements of faith healer and armchair Freud thrown in—running a semi-legitimate rest home for semi-eccentrics . . ." (69). He takes a special interest in Horner because he is the only patient who can be sent back into the world, living proof of the Doctor's superiority to the rest of the medical profession. Judged by the standards and practice of the profession the Doctor is illegitimate, but his success calls in question the concept of legitimacy. He has no other identity than the label "Doctor," which from the point of view of the "legitimate" would be translated "criminal," yet he is the only one who can make his life go as he wishes. His illegitimacy is therefore a parody of the other characters' values and his reality a threat and an insult to theirs. To the charge that his therapies are absurd he replies, "yes, so?"

The Doctor is a master of the "As-if" philosophy; to him the only relevant question about a therapy is how far is it life-sustaining, or life-furthering. Since Horner's paralysis is caused by nihilistic vision, the Doctor applies a therapy which will enable Horner to use this very nihilism as a basis for action. This is Mythotherapy, the therapeutic use of the representation of life as drama: put starkly, no action no life; for the individual this means, no choice no existence. "Choosing is existence: to the extent that you don't choose, you don't exist. . . . Everything we do must be oriented toward choice and action" (67). In this therapy all of the usual ethical standards attached to action are dismissed. "It doesn't matter whether this action is more or less reasonable than inaction; . . . it doesn't matter whether you act constructively or even consistently, so long as you act. It doesn't matter whether your character is admirable or not, so long as you think you have one" (67). Horner must learn that a man is free not only to choose his own essence but to change it at will:

> [As] everyone is necessarily the hero of his own life story . . . fiction isn't a lie . . . but a true representation of the distortion that everyone makes of life. This kind of role-assigning is myth-making, and when it's done consciously or unconsciously for the purpose of aggrandizing or protecting your ego . . . it becomes Mytho-therapy. Now many crises in people's lives occur because the hero role that they've assumed for one situation or set of situations no longer applies to some new situation . . . or . . . because they haven't the imagination to distort the new situation to fit their old role. . . . For you these crises had better be met by changing scripts as often as necessary. (70–73)

Horner learns his lesson easily; being a natural mimic he is glad to be able to use this talent to create personae for his many unpredictable moods. With the Doctor as director[7] Horner begins an action which is supposed to be a test run of his rehabilitated "I." The script calls for him to be a teacher of prescriptive grammar (the rules will make it occupational therapy, not merely occupation) and his first big scene is the job interview. In this scene he plays brilliant improvisations on the role of profoundly-committed-idealistic-young-teacher, but one of his audience, Joe Morgan the other major character in the book, is not engaged by his performance.

However, when Morgan makes his improvisations untenable by refusing to play along, Horner does not change scripts but adapts the one he's using to Morgan's role, thus upstaging him by rendering a parody of his scoutmaster mentality: " 'I sometimes compare it to a man making fire with flint and steel' I said calmly to Joe Morgan, knowing I was hitting him where he lived. 'He strikes and strikes and strikes, but the tinder lies dead under his hands. Then another strike, not a bit different from the rest, and there's your fire' " (17). Morgan, used only to being director and hero, is angered and yet fascinated by this performance and decides that he must know Horner better; that is, he must cast him in a suitable role. Morgan is a man who takes his script seriously, for he believes that there is no value in life but subjective value which must be coherently defined and justified in action; the threat of Horner's parody must therefore be met and mastered. But the difficulty in doing this is implicit in their first scene; in order to control one's role and others' one must be aware of role-playing, but that is almost impossible if one responds to a situation with emotion.

The difficulties of maintaining this awareness become clearer if we look at the audience aspect of the dramatic metaphor. How do we place the audience? With respect to others this is no great difficulty unless we identify with them too strongly, but what about our conscious selves? Do we view ourselves? We do, of course, for in terms of the dramatic metaphor the self is other and we can be and often are both actor and audience. But the problem of identification is profound. Because of it we are always on the verge of losing the crucial distinction between actor and audience and of being carried away with the role. Paradoxically, Horner's disease sharpens his awareness of this distinction and in fact enables him to perform the important function of critic. Even when most affected by Cosmopsis he can watch himself play the role of the sick man. As he follows the Doctor to his first therapy he notes, "I shook my head—at the same moment aware that I was watching myself act bewildered . . ." (63). And even when he's cast in a repugnant role, as in his first "love" scene with Peggy Rankin the aging school teacher, he enjoys the show. He finishes the ugly scene with Peggy, he says, because of ". . . a characteristic disinclination to walk out on any show, no matter how poor or painful, once I'd seen the first act" (27).

In the Morgan drama, however, Horner cannot maintain such detachment. Sometimes he consciously apes Morgan, though not always with any clear design; sometimes he unconsciously identifies with him, assuming Morgan's role in order to face up to difficult situations. Both attitudes demonstrate an intimate involvement and ". . . the more one learns about a given person, the more difficult it becomes to assign a character to him that will allow one to deal with him effectively in an emotional situation. Mythotherapy, in short, becomes increasingly harder to apply, because one is compelled to recognize the inadequacy of any role one assigns" (103). One should ignore a person's complexities—"*must* ignore them, in fact, if [one is] to get on with the plot . . ." (25).

In the early stages of the relationship Horner practices Mythotherapy assiduously and with enjoyment. Though impressed by the Morgans' forceful qualities he perceives enough that is ridiculous about them to give him plenty of material for a script. Given Horner's inclinations this leads to parody, which is evident in the first dialogue between him and Rennie Morgan; in it Horner skillfully mimics Morgan's style of arguing with his wife about absolutes and values: ". . . it doesn't follow that because a thing is unjustifiable it's without value. And you have to remember that *dispensing* with a convention, even a silly one, always involves the risk of being made to feel unreasonably guilty, simply because conventions *do* happen to be conventions. Take drinking beer for breakfast, . . . or going through red lights late at night, or committing adultery with your husband's approval . . ." (33). Rennie realizes that she is being put on and reports this to Morgan, but he takes Horner's parody as a cue for his own action. He values his marriage relationship above everything, but for it to remain valuable it must be taken seriously and "what one [partner takes] seriously both ought to be able to take seriously . . ." (50). Horner's parody therefore can be used as a test and Morgan sets it up by encouraging Rennie to give him horseback-riding lessons. Horner quickly realizes what Morgan is up to. "I don't see much . . . in this premeditated horseback-riding thing, [he says], anybody who didn't know better would think he was trying to fix me up with you." Rennie takes this calmly, but her reply lacks conviction: "he's so strong he can afford to look weak sometimes . . . and can even afford to be a caricature of his strength . . ." (52).

Morgan's ideal of Rennie, "self-sufficiency, strength, and privacy," is a role she cannot play. When she first fell short of the ideal early in their marriage he attempted to correct her misinterpretation of her role by socking her. This act shook Rennie's faith in Morgan, but he was confident it was called for. The reason, he says, is this: ". . . the more sophisticated your ethics get, the stronger you have to be to stay afloat. And when you say goodby to objective values, you really have to flex your muscles and keep your eyes open, because you're on your own. It takes *energy:* not just personal energy, but cultural energy, or you're lost. Energy's what makes the difference between American pragmatism and French existentialism—where the hell else but in America could you have a cheerful nihilism, for God's sake? I suppose it was rough slugging Rennie, but I saw the moment as a kind of crisis" (40). Morgan's thinking here is a parody of American Pragmatism, the frontiersman mentality mixed with the rationalist's faith in the abstractions of reason which, as the Doctor says, "can reach generality only by ignoring enough particularity" (65). Morgan ignores the particularity of Rennie and therefore never learns the inadequacy of Mythotherapy.

During the years of their marriage Rennie tried in every way to remake herself in Morgan's image and likeness, and during her scenes with Horner she laments her failure to do so: "I threw out every opinion I ever owned, because I couldn't defend them. I think I completely erased myself . . . right down to nothing, so I could start over again. And you know, I don't think I'll ever really get to be what Joe wants . . ." (51). Of course Morgan demands more of her than any man should, but instead of rebelling against him Rennie explains his behavior through a fantasy which depicts him as divine. "I think of Joe like I'd think of God," she says, and when Horner retorts that he's intolerant, she replies "so is God!" (51). Incredible as this fantasy is she persists in it because it is the only way she can deal with Morgan's script, especially now that he has added Horner. To reconcile herself to Morgan's test she casts the whole drama in cosmic, Manichaean terms: "I thought Joe had invited the Devil to test me . . . But this Devil scared me, because I wasn't that strong yet, and what was a game for Joe was a terrible fight for me. . . . Then when Joe saw how it was, he told me that the Devil wasn't real, and that he had conjured up the Devil out of his own strength, just like God might do" (56).

Unfortunately for Rennie, Horner chooses to play this role as if the Devil were real. Once Rennie gives him the cue to play Morgan's double he takes up the role with great enthusiasm and acts in both demonic and comic terms. The crucial scene in the book occurs when Horner gives the role the demonic interpretation of the threatening self bent on destroying Morgan's integrity. He takes his cue again from Rennie who has desperately overstated her argument for Morgan's superiority by claiming he alone is "real," that he wears no masks and has always the same identity. To disprove this, or at least qualify Rennie's perception of Morgan, Horner seizes on a chance opportunity to spy on him when he thinks he is alone. The drama becomes a peep show and what Horner sees and forces Rennie to see is Morgan presenting a grotesque parody of himself as scoutmaster and man. First he goes through a ridiculous pantomime of the military drill; then, caught by his reflection in a mirror he makes fun of the image in it, rendering a burlesque of Narcissus which is yet truly narcissistic in motive. Finally, he climaxes this grotesque dramatization of his self-love by ". . . masturbating and picking his nose at the same time . . ."(58).

Rennie's faith in Morgan is destroyed by this scene, but Horner continues to play the double until he supplants him in his bed. With Peggy Rankin Horner parodies Morgan's rationalization for hitting Rennie; he socks Peggy when she refuses him and then tells her he would not have done so if he did not take her seriously. This improbable logic wins Peggy once more and Horner takes her up to her room with "a mental salute to Joseph Morgan, *il mio maestro* . . ." (79). But there is a significant difference between the adultery scene and the one with Peggy. When he finally does put horns on Morgan he does not salute him in mock gratitude as he enters his bed, as one might expect. On the contrary, he claims he was unaware of any conscious intention to seduce Rennie. This claim is significant for the criticism of Mythotherapy because it underscores the problem of awareness involved. When Horner is most caught up in playing a role he is unaware of it and this has important ethical results. It is not until he is crushed by guilt and remorse that he becomes conscious of the role and can criticize it: "So, then, it seemed I had to admit that I *was* a coward after all: an adulterer, a deceiver, a betrayer of friends, and a coward. And now I was self-conscious again; I watched myself refuse to recognize that beside my bed was a telephone by means of which one could call Joe Morgan. . . . My curiosity returned with my self-consciousness. I placed my hand on the telephone and for some time studied with interest the blushing, uncomfortable fellow who would not pick it up" (85–86). From this point on Horner never again totally loses himself in a role; every action he participates in is complicated for him by his awareness of the role. This becomes clear to him when, in the aftermath of the adultery, he reflects on his response to Morgan: "[I was] . . . pretty satisfied at my ability to play a role that struck me as being at once somewhat abhorrent and yet apparently ineluctable. That is, I felt it to be a role, but I wasn't sure anything else wouldn't also be a role, and I couldn't think of any other possible roles for me anyhow. If, as may be, this is the best anyone can do—at least the best I can do—why, then, it's as much as can ever be signified by the term sincerity" (94).

But Morgan, nearly mad from the injury to his self-love, becomes fanatically committed to resolving this action in some acceptable way. The resolution must explain why it happened, and the only way he can see to bring this about is to replay the scene with each actor analyzing his feelings while playing it. This leads to the grotesque parody of the triangle situation, formed at the husband's urging and encouraged by him (a more convincing version of the situation in *The Floating Opera*); and from this follows the resolution in Rennie's pregnancy, abortion and death. Morgan directs the whole show and yet he insists the actors innovate as they play so that the action be resolved by free choice of ethical agents. Horner finally attempts such a choice and by tremendous effort manages to arrange an abortion by the Doctor who agrees to it as a last resort to save Horner's case. But a gruesome accident causes Rennie's death; the script and the actors are inadequate to the contingencies of life. The pain caused by this death is awful for both men, but worse pain comes from the realization that it is no resolution. The survivors become complements of the negative self: Morgan ". . . fixed in the delusion that intelligence will solve all problems" (99) and Horner ". . . not individual after all, any more than the atom is really atomistic" (114).

Together they create Barth's picture of nihilism. Morgan represents the older form which, setting itself in opposition to the transcendental, attempts to establish value in the rational will. He is destroyed because he does not see that man is ruled by other human factors. The new nihilists like Horner attempt to take these factors into account and their stance is that moral codes are nothing but matters of feeling or social pressure. But Horner is destroyed by Cosmopsis, the vision that begins with ironical detachment but ends in sheer bafflement. In Barth's words, Horner and Morgan "carry all non-mystical value thinking to the end of the road."[8]

II

Parody expresses the theme of nihilism in *The End of the Road* by forcing the characters to realize their unreality; in technique it expresses the unreality of literature, but not to further the theme of nihilism. Though Barth's purpose is to discredit the norms which the novel assumes he does this to render a more credible picture of reality through a more viable fictional form. And in so doing he is in the mainstream of fiction: as Frank Kermode so well puts it, ". . . .such new laws and customs as [fiction] creates have themselves to be repeatedly broken under the demands of a changed . . . reality. The extremest revolt against the customs or laws of fiction . . . creates its new laws, in their turn to be broken. . . . The history of the novel is the history of forms rejected or modified, by parody, manifesto, neglect, as absurd. Nowhere else, perhaps, are we so conscious of the dissidence between inherited forms and our own reality."[9]

The prototypes for Horner are not Doestoevsky's romantic nihilists, but figures like Musil's Ulrich and Kafka's K. Of course "Horner" is a surname, but it is a parody of the "naming-convention" which, says Ian Watt, is "the verbal expression of the particular identity of each individual person" in a novel.[10] Barth suggests that this "proper" name has an ambiguous double reference to both little Jack Horner, the childish rationalizer of the nursery rhyme, and the wife seducer common to literature.[11] Instead of giving him a particular identity the narrator's name parodically expresses his lack of one; he does not even have a particular literary ambience. In the novel the protagonist is a man of parts, but Horner's parts are those of the dramatic metaphor. Even in the role of lover he is segmented: ". . . the observing part of me now thought it pretty well understood the attracted part, [but] many, many other parts were totally unaffected one way or another" (55). The Doctor's title is similarly used. Since the Doctor remains nameless throughout the story Horner must think of him with a capital D in order to give him some sort of identity. (Barth evidently intends the name of his sinister receptionist-nurse Mrs. Dockey to underscore this aspect of the Doctor.) Yet, though he bears the label of the stock character, and even serves the function of the stock character necessary for the movement of plot, he is the most forceful and effectual person in the cast. The whole conception of the stock character is belied by the Doctor for he directs the destiny of the intelligence which presents us with the narrative and yet remains enigmatic to the end.

Barth locates the action of *The End of the Road* on the eastern shore of Maryland, but place is not "a pervasive operating force" as it tends to be in most novels.[12] In fact, though Barth mentions specific locations such as Baltimore and Philadelphia he intentionally fictionalizes the scene where most of the action takes place. The town is evidently Salisbury but he uses the name of the county, Wicomico, for the place of the action. No doubt the factor governing this choice was the sound of this name which puns so neatly on the mode of the book, but the emphasis on fictitiousness springs from the theory of imitation which informs the whole. Parody thus works on novelistic convention to transform normative "reality" into fictive vision.

The rooms where the greater part of the action takes place are treated similarly. The first described is the "Progress and Advice Room": "It is a medium sized room, about as large as an apartment living room, only high-ceilinged. The walls are flat white, the windows are covered by white venetian blinds, usually closed, and a globed ceiling fixture provides the light. In this room there are two straight-backed white wooden chairs, exactly alike, facing each other in the center of the floor, and no other furniture. The chairs are very close together—so close that the advisee almost touches knees with the adviser" (5). This room is obviously meant to ridicule the efficiency and sterility of the hospital interior, while at the same time reflecting the Doctor's scorn for the Victorian opulence of Freud's analysis room; but more important, it is a carefully structured parallel to the interior of the Morgan living room, thus emphasizing the fact that the Morgan-Rennie relationship is a parodical version of the Doctor-Horner alliance. In the Morgan living room "there were no rugs on the hardwood floors, no curtains or drapes on the polished windows, and not a piece of furniture above the necessary minimum; a daybed, two sling chairs, two lamps, a bookcase, and a writing table. . . . Because the walls and ceiling were white, the light pouring through the open venetian blinds made the living room blindly bright" (36). This parallelism emphasizes the magnitude of the effects of Mythotherapy, but it also calls attention to form; it is a strategy of form to break the novelistic illusion of a fictive world more or less like the one we experience.

Horner's room also functions as a kind of parodical setting, but it has an effect opposite to the others. In it every property shows up Horner's ineffectuality:

Six foot windows, three of them. Twelve foot ceiling. . . . An incredible bed three feet high, seven feet long, at least seven feet wide; a black, towering, canopied monster with four posts as thick as masts, fluted and ringed, and an elaborately carved headboard extending three feet above the bolster. The other furniture was a potpourri of styles and periods—one felt as if one had wandered into the odd-pieces room of Winterthur Museum—but every piece was immensely competent. The adjective *competent* came at once to mind, rather than, say, *efficient*. This furniture had an air of almost contemptuous competence, as though it were so absurdly well able to handle its job that it would scarcely notice *your* puny use of it. It would require a man indeed, a man's man, to make his presence felt by this furniture. (10)

Horner is not such a man. Rather, his perception of this setting allows him to lapse into vacuity, and let the objects assume a demonic life of their own. The description is evocative, but the intention is not, as Allen Tate says of description in the novel, "to put man wholly into his physical setting."[13] On the contrary, it shows him to be separate from, in fact alien to, his setting.

After these scenes are described once they are ignored. Horner's tendency is to ignore the physical world and concentrate on the mental world, but there is one object that figures importantly throughout the story. This is ". . . a plaster head of Laocöon done by a sculpting uncle . . . who died of influenza in the First World. . . ." Of Laocöon Horner says, "the set of that mouth was often my barometer, told me the weight of the day"(20). Sometimes it seems to him merely ugly, sometimes noncommital; on one rare occasion it is even Bacchic. But there is only one suitable role suggested by this property and that is the seer who is punished for his audacity in telling his vision. This object is thus Horner's link with the past—not with the immediate, local past as in a novel, the sculpting uncle remains insignificant—with a tradition of men who see too far and too much. The results of this in our time is Cosmopsis, the nihilism that paralyzes so that one ends like Horner, his limbs ". . . bound like Laocöon's—by the twin serpents of Knowledge and Imagination, which grown great in the fullness of time, no longer tempt but annihilate" (157). The use of this object as a symbol for Horner's predicament is typically ingenious. Unlike the objects in a novel which add authenticity to its world, Laocöon puts emphasis on the artifice in *The End of the Road*.

In Horner's retrospective narrative there is further emphasis on "the fullness of time," not the kind of time with which novels deal. Rather than seeking to impart the way lived time may feel, the time scheme of *The End of the Road* is manipulated in such a way that the action is shown to be outside the Aristotelian law. Though Horner seems to take us back to where it began he does not really demonstrate cause and effect. Or rather, because of the absence of first causes the whole story seems like a scene from some larger drama of which the beginning and end cannot be known. And even in the middle action which is recorded, the conventions of linear anecdote are distorted. Horner notes that his story begins in June of 1953, but before he gets more than a few paragraphs into it he digresses to point out that he is writing it "at 7:55 in the evening of Tuesday, October 5, 1955"(6). This precision of specification mocks the novel's serious treatment of time, yet it is not wholly gratuitous; if all Horner has is his role the present moment is his only point of orientation. (I will come back to the particular role he's playing in writing the story later.) He then takes the story through the summer of 1953, the period of his drama with the Morgans, but just before the adultery scene he stops again to spin out a long digression concerning his first meeting with the Doctor. This meeting took place on Tuesday, March 17 (the preceding Friday being the 13th), 1951, and Horner's digression on it shows once more that the summer of 1953 is only a part of a large action having no discernible beginning.

The scene of the adultery itself is played almost mindlessly by Horner so that in retelling it he has to put it into the broad context of human sexual behavior in order to give it significance. In the crucial action of the story the identities of the actors are reduced to the status of mere dancers in "the dance of sex." Under such conditions it is impossible to tell the dancer from the dance and human time becomes only the rhythmic pulsation of "the Absolute Genital." All such moments become more or less the same, which is the reason Horner relates his second tryst with Peggy before he describes the adultery, though it actually occurred five days after. And though from the adultery scene to the last the narrative moves in chronological order, the dates recorded do not point toward a last day. When Horner says the final word, "terminal," he is mocking the conventions of ending. The day on which it is spoken in early October, 1953 is not the last day; two years later he is writing about it, still trying to give it meaning. The shape that the novel gives to time, the Aristotelian order of beginning, middle, and end it asserts as real, is a conception of reality which Horner's ordering of time calls in question. Frank Kermode suggests that "in the middest, we look for a fullness of time, for beginning, middle, and end in concord. For concord or consonance really is the root of the matter, even in a world which thinks it can only be a fiction."[14] Horner does indeed look for such concord, but the whole of his experience, even the form in which he reconstructs it, insists it is a fiction.

Another of the narrative devices in *The End of the Road* that calls attention to its fictiveness is Horner's method of summarizing his lengthy arguments with the Morgans. In such summaries Horner reminds us of the narrator of *Murphy* as he calls attention to the fact that his report is a selection, a shaping of the originals to bring out their "meaning." He says of Morgan's first harangue that ". . . it may well be that Joe made no such long coherent speech as this all at once. . . . I put it down here in the form of one uninterrupted whiz-bang for convenience's sake, both to illustrate the nature of his preoccupations and to add a stroke or two to my picture of the man himself" (40). And when he presents Rennie's long, emotional confessions of her life with Morgan he begins with a statement that "this is what she told . . . edited and condensed." In a novel, *The Great Gatsby* for example, statements of this kind make the reader question the reliability of the narrator, but that question is not pertinent to Horner because Barth is in fact using the conventional first-person confessional narrative to attack the notion of the sincere "I." As the Doctor says, "*insincere* (?)—impossible word!" (73).

In every aspect Barth's technique is too artificial for the novelist, but for him there is "a different way to come to terms with the discrepancy between art and the Real Thing. [That is] . . . to affirm the artificial element in art (you can't get rid of it anyhow), and make the artifice part of your point. . . ."[15] Parody calls attention to itself as artifice because it ". . . emphasizes mechanics, especially prescriptive mechanics in executive technique, and greedily fastens on the merest possibilities of the material."[16] The most striking example of this in *The End of the Road* is Barth's handling of the convention of chapter headings. Fielding's famous statement in his chapter on chapters in *Joseph Andrews* may stand for the norm: ". . . What are the contents prefixed to every chapter but so many inscriptions over the gates of inns . . . informing the reader what entertainment he is to expect, which if he likes not, he may travel on to the next. . . ."[17] In *The End of the Road* what the reader finds are fragments of inscriptions (the first chapter being the only exception), broken off sentences which have no meaning unless he goes on with the chapter they begin. It is as if Horner, unable to maintain a sense of personal unity, must begin again with each chapter, in the hope that the narrative will provide him an identity.

But to talk about experience in order to create a self is to transform it into a fiction and that is the only possibility left for Horner. When Mythotherapy fails he withdraws from the world and is put on the therapies for the terminal case: "Philosophical Therapy" and "Scriptotherapy" (68). The former provides the attitude, the latter the medium for this last attempt to be a self; to be a Writer is what Horner tries to realize by means of his confession. "To turn experience into speech—that is, to classify, to categorize, to conceptualize, to grammarize, to syntactify it—is always a betrayal of experience, a falsification of it; but only so betrayed can it be dealt with at all, and only in so dealing with it did I ever feel a man, alive and kicking. It is therefore that . . . I responded to this precise falsification, this adroit, careful myth-making, with all the upsetting exhilaration of any artist at his work." But, though this myth-making is more adroit and careful than Mythotherapy, it still does violence to reality: "when my mythoplastic razors were sharply honed, it was unparalleled to lay about with them, to have at reality" (96). Scriptotherapy is an instance of the use of a poison as an antidote. Horner must destroy in order to reshape, he must criticize in order to create value. While engaged in Scriptotherapy he is preeminently in the role of critic.

In this role he criticizes not only the actors but the script, yet he recognizes the problematical in each and tries to inform his narrative with that recognition. It is only in the role of critic that articulation becomes truly precise because it is only in this role that one can recognize language itself as a falsification. As critic Horner knows that while it is indeed "enormously refreshing to articulate it all," it is also true that all feelings are completely particular and individual and that trouble starts when one attempts to label them with common nouns such as "love" or "abhorrence." Things can be signified by common nouns only if one ignores the differences between them; but it is precisely this difference, when deeply felt, that makes the nouns inadequate. . . . Assigning names to things is like assigning roles to people: it is necessarily a distortion, but it is a necessary distortion if one would get on with the plot . . ." (114). How can Horner put in words the complex feeling Rennie finally came to have for him? "Let us say she x-ed me, [he says], and know better than to smile" (114). Does Scriptotherapy end in the same nihilistic impasse as Mythotherapy then? Not quite. While Mythotherapy deals with people and attempts to control their lives, Scriptotherapy deals solely with form, with fiction. But in this self-conscious use of fiction it exposes our fantasies and reminds us of our propensity to regard them as reality, whereas Mythotherapy can only serve to enforce them.[18]

In describing Barth and the other writers he considers like him, Robert Scholes says that their work is ". . . a return to a more verbal kind of fiction. It also [is] a return to a more fictional kind, . . . a less realistic and more artistic kind of narrative."[19] And *The End of the Road* certainly shows the vitality of art in its ability to reshape old forms to create new ones. But such works cannot be pure artifice, they must deal with reality in some meaningful way or we dismiss them as trivia. Barth's way is to comment on reality by dealing with the problems of fiction. In this way he can explore what we can know of life and what we can make of it. This kind of knowledge does not come from the identification evoked by the novel; it is the result of a harder, more critical response that keeps us aware of the illusion as well as the truth of art.

In many ways *The End of the Road* resembles traditional satire.[20] Both the emphasis on mental attitudes rather than character psychology and the use of parody to telescope into a single symbol the polar opposites of truth and illusion are typical of satire. So too is the alien stance the book takes to our cultural norms and the questioning of the very language by which they are communicated. But there is an entirely different mood in this satire, if we would call it that. Though an anti-book that parodies form it is yet as esthetically sure as its predecessors; but it does not have the certainty of the ideal. In that respect it is paradigmatic of art in our time. As Herbert Mercuse says, in the past ". . . within the limits of esthetic form art expressed, although in an ambivalent manner, the return of the repressed image of liberation; art was opposition. At the present stage . . . even this highly ambivalent opposition seems no longer viable. Art survives only where it cancels itself, where it saves substance by denying its traditional form and thereby denying reconciliation. . . . Otherwise, art shares the fate of all genuine human communication: it dies off."[21] Barth's esthetic is an attempt to avoid an end such as this and yet, as he says, ". . . to speak eloquently and memorably to our still-human hearts and conditions, as the great artists have always done."[22]

Notes

1. "The Literature of Exhaustion," *The Atlantic Monthly* (August 1967), 32–33.

2. See for example Robert Scholes' fine analysis of *Giles Goat-Boy* in which he shows Barth ". . . militantly fabulative, insisting on its fabulous dimension, its unreality." *The Fabulators* (New York, 1967), p. 136.

3. See Alan Trachtenberg "Barth and Hawkes: Two Fabulists," *Critique*, VI (Fall 1963), 4–19, and Richard W, Noland, "John Barth and the Novel of Comic Nihilism," *Wisconsin Studies in Contemporary Literature*, VII (Autumn 1966), 239–257.

4. See, for example, Ian Watt, *The Rise of the Novel* (Berkeley, 1957) and Maurice Z. Shroder, "The Novel as Genre," *The Massachusetts Review*, IV (Winter 1963), 291–309.

5. "The Literature of Exhaustion," 33.

6. *The End of the Road* (New York, 1964), p. 5. Hereafter reference will be cited by page in the text.

7. In my discussion of the dramatic metaphor I am indebted to Morse Peckham's incisive commentary in *Man's Rage for Chaos: Biology, Behavior and the Arts* (New York, 1967), pp. 49–59.

8. Quoted in George Bluestone, "John Wain and John Barth: The Angry and the Accurate," *The Massachusetts Review*, I (May 1960), 586.

9. *The Sense of an Ending* (New York, 1967), pp. 129–130. Though Kermode does not discuss Barth his excellent analyses of the way our fictions change in relation to our conceptions of reality illuminate Barth's art as they do all of modern fiction.

10. *The Rise of the Novel*, p. 18.

11. "John Barth: An Interview," *Wisconsin Studies in Contemporary Literature*, V (Winter-Spring 1965), 12.

12. *The Rise of the Novel*, p. 27.

13. "Techniques of Fiction," *On the Limits of Poetry* (New York, 1948), p. 143.

14. *The Sense of an Ending*, p. 58.

15. "John Barth: An Interview," 6.

16. R. P. Blackmur, "Parody and Critique: Mann's *Doctor Faustus*," in *Eleven Essays in the European Novel* (New York, 1964), p. 110.

17. *Joseph Andrews*, ed. Martin C. Battestin (Boston, 1961), p. 74. In *The Sot-Weed Factor* Barth returns to Fielding's practice.

18. A comment of Kermode's seems especially relevant here. He says: "Fictions are finding things out, and they change as the needs of sense-making change. . . . Myths call for absolute, fictions for conditional assent" (*The Sense of an Ending*, p. 39).

19. *The Fabulators*, p. 12.

20. Scholes notes that ". . . it is surely better to think of Voltaire and Swift when reading . . . Barth than to think of Hemingway and Fitzgerald" (*ibid.*, p. 40).

21. *Eros and Civilization* (Boston, 1966), p. 145.

22. "The Literature of Exhaustion," p. 30.

The Sot-Weed Factor

The Joke is on Mankind

Edmund Fuller*

John Barth's "The Sot-Weed Factor" is a brilliantly specialized performance, so monstrously long that reading it seemed nearly as laborious
as writing it. Obviously Barth (author previously of "The End of the
Road" and "The Floating Opera") believed he needed these approximate-
ly 500,000 words to achieve his effects. Few will agree with him, for
though he abounds in excellent satirical devices he is addicted to repeating
them.

For "Sot-Weed Factor" read tobacco merchant. The settings are
England and the province of Maryland. The time is late seventeenth century, the reign of William and Mary. The book is a bare-knuckled satire
of humanity at large and the grandiose costume romance, done with
meticulous skill in imitation of such eighteenth-century picaresque
novelists as Fielding, Smollett and Sterne. For all the vigor of these
models, we have to go back to Rabelais to match its unbridled bawdiness
and scatological mirth. But the book is not pornographic. Rather than
arousing to venery, Barth reduces human sexuality to a raucous pest and
occasion of folly, employing a variety of fresh, vivid verbs for its functions. He does sometimes cross the line to the simply ugly in both act and
attitude.

The plot itself is a parody in incalculable complexity; a tissue of intrigue and counter-intrigue, ludicrous mock-heroic adventure, masquerades and confusions of identity. Its three major figures among a huge
gallery are Ebenezer Cooke, his twin sister, Anna, and one Henry Burlingame, once tutor to both and, in a manner of speaking, suitor to both.

Ebenezer, self-styled poet and virgin, whose Hudibrastic couplets
subjected to much solemn analysis are among Barth's triumphs, goes to
Maryland to be proprietor of his father's tobacco plantation on the Choptank River. He supposes himself commissioned by the third Lord
Baltimore as poet and laureate of Maryland to write an epic "Marylandiad." He finds life and limb in constant danger from political intrigues.
Burlingame, intricately involved in the plotting, constantly helps or saves
Ebenezer, but anybody having Burlingame for a friend doesn't need an
enemy.

*Reprinted by permission of *The New York Times*, Aug. 21, 1960.

111

Ebenezer has a mystical sense of his dual calling. His desperate struggles to preserve virginity against man and woman alike are a primary comic device, while defecation, voiding and vomiting are prominent. The descriptive chapter headings are entertaining. A sample: "The Laureate is Exposed to Two Assassinations of Character, a Piracy, a Near-DeFlowering, a Near-Mutiny, a Murder and an Appalling Colloquy Between Captains of the Sea. All Within the Space of a Few Pages."

Barth's masterstroke is an outrageously funny, villainously slanderous, alleged secret journal of Capt. John Smith. Its version of the Pocahontas story and other events is truly Rabelaisian and marvelously executed. In the author's apology Barth observes, against the charge of abusing the Muse of history, "This Clio was already a scarred and crafty trollop when the Author found her."

He is fond of tours de force in the form of itemizations, or displays of vocabulary or esoteric knowledge. One such is several pages of traded invectives, alternately French and English, between two prostitutes, appropriate to their calling. Another is an anthropological discourse on twin-lore partly anachronistic in its inclusiveness. A high spot of the pseudo John Smith manuscript is the detailed inventory of stuffs consumed in an eating match to the death. There is also a fantastic aphrodisiac recipe which may do for the eggplant what Hemingway was said to have done for sleeping bags.

All is summed up in the full title of Ebenezer's magnum opus: "The Sot-Weed Factor: Or, a Voyage to Maryland. A Satyr. In which is describ'd, the Laws, Government, Courts and Constitutions of the Country; and also the Buildings, Feats, Frolics, Entertainments and Drunken Humours of the Inhabitants of that Part of America." Though it is not for all palates, it is possible that Barth's book may be cherished by its true audience for some time to come.

Worth a Guilty Conscience

Denham Sutcliffe*

If the *Review* were a learned journal, and if your reviewer were a scholar, *The Sot-Weed Factor* would occasion a field day among sources and analogues. We might indicate some of its literary origins and effects by saying that it was begotten by Don Quixote upon Fanny Hill; or perhaps with equal justice that it is by Rabelais out of Moll Flanders. Completeness would require us to say that our author had been soused in Sterne and pickled in Fielding; that we suspect him of knowing *Candide* pretty well and of having a commendable love of Chaucer. Of actual sources employed by our author, we should say nothing, knowing nothing. But we would refer joyfully to his brilliantly impudent manufacture of sources, such as the heretofore lost journals of Lord Henry Burlingame and of Captain Jn° Smith, which considerably revise the familiar story of Pocahontas. We might have to wonder whether it was indeed a practice of the late seventeenth century to send boatloads of whores to the Colonies, but granted that they did, we are not surprised to learn what happened when one of those vessels was boarded by pirates. It is of course mandatory, in writing about literary London of this period, to discuss coffeehouses, and our review would have to say that Addison apparently did not tell us the whole truth about them.

What is the truth about Pocahontas? The truth is that she had a most curious queynte which the best-equipped braves of her community had attempted in vain. Smith, who never tired of boasting of his abilities in this art, was assured of his freedom if he could publicly relieve her of a superfluous bit of tissue. Another truth is that Smith was not himself prodigiously equipped, but by judicious use of a secret potation (the recipe is unfortunately not revealed; perhaps even our author doesn't know what it was; it included eggplant, which suggests sympathetic magic) he managed to induce "a weapon of the gods." When Pocahontas saw the frightful engine she leered with delight—only to swoon dead away while the Captain proceeded to his duty, from which her father had finally to beg him to desist. All this is true, for it is here quoted from the journals of Henry Burlingame.

Also revealed is the practice of certain aborigines of Maryland who, when they were about to burn a man in the morning, would tether him in a hut with the unmarried girls of the village. It was thus that they tethered a Jesuit missionary, with half a score of mirthful young things. Despite his struggles, one of them

> lays hands upon the candle of the Carnal Mass, and *mirabile*, the more she trims the greater doth it wax! Father Fitzmaurice sets to saying *Paternosters* with all haste, more concerned now with the preservation of his own grace than the institution of his wards. But no sooner is he thus engaged than *zut!* she caps his candle with the snuffer priests must shun, that so far from putting out the fire, only fuels it to a greater heat and brilliance.

Father Fitzmaurice, concluding that he is promoting with the heathen a rapport that must precede conversion, labors with a will and "ere dawn, with the help of God, he hath persuaded every woman in the hut of the clear superiority of the Faith."

Now I am aware that some novelists have in recent years shown an interest in sex. D. H. Lawrence did, for example, and Henry Miller. Even Hemingway's books were accused of "smelling of the boudoir." But these are pallid fellows beside our present author, who gives us what I don't remember to have seen in an American writer or in a modern British one. That is, bawdry. While I am working so hard to sound scholarly, I remind myself that in Old French "baud" signified "merry." Bawdry drains sex of all moral concern; it never moons about love and beauty; it simply inverts all the ordinary conventions surrounding the subject and presents us with the ludicrous, as "The Reeve's Tale" presents us with the ludicrous. (As mater of fact, "The Reeve's Tale is retold here, with interesting variations.) Bawdry sees no virtue in virginity; it prefers, instead, the stratagems that bring it down. The hero of our story, Ebenezer Cooke, constantly describes himself as "poet and virgin," clearly indicating his conviction that these are professions of equal worth. But between the stratagems of his friends and the assaults of nature, he gets into situations that provide the reader with more fun than an actual swiving would. One of these situations involves Henry More (which recalls to your scholarly mind "the Cambridge Platonists") and Isaac Newton, who may be libeled for all I know, but whose tastes in sex, it is suggested, were on the bizarre side.

Folklorists will find the book a mine of proverbial sayings. I didn't count them, but there must be scores, including some gems. I suspect that, along with the historical documents, they are gay fabrications. "Who traffics with strumpets hath a taste for the pox." "More history's made in the bedchamber than in the throne room." The volume includes a "Pandect of Geminology" (the unlearned are to understand "a digest of the lore of twins") which recalls Slawkenbergius on noses. There is a fliting in which a French whore and an English one exchange insults descriptive of their trade. When the list ends after six long pages one feels that the characters are exhausted, not the author. There is a contest which requires the losers to take turns walking close behind a flatulent horse.

What we are dealing with, of course, is a picaresque which is also a burlesque of the historical novel. Ebenezer, "poet and virgin," is commissioned by Lord Baltimore (or so he thinks) to write a Marylandiad, and in anticipation of a happy result he is given the title "Laureate of Maryland." He writes a good share of the poem before his embarkation, celebrating the delights of the voyage and the pastoral happiness of the colony. Sad reality destroys his dream and what was to have been a paean comes out as an Hudibrastic satire titled *The Sot-Weed Factor* (i.e. a tobacco agent). We are even treated to several good pages on the theory and practice of Hudibrastics, which Ebenezer regards as a more artful form than we had ever supposed it to be. "Good rhymes," he argues, "are mere embroidery on the muse's drawers." It is a pity that after we have gotten to like him so well, we must declare the laureate to be an indifferent poet.

The mark of style in this novel is untiring exuberance, limitless fertility of imagination (fancy, if you prefer), a breathless pace of narrative that never lets the reader rest or want to rest. Superficially one might say that our author "imitates" seventeenth-century style, but he doesn't really; he only makes one think he does. He thereby avoids the stiffness of pedantry and at the same time gets a flavor of the antique. The aim, as I have said, is burlesque—even the apparently inordinate size of the book is a joke. It was a dangerous joke, but he gets away with it. He burlesques the aged conventions of fiction—mistaken identity, "the search for a father," true love, and all the rest—with merciless ingenuity. No moral purpose is discoverable, no arcane "significance," simply fun. I suppose it's as dirty as the devil, but as a priest is made to say in the book, "A good tale's worth a guilty conscience." We may be allowed to hope that our author has restored to common usage a word that has been too long in desuetude: "swiving." That is unashamedly his principle subject.

I rejoice to concur in the opinion of the trapper who says:

"No pleasure pleasures me as doth a well-spun tale, be't sad or merry, shallow or deep. If the subject's privy business, or unpleasant, who cares a fig? The road to Heaven's beset with thistles, and methinks there's many a cow-pat on't as well. And what matter if your folk are drawn from life? 'T is not likely I'll ha' met 'em, or know 'em from your telling if e'er I should. Call 'em what names ye will: in a tale they're less than themselves, and more. Besides which, if ye have the art to make 'em live—'sheart!—thour't nowise liable for what the rascals do, no more than God Almighty for the lot of us. [*Vide* Chaucer.] As for length, fie on't. A bad tale's long though it want but a single eyeblink for the telling, and a good tale short though it takes from St. Swithin's to Michaelmas to have done with't. Ha! And the plot is tangled, d'ye say. Is it more knotted or bewildered than the skein o' life itself, that a good tale tangles the better to unsnarl? . . . A tale well wrought is the gossip o' the gods, that see the heart and hidden point o' life on earth; the seamless web o' the world; the Warp and Woof. . . . I'Christ, I do love a story, sirs! Tell away!"

The Novel as Parody:
John Barth

Earl Rovit*

John Barth's *The Sot-Weed Factor* (1960) is, in a sense, a kind of prolonged academic joke; it is wonderfully adroit, as sophisticated as a modern reproduction of "authentic" antiquarianism, and is somewhat perversely fixed on a puristic conception of the factuality of source materials. This last factor gives it a special interest for my purposes, since the novel exhibits most clearly an eccentric faith in the imitations (rather than the possibilities) of the imagination and the creative process. I shall be manifestly unjust to Barth's novel—which injustice it can surely bear—because I think it represents one of the directions which contemporary fiction has resorted to since *Finnegan's Wake*—a direction which I fear can lead only to a *cul de sac*. And if I attribute to *The Sot-Weed Factor* some of the perversities writ much larger in other fictions than itself, I plead excuse out of a recognition of the extremely trenchant powers as a novelist which Barth so obviously possesses.

In *The Floating Opera* (1956), Barth's first novel, the major character pronounces the truism of our age: "Nothing has intrinsic value." On the basis of this perception, that first novel flirts with the possibilities of suicide, ultimately rejecting purposive negation on the grounds of absurdity. If Todd Andrews, the hero, should choose death because there is no meaning in life, he would be caught in the absurd contradiction of ascribing intrinsic value to something—in this case, suicide. Logic, itself valueless, shows him the ridiculousness of his position and the novel ends in an affirmative snicker which accepts chance confusion as the only viable life-principle which can make sense or non-sense to the hero. The structural response of the novel to this thematic base is a wandering digressive form, patterned on the consciously haphazard reminiscences of a single day in the life of the narrator. If the ghost of Laurence Sterne haunts the literary locale of the novel a little too heavily, and if the digressive material is somewhat too strenuously pasted into its proper places, *The Floating Opera* is still very much a "promising" first novel—deft in its handling of humorous incongruity, and impassive in its

*Reprinted by permission of *Critique*, vi, No. 2 (Fall 1963), 77–85.

116

cynical attachment to the sentimentalities of the local-color of Maryland's Eastern Shore. But its preoccupation with the problem of *value*—and its literary synonym, *form*—prefigures the kinds of difficulties with which *The Sot-Weed Factor* will have to struggle.

If "nothing has intrinsic value," then the harrowing problem for the artist will be the problem of form. Regardless of the metaphysical quiddities which our contemporary debate over Existentialism entails, the novelist is still faced with the old Aristotelian injunction to make a beginning, a middle, and an end—to start somewhere and conclude with some artifice of finality. The line of movement which the reader traces in the novelist's wake—whether it be serpentine or linear, whether it circles back on itself or climbs far from its point of origin—will indelibly delineate the artist's resolution of *form* and his statement of *value.* Nihilism, absurdity, all the variants of humanism or super-naturalism—one of the infinite varieties of valuation must be resonant in the form of the finished novel if the novel is to be taken at all seriously. And no contemporary novelist can evade the moral and aesthetic challenge that this problem of form brings with it.

To put it in an over-extreme way, the modern novelist is forced into a choice of subjugation to one of two literary techniques—to the externally structured universe of an Alexander Pope or to the dream-emergent rhythms of an Edgar Allan Poe. Word and image, character and action swirl in an inchoate limbo-world, requiring the imposition of design in order to be brought into literary life. But our age offers no readily acceptable design; the babble of our confusion of values drowns out both the still, small voice within and the thundering command from the misty top of the volcanic rock. The novelist has every right—perhaps, indeed, every obligation—to begin with the axiom that "nothing has intrinsic value," but the end of his novel must make a tacit declaration of value, or it will have failed to have achieved an aesthetic form. Hence the popularity of two opposite strategies in contemporary fiction; on the one side is the faith in a superimposed intellectual system with its self-contained logicalities, and, on the other side, the irrational faith in the dark currents of the passional life. The constructed concept and the fragmented dream, the completely conscious abstraction and the dangerous world of the marginal consciousness—these are the two major paths which the artist can choose between, and, with rare exceptions, the choice of one will exclude a significant influence from the other. *The Sot-Weed Factor* is exemplary of the choice for Pope rather than for Poe, for a faith in the limited powers of the human capacity to make abstractions rather than a faith in the irrational urge toward what is unknown and unknowable.

Barth's *The Sot-Weed Factor* is an almost pure specimen of that group of novels which I would call "parodies"—even as I recognize the inadequacy of the particular term. In such novels, there is an arbitrary selection of a closed system of some sort or other—either the imitation of a well-known form, or the invention or adaptation of some technique for organizing disparate material into consciously manageable order. In this sense, such recent fictions as Durrell's *Alexandria Quartet,* Nabokov's *Pale Fire,* and Jorge Luis Borges' *Labyrinths* may indicate the variety and range of the "parody-novel." The emphasis in all these fictions is on *control*—a firm and unyielding regimen of subordination in which every element of the fiction—prose style, narrative point of view, theme and action—is resolutely manipulated under the guidance of a single shaping design. In spite of the various artifices of concealment which the parodists practice (the pseudo-lyricism of Durrell or the brilliant ironic displacement which Nabokov has perfected), the result is the Novel as Jig-Saw Puzzle. The design has been engineered in the factory, the instructions are on the box, and the job of the novelist and the reader is to put the pieces together in the one correct way which the blueprint demands. However, lest this appear more simple than it really is, there is usually a radical variable built into the design at one place or another. The puzzle-maker may take great pains to deceive the reader into mistaking the blue of the sky with the blue of the water. He may juggle his focus of narration into an ultimate blur through the device of multiple lenses, as in Durrell's *Quartet;* or, he may shape his controlling consciousness in such a way as to make it ultimately ambiguous, as with Nabokov's Charles Kinbote. The parody-novel runs the constant danger of becoming a bewildering plaything in which its own obsessive order operates on the principle of a Rube Goldberg machine, each part frenetically fulfilling its own function, while the function of the total mechanism is one of self-enclosed uselessness.

Now parody has always been a significant element in the shaping of the novel—from Cervantes to Defoe, from Fielding to Flaubert, from Mark Twain to Joyce and Mann. But, at its best, parody begins in caricatured imitation and ends either in the vitriolic vein of criticism or the ornate brocade of a poetic vision; in both cases imitation transcends itself to become original creation. The devices of parody are absorbed into the valences of the new form as though the stammering novelist had first to lisp his alphabet in mocking echo of what he has read in order to pronounce his own new word. In this sense the novel has always been involved with parody to some degree. However, the parody-novel makes parody less an instrument than an end. Confronted with an unlimited choice among equally cogent values, the parodist resorts to the devices of parody for his final answers instead of using it as a means for further questionings Nabokov has a character describe our time as "a comic age/That sees in Dr. Schweizer a great sage." In these circumstances parody should ideally regiment itself into a satirical exposure of the false, the ugly, the affected, and the hypocritical. But the keystone pediment—in this case, the major *im*pediment—in the creation of any system of values is the horrifying perception that "nothing is of intrinsic value." The false, the ugly, the meretricious, and the hypocritical are neither more nor less ridiculous than their classical opposites. Hence parody becomes employed without the rigorous passion that can make effective satire. And the twentieth-century parody-novel which shapes itself under the superimposition of an external order will run the desperate danger of being a hollow vessel, a cosmetic rather than a cosmic design, decorative, playful, ultimately turning upon itself in bitterness, its ambiguities forced and mendacious because unrooted in the concrete ambiguities of human experience.

The Sot-Weed Factor pretends to be a recreation of the life of Ebenezer Cooke, an obscure Englishman who published in 1708 a twenty-three page satirical poem (entitled *The Sot-Weed Factor*) on his unhappy adventures in Maryland. Nothing is known about Cooke, although it is assumed that his poem gives a Hudibrastically exaggerated rendition of his own abortive emigration to Lord Baltimore's colony in the late years of the seventeenth century. The original poem is savagely ebullient and clever, and its meager life has been that of a literary curiosity enjoyed by specialists in colonial American literature and history. Barth's novel is an eight hundred page commentary on the poem—a fictional biography of Cooke and his misadventures in England and in the colonial settlements centering around the Eastern Shore of Maryland. The controlling devices of the parodistic form of the novel are the factual history of the Palatinate of Maryland and the literary conventions of the eighteenth-century novel. It is possible that Barth transgresses known historical fact in his exposition of the intrigue and counter-intrigue which seem to have marked the attempts of the three Lords Baltimore to found a unique colony in the New World. If he has done so, however, none but an absorbed scholar in early Maryland history would know. The alleged machinations of William Claiborne, John Coode, Edmund Andros, William Penn, and Francis Nicholson are played against a shifting shadow-screen in which the problem of spurious identity becomes so complicated that even the existence of Charles Calvert, the third Lord Baltimore, is thrown into doubt. The suspicious fact of Baltimore's Catholicism in the Protestant New World, the greeds and frustrations of the tobacco planters, and the mercurial shifts of policy on the part of the English Crown provide a historical background which frames the novel like a very elaborate double acrostic. And Barth's minute knowledge of the geography and topography of the Choptank River area of Maryland's Eastern Shore gives him an additional limiting factor in the illusion of authority with which the novel is narrated.

The literary conventions of the eighteenth-century novel (most particularly, *Tom Jones*) provide the other parodistic control for *The Sot-Weed Factor*. Barth's novel is almost a compendium of the eighteenth-century picaresque form; there are two interrelated main plots (Cooke's and Henry Burlingame's respective quests for identity), interlaced by literally dozens of supporting sub-plots. While the main action of Eben's life—his upbringing, his resolution to become the poet laureate of Maryland, the loss of his Maryland estate and his virginity, and the regaining of the estate, although not the virginity—proceeds in a relatively direct line, the Henry Burlingame plot and the total reconstruction of life in Maryland in the last part of the seventeenth-century are interthreaded into the novel in leisurely fits and starts, feints and parries, false clues and deceptive coincidences. Digressions and stories-within-stories determine the structure of the novel, so that although Cooke's plot-line is reasonably straight, the overall structural impact of the novel reminds one of a pack of hounds with stuffed noses frantically sniffing out a nonexistent covey of quail. All this is very comic, of course, and the comedy is rendered even more effective when the reader realizes at the end of the novel that no detail has been accidental; each seemingly digressive flight of fancy and each wildly invented anecdote are seen to fit into their proper places. Barth's comic parody turns upon the reader as a conjuror's trick of deception. The entire novel is a joke upon the reader; he was persuaded to show his courage by plunging into a literary swamp and the swamp turned into an elaborately designed swimming pool, replete with interior lighting, automatic drains, and cleverly concealed filter systems.

But even as the structure of the picaresque is meticulously parodied, so also are the major themes of eighteenth-century fiction. Uncertain parentage, incest, the difficulty of differentiating between reality and appearance, the masquerade of disguises, and the regular unpredictability of Fortune's largesse—all these are represented with laborious proliferation. And Barth accepts one final limitation as well, and perhaps this is the ultimate perversity of his *tour de force:* he elects to write his novel in the eighteenth-century manner, using no words, images, illusions, metaphors, or other figures of speech not current and available to the English novelist writing in Fielding's time. It is possible that here again there may be minor transgressions, but I did not find any. There are some remarkable verbal pyrotechnics in Barth's mastery of eighteenth-century slang as well as formal diction. His invention of *The Secret Diary of John Smith*, his rendition of the scholastic arguments between the followers of the Platonist Henry More and Isaac Newton, and the seven-page badinage of French and English synonyms for "prostitute" which is held between two colonial ladies of joy are some of the scenes in the novel which exhibit this verbal dexterity most completely. But, for a twentieth-century writer to present an eight hundred page novel while denying himself access to the speech of his own time is to suggest that parody has become that kind of imitation which is frozen into the inflexible forms of that which it is meant to ridicule or use as a means of ridicule.

To be sure, there are indications that *The Sot-Weed Factor* attempts a satirical range beyond this. Especially in the characterization of Henry Burlingame, the consummate master of disguises who seems to be without any essential face of his own, Barth would seem to be grappling with the question of identity so common to the concerns of contemporary fiction. Burlingame, Eben Cooke's young tutor and the grandson of John Smith's ill-fated companion, Sir Henry Burlingame, is reminiscent of Melville's Confidence Man; he changes personalities and identities like a chameleon, but the author never divulges the purposes of his incessant schemes and espionages. And the secret of his energy and his genius (for he is a genius) is likewise never discovered by the reader. Perhaps Burlingame is meant to represent Modern Man, and Barth leaves him basically mysterious since he must reject any order at the roots of human behavior save the principle of disordered confusion. All this is legitimate enough, and the short discussion on aesthetics in which Burlingame refutes Eben's argument for "merit" in things in favor of his own position of "interest" reminds us of Barth's earlier advocacy of intrinsic valuelessness. Other areas as well are probably meant to be satirized—Eben's cocksure certainty in his own perceptions (which is again and again proved false), the metamorphic changes in personality which Eben undergoes in spite of his belief in essential selfhood, the unbridgable gap between ideal and action, the indeterminacy of all things—these are surely matters of current interest, whether narrated in eighteenth-century form or not. And yet they fail to engage our attentions because of the excessive paraphernalia of authentic antiquarianism in which they are smothered. The parody imprisons the reader instead of liberating him; and in his prison he can only remark upon the highly wrought mosaic-work which keeps him from breathing free.

And finally, something must be said about the treatment of sex or sheer physicality in the novel. If the artifices of mind and spirit—philosophy and art—are insufficient in themselves to bring "merit" or value into being, then perhaps the sensuous responses of the neural system may offer a hope for Barth and his readers. In *The Floating Opera*, Todd Andrews had witnessed his initiation into sex in an unusually large mirror next to his bed, and he had concluded in his seventeen-year-old wisdom that "Nothing is *intrinsically* funny, to be sure, but to me nothing is so consistently, profoundly, earth-shakingly funny as we animals in the act of mating." The Barth of *The Sot-Weed Factor* enlarges Andrews' mirror to reflect almost every variety of copulation and near-copulation that is humanly (and sometimes superhumanly) possible. Rapes and orgies, seductions and impotencies, and God's plenty of what used to be called in a gentler age "unnatural" practices are described with neo-classical precision. And yet, although many of the individual scenes are funny in themselves, the cumulative effect of the sexual athletics of the novel is one of sour sweat and glandular depression. Nor is this feeling mitigated by the non-erotic physical functions of the human animal at work and play. Characters befoul themselves, eat and drink into gluttonous stupors, belch, break wind, and decay perceptibly from syphilis and the pox. And here too, although many of these scenes are individually comic in their grotesquerie or incongruity, the overall effect is the same sour staleness that sees in the tincture of human flesh nothing but the ordure of rotting meat.

I do not think that *The Sot-Weed Factor* is the novel that John Barth intended to write. It seems to me quite possible that in this, his third novel, he meant to use a parody-form in order to make a more positive statement of the possiblity of *value*, perhaps in terms of his recognition that chance or confusion is the disordering pulse at the heart of human existence. And it is for this reason that *The Sot-Weed Factor* possesses "interest" for the student of contemporary fiction. Barth's conscious decision to organize his talents within the circumscribing frame of a rigorous parody leads him inevitably to surrender his own moral opportunity to create values. The form which he arbitrarily selects denies him the chance to project his own unique metaphor of existence, and denies his novel the necessary illusion of engagement in human affairs which it must have in order to live. The intellectual design becomes the factor of paramount importance and the novelist's vision is pressed between the pages of his heavy book like the pale wings of a withered insect. The parody drones without passion, without even the desperate revulsion which still makes *Gulliver's Travels* so much alive. The novel ends in the last analysis as a shallow parody, an intellectual gymnastic, a mechanical puzzle in which Barth can flex the muscles of his extraordinary dexterity. The reader admires the labor and the craft, enjoys the well-wrought gimcrack, but finds his world unchanged, his experience unenhanced. He has been entertained, to be sure, but he has been cheated of the honest confrontation with the basic questions of his own secret soul that Barth's talents had led him to expect. And he has been doubly cheated, because Barth had perhaps deceived himself while deceiving his reader.

It may be that Vladimir Nabokov expresses best the problems that the parodist must successfully resolve if his novel is to attain that moral seriousness which all responsible art aims at. A character in *Pale Fire* who seems clearly to be speaking for his author explains why he is a true artist even though he works through the means of imitating other writers' styles: "I can do what only a true artist can do—pounce upon the forgotten butterfly of revelation, wean myself abruptly from the habit of things, see the web of the world, and the warp and weft of that web." Barth's powers as a novelist are large and his technical mastery of the difficult art of parody is beyond question. And one senses that he has dreamed the revelation and seen it soar in irrational flight. But if he is to employ parody as a willing instrument of his vision, he must learn to let his butterfly have a life that transcends his capturing design. Otherwise, his work will suffocate within his designs, old and musty at the moment of its birth.

"What Marvelous Plot . . . Was Afoot?": John Barth's *The Sot-Weed Factor*

Alan Holder*

John Barth has said that his starting point in composing *The Sot-Weed Factor* was the poem of the same name written by Ebenezer Cooke, and published in 1708, a work of interest to students of early American literature.[1] But going far beyond that satirical account, and drawing heavily on the raw historical record as preserved in the *Archives of Maryland*, Barth produced a massive novel about Cooke's adventures in England and America which dwarfs the seven hundred-odd lines of the poem. Combining the suggestions of a number of these lines, facts gathered from the *Archives*, and characters, events and documents of his own invention, Barth has attempted to put colonial Maryland on the map of the American literary imagination, to work with a region that has been for the most part, like the territory originally granted to Lord Baltimore, *"hactenus inculta"*—hitherto uncultivated. Leslie Fiedler noted in his review of *The Sot-Weed Factor* that Maryland "has less ready-made mythic import for other Americans than almost any region to which Barth might have been born."[2]

Early in the novel, Ebenezer proclaims that his virginity is part of his essence and must be preserved. That virginity, which Eben and the book identify with innocence, will in turn preserve him from time, death and history, or so he absurdly thinks. (It is no surprise to have a character tell him " 'tis not simply love ye know naught of, 'tis the *entire great real world!*' "[3]) Eben's preoccupation with his virginity gives particular weight to his declaration that as a subject for poetry, the accomplishments in Maryland of " 'the noble house of Calverts, the Barons Baltimore' " is " 'virgin territory!' " (p. 87). He proposes writing a *Marylandiad:*

> An epic to out-epic epics. . . . The courage and perseverance of her settlers in battling barb'rous nature and fearsome salvage to wrest a territory from the wild and transform it to an earthly paradise! The majesty and enlightenment of her proprietors, who like kingly gardeners fostered the tender seeds of civilization in their rude soil, and so husbanded and cultivated them as to bring to fruit

*Reprinted by permission of *The American Quarterly*.

a Maryland beauteous beyond description; verdant, fertile, prosperous, and cultured; peopled with brave men and virtuous women, healthy, handsome, and refined: a Maryland, in short, splendid in her past, majestic in her present, and glorious in her future, the brightest jewel in the fair crown of England . . . (pp. 87–88).

Lord Baltimore (actually Eben's friend Henry Burlingame in disguise) tells the would-be epic writer that he is " 'all innocent of Maryland's history' " (p. 89), and fills him in on Maryland's past (Eben is about to embark for that colony). In listening to "Baltimore," Eben, together with the reader, is confronted by a bewildering proliferation of names and a profusion of events. Later giving a supplementary history lesson to Eben, Burlingame—not in disguise this time—says " 'Tis not so deadly long a story, but I must own 'tis a passing tangled one, with much running hither and thither and an army of names to bear in mind' " (p. 152). For early as the novel is set—the 1690's—America seems to have acquired a considerable history by the time Eben sets foot on the Maryland shore. There is virtually no primeval forest, no virgin land to be contemplated; such a domain is not within the book's sensibility. Indeed much of the comedy of the story, as well as its serious developments, comes from the collisions between Eben, the self-proclaimed virgin, and a territory that is something less than intact. It is significant that when he lands on what he assumes is an uncharted island, it turns out to be, in the words of a planter settled there, " 'but poor shitten Maryland . . .' " (p. 312).

This phrase, which does not dampen Eben's enthusiasm for the place (it takes much to dent his innocence), serves as a capsule characterization of much of the world of the book (and one particularly appropriate to a story which has a good deal of fecal humor). For *The Sot-Weed Factor* displays a strong tendency to debunk the past, finding in colonial America not a spirit of courage, admirable endurance and daring, but seeing our early history as made up of selfish motives and unheroic behavior, conceiving of its participants as a collection of scoundrels and perverts together with their victims. (This tendency is already present in the English setting where the novel begins, as we find Sir Isaac Newton and Sir Henry More characterized as homosexuals, the quarrel between them, originating in philosophical disagreement, coming to a head because of their competition for the favors of Burlingame.) Two of the first people Eben encounters are a slave who was thrown off a ship to drown, and a displaced Indian king. The Maryland landscape is strewn with hovels and brothels. Its courts are a travesty of justice, the standard of honesty being that nobody gets a verdict he has not paid for.[4] Its indentured servants are the victims of a "redemption" racket. (All this is consistent with the spirit of Cooke's original poem.[5]) The estate of his father that Eben has come to America to manage operates as a combination "gambling house, tavern, brothel, and opium den . . ." (p. 485).

The unglorious was present from the very early appearance of the white man in America, according to a pair of "documents" that Barth introduces, which purport to give the real story behind Captain John Smith's self-celebratory descriptions of his Virginia ventures, particularly his encounter with Pocahontas. One of them, *"A Secret Historie,"* was supposedly written by Smith himself, while the other, *"The Privie Journall of Sir Henry Burlingame"* (a pun on "privy" being undoubtedly intended by Barth), was allegedly kept by one of Smith's company. The first of these presents, among other things, an hilarious picture of Smith's crew seized by diarrhea and consequently unable to make much progress in sailing their boat because they " *'must continuallie hang there bummes abeame . . .'* " (p. 391). The *"Journall"* portrays Smith as carrying a pack of pornographic cards, gorging himself in swinish fashion, satisfying a sexually voracious Indian queen, and meeting successfully a challenge to pierce Pocahontas' hitherto impenetrable vaginal membrane. These documents would seem to confirm one of the many proverbs appearing in the book, namely, *"More history's made in the bedchamber than in the throne room"* (p. 261). All in all, Barth's descriptions of Captain Smith and of early Maryland may be said to serve as the antithesis to the romantic, chivalric self-portrait emerging from Smith's own writings, and to the picture of a colonial South embodying these qualities found in such American historical novelists as John Esten Cooke and Mary Johnston. (Though obviously very different from him, Barth displays something akin to Washington Irving's humorous, irreverent approach to the past.)

It is not only the white man who is made to look ridiculous in Barth's rendering of early America. While the first Indian we encounter is a dignified chieftain, a victim of the English, the Indians in general do not figure as nature's noblemen in the novel.[6] Smith's secret history tells of Sir Henry Burlingame being made to enter into an eating contest with an Indian, a ritual based on the tribe's assumption that the heavier a king the more secure will his followers be against enemies. One of the tribe's former kings was called *"Kekataughtassapooekskunoughmass, for that he did eate ninetie fish on the daye he became there King,"* Ahatchwhoop, the tribe's name, signifies *"a belch of gass. . ."* (p. 594). The description of the eating contest between Burlingame and the Indian Attonce is in keeping with the tone of these etymological tidbits. ". . . *Attonce, sitting cross-legged, did bump his buttocks up & down upon the earthe, farther to appetyze him selfe; Burlingame also, that he give his foe no quarter, and the verie grownd shudder'd beneath these awful bummes."* After consuming an enormous amount of food, Attonce was struck upon the gut as an aid toward getting down some last morsels, whereupon he *"did let flie a tooling fart and dy'd upon the instant where he sat"* (pp. 597, 598). (Not only is history, the red man's as well as the white man's, rendered in comic, reductive terms by Barth's narrative, but so, too, is myth, or what might potentially serve as myth. Compare the reverence and awe surrounding the encounter of man and animal in Faulkner's *The Bear* with Barth's account of the Indian Billy Rumbly killing a bear by thrusting a stick deep into its anus.)

There is not much new about Barth's New World in relation to the Old, except for the intensity of its dubious activities. Maryland is a place much trampled by the busy feet of European settlers, and embroiled in conflicts having their source in Europe. Eben's friend Burlingame (a descendant of the keeper of the *Journall*) describes it as " 'just a piece o' the great world like England—with the difference, haply, that the soil is vast and new where the sot-weed [tobacco] hath not drained it and oft will sprout wild seeds of energy in men that had lain fallow [in England]' " (p. 180). Eben, reacting to summaries of Maryland's history, thinks of the "strange and terrible energy" of the men he has been told about, "figures awful in their energy and purpose . . ." (pp. 114, 162). William Claiborne, holding sway over the Isle of Kent, is prominent among these persons, and he is no sooner dead in the account Eben hears than John Coode is on the scene, stirring up strife. (Both of these men are based on actual, historical personages.) It is as though there had been an implicit legacy of disruptive force passed on from the one man to the other, the transmission of an Iago-like genius for creating disorder. Eben refers to Claiborne as Coode's " 'spiritual father' " (p. 372).

What is the precise form that the energy of men like Claiborne and Coode takes? In Barth's conception of them they are deeply and continuously immersed in *plots*. Burlingame, posing as Lord Baltimore, tells Eben that Maryland's history is the tale of his family's " 'struggle to preserve her, and of the plots of countless knaves to take her from us . . .' " (p. 90). After listening to the account of this struggle, Eben is moved to exclaim: " 'Ne'er have I encountered such a string of plots, cabals, murthers, and machinations in life or literature as this history you relate me—it sets my head a-twirl, and chills my blood!' " (p. 106). (This, of course, serves as a counter-statement to his earlier assumption that the history of Maryland has been "glorious," a fit subject for a *Marylandiad*.) The word *plot* appears again and again in the book, with, e.g., William Penn described as engaged in manipulations to have the borders of his colony extended to take in what was originally a part of Maryland, while Claiborne and Coode are seen as maneuvering tirelessly to undermine Baltimore's authority and control. Burlingame, supposedly an agent of Baltimore, plots against Coode (whose energy his own rivals). At one point he tells Eben that " 'There is a wondrous wicked plot afoot to ruin the Province with pox and opium, the better to overthrow it' " (p. 476). Later it turns out that Baltimore himself may be engaged in a plot to enervate the English in America with opium in the hope that they will succumb to the French and Indians; the colonies are to be turned into a Catholic domain with Baltimore to be crowned Emperor of America and made a saint upon his death. (Here Barth may be drawing upon rumors of

Indian-Catholic alliances that frightened Protestants in seventeenth-century Maryland.)[7] Intrigue appears to be operating in Eben's own affairs, and he wonders at one point: "What marvelous plot . . . was afoot?" (p. 287).

To heighten the effect of inexhaustible colonial energies being channeled into devious plots, Barth has taken some liberties with the historical records as these appear in the *Archives of Maryland*. He has either altered the facts or linked them together in the shape of a plot. So, for example, he has Burlingame attribute to Claiborne an accusation against a colonial official that was actually made by a woman.[8] Also, Burlingame claims that Claiborne arranged to have two commissioners lost at sea, a charge for which there is no evidence in the record. Again without a basis in the book's sources, it is indicated that William Fuller and Josias Fendall, officials who had turned against Baltimore, urged a rebellion in Maryland similar to that of Bacon's rebellion in Virginia. Fendall is accused of further conspiring against Baltimore, this time with John Coode. The latter, in turn, is arbitrarily described as the associate of several other men, and Jacob Leisler, New York's equivalent of Coode, is reported as coming south for the purpose of conniving with him. This conjoining appears to be Barth's own invention. Another apparent fabrication of Barth's is the alleged plot by Indians and escaped slaves to massacre every white man in Maryland.

What emerges from these alterations of and additions to items in the *Archives* is the conception of early American history as intrigue, the sense of historical events as the products of plots and counterplots. There is enough in the documentary record to suggest that considerable truth inheres in this view (Howard Mumford Jones has written that "if Machiavelli had known as much about the performance of Europeans in America as he knew about the performance of Italian rulers, he could have drawn his illustrations quite as richly from the one case as he did from the other.")[9] But Barth has chosen to go from suggestion to assertion, supplying linkages where the record supplies only lacunae. However, one is not sure whether he is seriously offering the various plots as his conception of the actual shape of events, or whether he is simply indulging a storyteller's desire to tidy up the clutter of history and mold it into a neat narrative pattern, a plot in the literary sense of the term. The latter may well be the case. Certainly, one of the striking features of the book is Barth's ingenuity in weaving together plot developments that at first seem to have little to do with each other. But if he busily arranges his historical materials into orderly patterns, he also displays a very different tendency in his treatment of the past, one that renders history as problematical.

For Burlingame's and Ebenezer's judgments of the alleged plots modulate from condemnation of Coode to a consideration of the possibility that Baltimore might be a villain, and his various antagonists—Fendall, Penn, Claiborne, Coode—heroes. The compilers of the *Archives* side unequivocally with Baltimore, but the *Archives* themselves contain materials that do not encourage such a black-and-white judgment. There is, for example, a long, vigorously written document, which sees Baltimore as a Catholic oppressing Protestants, acting imperiously and taxing excessively.[10] This the compilers arbitrarily dismiss as the "grotesque tirade of some illiterate fanatic. . . ."[11] There are also documents that give a picture of Claiborne as a constructive, helpful man.[12] We can find, too, evidence to indicate that Coode was respected by his fellow members of the House of Burgesses.[13] Barth, then, is being true to the records when he has his book indicate the difficulty, if not the impossibility, of assigning with certainty the labels of good and evil to the conflicting parties in Maryland's past. But as in his treatment of history as plot, Barth is not content to stay within the limits of his documents. He will not rest with the notion that judgments about the past are difficult, but must introduce an additional complication by having Burlingame suggest that Coode and Baltimore may not exist at all. After having heard of their activities in detail, and from Burlingame himself, this suggestion strikes one as an arbitrary turn of the screw and a piece of obscurantism, mystification rather than earned mystery. (This might be considered an example of Barth's *playing* with history, a matter that will be considered more fully a little later.)

Burlingame does not seem oppressed by the difficulty of deciding which of the two warring parties, Coode or Baltimore, represents the good and which the evil. The important thing for him is a commitment to *doing*. He characterizes Coode as loving intrigue for its own sake, and he vows to match wits with him. He proceeds to do so with such energy that Eben declares: "Good heavens, Henry, thou'rt a plotting Coode thyself!' " (p. 178). (It is appropriate that at times he has posed as Coode.) Burlingame wishes to avoid what he has seen occur in Eben, the paralysis of will, the falling into a state of suspended animation. This is the condition that Jacob Horner, the protagonist of an earlier Barth novel, *End of the Road*, suffers from. He is told by another character that " 'Choosing is existence: to the extent that you don't choose, you don't exist. . . . It doesn't matter whether you act constructively or even consistently, so long as you act.' "[14] Burlingame appears to subscribe to the same principle, saying: " 'one must choose his gods and devils on the run, quill his own name upon the universe. . . . One must *assert, assert, assert*, or go screaming mad. What other course remains?' " (p. 365).

Given Barth's concern with the notion of action as a good in itself, one can understand his fascination with Claiborne and Coode, who, whatever their motives, were such *busy* personages, continually in movement. The conditions of the time and place in which they lived allowed their energy and resourcefulness repeated opportunities for great impact, for causing government to totter, and it may be their displays of the potency of the individual will engaged in persistent action that commands

Barth's interest in these men. We might note that the book's general spirit of debunking is replaced, in its treatment of Coode, Claiborne and Burlingame, by a tendency to admire. Responding to Burlingame's suggestion that Baltimore and Coode may be only rumors and tales, Eben says: " 'If that . . . is so . . . Heav'n knows 'twere a potent life enough!' " (p. 753).

Burlingame believes that it is Maryland's relative lack of history that allows men like Coode and himself to subordinate goals to action, even to reverse the direction of their efforts (Barth presents Coode as a Catholic priest who has turned against his co-religionists, although the *Archives* indicate he was an Anglican cleric.)[15] This lack of history, Burlingame says, confers " 'philosophic liberty' " upon a man, makes him in effect a spiritual orphan (p. 181). Burlingame *is* an orphan, a condition he is originally happy in. When Eben says that a man's father is his link with the past, Burlingame rejoins: " 'Then . . . I thank Heav'n I'm quit of mine'. . . . 'It leaves me free and unencumbered' " (p. 42). This freedom, the book seems to imply, is exercised in Burlingame's impersonations—he poses not only as Coode and as Baltimore, but also as Governor Frances Nicholson, and as Monsieur Casteene, a French intriguer. In doing so, he is displaying Coode-like behavior. Coode, says Burlingame, " 'is whate'er he chooses to call himself' . . ." (p. 161).[16] But while Burlingame at first cherishes this same freedom in his life, he later tells Eben that he envies him his father: " 'what a burden and despair to be a stranger to the world at large, and have no link with history!' " (pp. 145–146). He eventually embarks upon a quest to discover who his own father was. The connection between his orphan state, (the "philosophic liberty" conferred by this severance with the past), and the metamorphoses of both Coode and himself, is suggested on his learning that events had so transpired that " 'the search for my father and the search for ways to put down Coode were now the selfsame search!' " (p. 176). Barth appears to be indicating here that to search for one's father, that is, to discover one's connection with the past, is to discover moral boundaries and limits of identity, thereby relinquishing the role-playing, changes of allegiance, and unrestricted choices that the "orphan" enjoys. Learning that he is a member of the Ahatchwhoop tribe, Burlingame goes off to join it and try to dissuade its chieftain, his father, not to carry out a planned massacre of the English. He returns garbed like an Indian to see Eben and Eben's sister, Anna, but then leaves for good. Burlingame had been sexually attracted to both siblings, and desirous of having relations with them both (and simultaneously!). His androgynousness may be seen as a particular example of the "philosophic liberty" he has enjoyed prior to his discovery of his paternity. Having Burlingame cut himself off from both Eben and Anna might be Barth's way of dramatizing the assumption of limits by a man who had earlier declared himself the " 'Suitor of Totality, Embracer of Contradictories, Husband to all Creation, the Cosmic Lover! . . . I have no parentage to give me place and aim in Nature's order: very well—I am outside Her, and shall be Her lord and spouse!' " (p. 526). At the end of the book, the Cosmic Lover has renewed his connection with his past, taken on a particular task, given up his plan to enjoy both brother and sister, and disappeared into the murk of history.

But Barth makes Burlingame's ultimate fate ambiguous, suggesting the possibility that he has assumed yet one more identity, that of Nicholas Lowe. It would not be entirely inconsistent for Burlingame to have done this, for his statement that it is " 'a burden and despair' " to be an orphan, to have " 'no link with history,' " had not been his final word on the matter. Moreover, his adoption of an Indian identity was motivated by his commitment to serving the *English* in the New World. That commitment, in turn, cannot easily be seen as constituting a final position for Burlingame. Eben thinks: "how slight and qualified were Henry's ties to the cause of Western Civilization (to say nothing of English colonialism!), than which his mind and interests were so enormously more complex that it seemed parochial by comparison!" (p. 754). There appears to be a dialectic of emotion within Burlingame, now pulling him toward establishing a particular identity, now returning him to his status of Cosmic Lover.

The Sot-Weed Factor's own relation to the past would appear to be that of a Cosmic Lover as well, in the sense that the book refuses to commit itself to a particular conception of the past, of historical truth, but wants the freedom to embrace simultaneously a variety of possibilities —that the heroes and villains of the orthodox view were indeed such, that the application of these terms should be reversed, that the men did not exist at all. At one point, Barth talks of Eben's difficulty in realizing the "finality" of the real world. He feels nervous and irritable at the thought of "the whole business of Greece and Rome" being "the *only* way it happened" (p. 19), and is unable to "acknowledge in his heart that there really *had* been a Roman Empire" (p. 289). In his approach to history, as well as to literature and philosophy, Eben is "dizzy with the beauty of the possible . . ." (p. 21). He appears to possess sentiments close to those of his creator. For in an interview published in 1965, Barth is reported as saying that

> a certain kind of sensibility can be made very uncomfortable by the recognition of the *arbitrariness* of physical facts and the inability to accept their *finality*. . . . it seems to me that this emotion, which is a kind of metaphysical emotion, goes almost to the heart of what art is, at least some kinds of art, and this impulse to imagine alternatives to the world can become a driving impulse for writers. I confess that it is for me. So that really what you want to do is re-invent philosophy and the rest—make your own whole history of the world.[17]

Barth is apparently reluctant to commit himself to a final image of history, even if the image is of his own making. This does not, I think, derive so much from a brooding skepticism about the inability to arrive at the truth of the past (the attitude present in works, say, like Ezra Pound's

"Near Perigord" or Faulkner's *Absalom, Absalom!*), but from a desire to *play* with history, and with ideas about it. There is a symptomatic passage in the book in which Eben speaks of

> sundry theories of history—the retrogressive, held by Dante and Hesiod; the dramatic, held by the Hebrews and the Christian fathers; the progressive, held by Virgil; the cyclical, held by Plato and Ecclesiasticus; the undulatory, and even the vortical hypothesis entertained, according to Henry Burlingame, by a gloomy neo-Platonist of Christ's College, who believed that the cyclic periods of history were growing ever shorter and thus that at some not-unpredictable moment in the future the universe would go rigid and explode, just as the legendary bird called *Ouida* . . . was reputed to fly in ever-diminishing circles until at the end he disappeared into his own fundament (p. 728).

The comparison of the historical cycle to the path of the Ouida bird is in keeping with what has already been referred to as the fecal humor of the book. But the display of learning ending in a gag points up Barth's intellectual frivolity. Ideas in *The Sot-Weed Factor* are generally not serious or passionate attempts to give shape to experience, but things to play with, as Coode and Burlingame play with governments. There are exceptions to this, as when Eben thinks of his being in a particular predicament because of the totality of the world's history, acknowledging that "as an educated gentleman of the western world he had shared in the fruits of his culture's power and must therefore share what guilt that power incurred." At the same time he feels it was as human for the white man to exploit as it was for the red and black "to slaughter on the basis of color alone. . . ." But Barth has Eben arrive at these conclusions, which move him as few things had done, "more by insight than by casuistical speculation . . ." (p. 579). The use of "insight" is a cover-up for the abruptness with which the ideas appear in (and disappear from) the text.[18] They are just more items among many, islets of ideation in the book's narrative stream, though Barth appears to be claiming great importance for them.

The trouble is that the book's ideas, even when offered in seriousness, may be said to be inadequately felt. They are, rather, simply tossed off, giving the effect that they are merely further proof of the mastery the book is so intent on conveying, part of its character as a *tour de force*. For *The Sot-Weed Factor* is a formidable performance, one which exhibits a knowlege of minute historical detail and esoteric lore, which invents whole documents of bawdy humor, which abounds in linguistic energy, and which spins an immensely sinuous plot.[19] Barth said that one of his intentions in writing the novel "was to see if I couldn't make up a plot that was fancier than *Tom Jones*."[20] (He might also have said he wanted to make up a plot more ingenious than any John Coode ever put together in real life.) Of a story within the story, a character asks: " 'Is't more knotful or bewildered than the skein o' life itself, that a good tale tangles the better to unsnarl?' " (p. 625). The book reads too much as though it were indeed a carrying out of such complex plotting, an abstract exercise in form. Unlike somebody like Faulkner, for whom the past is a burden, and who strains to cope with it in *Absalom, Absalom!* or *The Bear*, Barth appears to stand outside history the way Burlingame, as orphan, stands outside Nature's order. Like Burlingame, Barth would be history's "Lord and Spouse," mastering its facts, trying them on, rejecting them and making up alternatives, as in his invention of Smith's *A Secret Historie*. Barth might offer, in defense of this, his narrator's observation that "we all invent our pasts, more or less, as we go along, at the dictates of Whim and Interest; the happenings of former times are a clay in the present moment that will-we, nill-we, the lot of us must sculpt" (p. 793). But one wishes *The Sot-Weed Factor* conveyed more of a sense that Barth *had* to sculpt the past in the first place—that he did not stand outside it, but felt it impinge strongly on him. Without the sense of such a pressure, one tends to assume a stance towards *The Sot-Weed Factor* similar to that ascribed by Barth to commentators on Ebenezer's poem of the same name: "Critics spoke of it as a fine example of the satiric extravaganza currently in vogue; they praised its rhymes and wit; they applauded the characterizations and the farcical action—and not one of them took the poem seriously!" (p. 803).[21]

There *are* things in the story that do appear to nag at Barth's imagination—the aging of the characters, violence (particularly in the form of rape), his protagonist's betraying his beloved—but these do not become part of any deeply-felt, comprehensive conception of, or response to, the past. Perhaps Barth is attempting to create such a conception in his focus on Eben's innocence (is this supposed to represent a foolish national dream?), its capacity for adding, albeit unknowingly, to the sum of human confusion and misery. Near the end of the book, Eben says: " 'That is the crime I stand indicted for' . . . 'the crime of innocence, whereof the Knowledged must bear the burthen. There's the true Original Sin our souls are born in: not that Adam *learned*, but that he *had* to learn—in short, that he was innocent' " (p. 788). But the solemnity of this statement is not in keeping with the dominant tone of the novel or with its self-delighting narrative ingenuities. In its mockery of Eben's innocence, *The Sot-Weed Factor* offers us history as pure selfishness, or history as bawdy. But ultimately, history exists in the book as a repository of details and plots that Barth wants to master and outdo, ending up as a literary John Coode or Henry Burlingame.

Notes

1. See "John Barth: An Interview," *Wisconsin Studies in Contemporary Literature*, VI (Winter-Spring, 1965), 7.

2. Leslie Fiedler, "John Barth: An Eccentric Genius," *New Leader*, XLIV (Feb. 13, 1961), 22.

3. *The Sot-Weed Factor* (New York, 1964), p. 74. This is the edition of the book I have

used in writing this chapter (the novel was first published in 1960). Subsequent quotations from the book will be followed in the text of the chapter by the relevant page numbers. Italics in the quotations appear in the original. Barth has brought out a revised version of *The Sot-Weed Factor* which differs only slightly from the original version.

4. Here Barth may have been deliberately debunking an image of Maryland justice put forth in George Alsop's *A Character of the Province of Maryland* (1666). Alsop claimed that lawyers had little to do in Maryland, and that "the turbulent Spirit of continued and vexatious Law, with all its quirks and evasions, is openly and most eagerly opposed. . . ." See *Narratives of Early Maryland 1633–1684*, ed. Clayton Colman Hall (New York 1910), p. 351. This is volume ten of the *Original Narratives of Early American History*.

5. Of that poem, Lawrence C. Wroth has written that among the types it depicts "one looks in vain for an upright or a literate judge, an honest merchant, a decent woman or a sober planter." This remark is found in Worth's introduction to a facsimile reproduction of *The Maryland Muse* in *Proceedings of the American Antiquarian Society*, XLIV, New Series (April–October, 1934), 281.

6. Moreover, late in the book, when Eben is trying to avert a massacre of the whites, he puts forth the following argument to an Indian, who apparently accepts it: " ' 'tis not the English case I plead: 'tis the cause of humankind, of Civilization *versus* the Abyss of salvagery . . . I grant the English have used you ill, but to drive them out is to drive yourself back into darkness . . .' " (pp. 707–708).

7. See Herbert L. Osgood, *The American Colonies in the 17th Century*, III (New York, 1926), 493–494.

8. See *Archives of Maryland*, III, 166–170.

9. Howard Mumford Jones, *O Strange New World* (New York, 1964), p. 127.

10. *Archives of Maryland*, V, 134–149.

11. *Ibid.*, vii.

12. E.g., *ibid.*, 220ff.

13. E.g., XIX, 476.

14. John Barth, *End of the Road* (New York, 1964), p. 67. The book was originally published in 1958.

15. *Archives*, XX, 491.

16. Cf. Frances Nicholson, Governor of Maryland, as Eben describes him: " 'He is neither this nor that . . . he is no Papist, yet he fought for James at Hounslow Heath; he was Edmund Andros's lieutenant, and so differed with him that the two despise each other yet; Lord Baltimore chose him to be commissioned Royal Governor, thinking Nicholson shared his sympathies, but albeit Nicholson seems concerned with prosecuting Coode, he governs as if Lord Baltimore did not exist . . .' " (p. 701). Burlingame and Nicholson appear to get on very well together.

17. "John Barth: An Interview, " *op. cit.*, 8. Italics in original.

18. The notion of a shared guilt does make an earlier appearance in the book, but it is a very brief one, and occurs about eighty pages before the passage in question. Another idea that seems to be important to Eben also makes a brief appearance and is attributed to "insight" (pp. 644–645).

19. The plot is so intricate it may have gotten away from Barth himself at one point, with Burlingame giving what looks like inconsistent accounts of how he came upon *The Privie Journall of Sir Henry Burlingame*.

20. "John Barth: An Interview," 7.

21. In talking of not, ultimately, taking the book seriously, I speak only for myself. Some critics have taken *The Sot-Weed Factor* quite seriously. See, e.g., Leslie Fiedler's piece cited in footnote 2.

John Barth's *The Sot-Weed Factor*: The Pitfalls of Mythopoesis

Manfred Puetz*

> Or is't that what the cosmos lacks
> we must ourselves supply?
> John Barth
>
> I must Create a System, or be
> enslav'd by another Man's
> William Blake

John Barth's writings are epitomes of contemporary American fiction; they expose some of its key problems and they test representative strategies for solving them. Barth belongs to a new school of fabulators[1] whose inventiveness, whose unexpected fantasies and whose renewed love for old tales have dominated the fictional landscape of the past decade in America. But beyond mere inventiveness and wit, ostentatious glibness and stylistic idiosyncrasies, Barth has a keen awareness of topicality—not in the derogatory sense—and offers in his novels of ideas (a sub-genre long despised) prototypical formulations of present day pathology. Thus Barth's early fiction takes off on a statement of contemporary nihilism and absurdity. It puts variations of existentialist thought concerning the possibility or impossibility of stringent self-definition to a test. His later works increasingly concentrate on the function of the imagination in the self-defining process. It is in these works that Barth explores the dangers inherent in a reapplication of mythical schemes to history and everyday life and in the practice of storifying human experience.

In 1964 Barth announced that *The Sot-Weed Factor*, a seventeenth-century mock epic, was planned as one of three amusing novels sounding the depth of nihilism in our time. He added: "I had thought I was writing about values and it turned out I was writing about innocence."[2] The heroes of Barth's earlier novels *The Floating Opera* and *The End of the Road* were forever seen coping with questions of "ultimate" sense and "absolute" value. Their answer to such questions consisted, simultane-

---

*Reprinted by permission of *Twentieth Century Literature*.

134

ously, in a gesture of futility and a relative affirmation. Ebenezer Cooke, central character of *The Sot-Weed Factor*, is preoccupied with the same set of questions, but tends to try out more radical responses to the problem. In the absence of all clear-cut answers, Cooke chooses to create the absolutes he will henceforth build and rely upon: a decision which puts him into the favorable position of someone who is no longer forced to cope with "fundamental" and "ultimate" values, but rather with the technicalities of what follows from his first, arbitrary choice.

The opening gambit of Barth's novel is a familiar one. It is almost identical to that in *The End of the Road*; it has outlines similar to the opening of *The Floating Opera*; and it is reminiscent of the situation so many fictional characters in the American novel of the sixties find themselves in. In a letter to his sister Anna, Ebenezer writes: "All Roads are fine Roads, beloved Sister, none more than another . . . to choose one, impossible! . . . I cannot choose, sweet Anna: twixt Stools my Breech falleth to the Ground."[3] To which the narrator adds: "The man (in short), thanks both to Burlingame and to his natural proclivities, was dizzy with the beauty of the possible; dazzled, he threw up his hands at choice, and like ungainly flotsam rode half-content the tide of chance" (p. 21). In other words, Eben's situation indicates that he suffers from the very "cosmopsis" Jacob Horner in *The End of the Road* had discovered, named, and learned to hate. The consequences for the lives of these two characters are similar. Like Horner, Eben is subject to fits of total immobility. He is characterized as "consistently no special sort of person" (p. 21), and (somewhat unlike Horner's case) immobility and lack of decision determine even the most intimate specifics of his love-life. What Ebenezer has detected in his comic explorations of life is the curious reversal of a state the nineteenth century had seriously fretted over. In *The Sickness Unto Death* Søren Kierkegaard stated that human beings inevitably fall into despair when they lack possibility. Ebenezer Cooke has found out—representative for many characters of contemporary fiction—that the reverse is valid too: human beings invariably fall into despair when confronted with too many possibilities.

In this quandary Cooke unwittingly takes to a solution which seems to resolve his problems with a stroke of genius. True to a maxim which he only later is able to state explicitly, namely "that what the cosmos lacks we must ourselves supply" (p. 660)—a maxim which seems to have sprung straight out of Shelley's *Defence of Poetry*—he creates his own essence and decides to hold on to it no matter how adverse conditions might become. Creating his essence means in practice little else but creating a role; and the ensuing complications of the novel, from Eben's first collisions with experience to the disappointment of the end, are all planted together with the initial choice. This choice, in turn, seems to precede the chooser. Born out of the innocence of new beginnings, this is Eben's decision and argument:

> Faith, 'tis a rare wise man knows who he is: had I not stood firm with Joan
> Toast, I might well ne'er have discovered that knowledge! Did I, then, make a
> choice? Nay, for there was no *I* to make it! 'Twas the choice made *me:* a noble
> choice, to prize my love o'er my lust, and a noble choice bespeaks a noble
> chooser. What am I? What am I? *Virgin*, sir! *Poet*, sir! I am a virgin and a
> poet . . . (p. 70/71)

In the course of the ensuing events, Eben's original fantasy generates other fantasies. These he easily incorporates into the grandiose dream he pits against the bleak world of the given. Since he is the poet per se, later specified as the celebrated Poet and Laureate of Maryland, there must be a land worthy of his labor and praise. Since his love is pure and untainted by what he considers base motives, there must be a woman worthy of it. Thus the myth of Maryland, the perfect, and the fantasy of Joan Toast, his eternal love, are born. In sum, the hero turns to the panacea of mythopoesis and creates fictional schemes and mythical worlds around himself which in turn support the very self-concepts from which all interpretations of self and world have sprung. In *The Sot-Weed Factor* not even the hen knows which came first, she or the egg.

What is spontaneous, almost instinctive, reaction in Ebenezer gains the status of a philosophical program in Burlingame, legendary tutor and counterpart to the title figure of the novel. Where Cooke blindly gropes for solutions, Burlingame has reasoned out in advance what might be attempted, what should be done, and what can be justified. As the teacher of Ebenezer and his twin sister Anna he enthusiastically seizes on the children's natural talent for playacting. He encourages them to assume various identities, to try on different roles for size, and to approach an understanding of history and historical personalities through a reenacting of the past. His is an attitude toward history and tradition that partly imitates attitudes of the Romantics: if you want to know who you are, search for the historical models from which you have been cast. Moreover, if you cannot find any suitable models which will facilitate an understanding of yourself, then invent them, create them, and impose them on an existence whose chief characteristic has always been lack of essence. "One must needs make and seize his soul," Burlingame instructs Ebenezer,

> and then cleave fast to't, or go babbling in the corner; one must choose his gods
> and devils on the run, quill his own name upon the universe, and declare, " 'Tis
> *I*, and the world stands such-a-way!" One must *assert, assert, assert,* or go
> screaming mad. What other course remains? (p. 360)

About the necessity and justification of such an act of self-creation there can be no doubt. In an earlier discussion between Eben and Burlingame, which took the shape of an extended treatise on the question of identity, the latter has laid the philosophical foundations for his beliefs. The knotty problem of identity, Burlingame held, arises because "The world's indeed a flux, as Heraclitus declared: the very universe is naught but change and motion" (p. 137). In this sea of change there seems to be only one guarantee for a continuous sense of sameness in the life of the individual:

> 'Tis the house of Identity, the Soul's dwelling place! Thy memory, my memory, the memory of the race: 'tis the constant from which we measure change; the sun. Without it, all were Chaos right enough. (p. 137)

But the individual's memory, as Burlingame quickly points out, is not truly a reliable foundation. Is it sometimes faulty? Does it not tend to color everything it holds? Hence Burlingame—who in this passage alternately sounds like Heraclitus, a phenomenologist, and an existentialist philosopher—warns that nothing is truly reliable except a man's ability to alter himself and to hang on for a while to the self-concepts he has defiantly created. Only the double acts of creation and faith, to both of which Eben will later cling as artist and quester, are worthy of our pursuit. Yet, for the moment our hero is more confused than reassured. "Marry," he exclaims, "your discourse hath robbed me of smiles: I know of naught immutable and sure! (p. 140).To which Burlingame, the archetypal "Suitor of Totality, Embracer of Contradictories, Husband to all Creation" (p. 516), prophetically answers: " 'Tis the first step on the road to Heaven" (p. 140).

In yet another way the figure of Burlingame dominates the intellectual landscape of the novel. Barth uses him in order to demonstrate the dangers inherent in a strategy devised by many contemporary novelists for the benefit of their fictional characters. The novel of the sixties has celebrated with unsubdued enthusiasm the second coming of Proteus, the archetypal shape-shifter, and the maxims of Protean existence have been elevated to the status of a new philosophical program in our time. If change itself is the defining feature of human existence, the argument goes, then why not seize the opportunity to transcend the concept of the unitary self and become a whole spectrum of varying selves?

Barth, who has a knack for conceiving characters whose material situations become metaphorical equivalents for their spirited plights, has put Burlingame in the perfect position to explore the overwhelming potentials of Protean existence. (Another of these allegorical homunculi familiar from Barth's fiction is the child-hero Ambrose, who appears in three sections of *Lost in the Funhouse* and whose queer personal fate of receiving no name at birth epitomizes, maybe too demonstratively, the American hero's plight of being born without a clear identity.)[4] Burlingame is a foundling, fished, like Moses, out of the water, or as he puts it himself, "sprung *de novo* like a maggot out of meat, or dropped from the sky" (p. 142). Since he has thus no demonstrable link with history, no fixed position in the world, he can feel free to create his own identity from whatever materials he appreciates, *"ex nihilo* and without travail" (p. 503). As it happens, he is also convinced that all existence is "a

Heraclitean flux" (p. 345) of which he wants to partake in its totality. Of his own ambitions he says: ". . . I love no part of the world, as you might have guessed, but the entire parti-colored whole, with all her poles and contradictories" (p. 508). From both premises together he draws conclusions which instantly make him the paradigm for a modern existence of self-regulated change. First, "When I reflect on the weight and power of such fictions beside my own poor shade of a self, that hath been so much disguised and counterfeited, methinks they have tenfold my substance!" (p. 744). Second, "I have no parentage to give me place and aim in Nature's order: very well—I am outside Her, and shall be Her lord and spouse!" (p. 516). It is this intention to test the limits of a radical program in new forms of self-discovery and not the simple thrills of endless travesties which Burlingame acts out in the course of the novel. Slipping alternately into the roles of Lord Baltimore, John Coode, Peter Sayer, Timothy Mitchell, Nicholas Lowe, and even Ebenezer Cooke himself, Burlingame makes travesty the backbone of a new philosophy. There is a suggestive little episode in Barth's latest book, *Chimera*, where somebody tells the story of a species of snails common in the Maryland marshes:

> There's a special kind of snail in the Maryland marshes—perhaps I invented him—that makes his shell as he goes along out of whatever he comes across, cementing it with his own juices, and at the same time makes his path instinctively toward the best available material for his shell; he carries his history on his back, living in it, adding new and larger spirals to it from the present as he grows.[5]

Apparently Burlingame, too, is such a snail except that his efforts at self-creation go even further: for Burlingame does not hesitate to shed, once in a while, his self-assembled house and exchange it for a brand-new one.

As Burlingame is quick to notice and Barth is eager to emphasize, Burlingame's philosophy compels him in practice to walk a tightrope without a net. As long as he has no link with the past and the world, he is free to embrace experience in its totality and to choose or even to create any number of roles. But at the same time this freedom makes him utterly diffuse and somehow nullifies him as an individual. Embracing everything, he eventually embraces (like Thomas Pynchon's heroine V.) nothing. Alternatively, if he establishes a clear link with the world (as he finally does when he finds out and accepts that he is the son of the Tayac Chicamec of the Ahatchwhoops Indians and the brother of Charley Mattassin and Cohunkowprets), he finds the one identity that substantiates him as a person, but he loses touch with the all-inclusive possibilities which constituted his freedom. There can be no satisfying solution to such a quandary, a fact of which Burlingame himself is aware.

> There is a freedom there that's both a blessing and a curse, for't means both liberty and lawlessness. 'Tis more than just political and religious liberty—they come and go from one year to the next. 'Tis philosophic liberty I speak of, that

comes from want of history. It throws one on his own resources, that freedom—makes every man an orphan like myself and can as well demoralize as elevate. (p. 178)

Barth attempts to offer a solution, though. But he can only do so at the price of sacrificing philosophical stringency to superficial speculation. In the end, we witness Eben and his sister fleetingly speculate that Burlingame probably did not accept the verdict of his true identity and again slipped into one of his disguises, namely that of Nicholas Lowe.

Ebenezer Cooke's complementary quest for self-definition illustrates yet another problem that arises when the imagination gains undisputed dominance in life. As he loses touch with the realities in and around him, and as he methodically transcends the boundaries of actual experience, both reality and experience are converted to mere substrata of art. Ebenezer's mythopoeic view becomes a lens that distorts reality by refracting it as a potential or actual work of art. The realm of facts becomes by analogy the realm of aesthetic appearances: what Ebenezer surrenders in actual experience he gains back as the subject of his poetry. The poem he intends to write is only the most obvious token of this transformation. It is more important that in the same process Ebenezer's whole life is slowly converted into a unique work of art. By letting go of the world and the self he gains the momentary freedom to recreate both as autonomous objects. But by the same act he plants the seeds of a potential collision with experience which is likely to refute the very precepts on which his artistic creations were based. Ebenezer seems to be dimly aware of such a danger. Hence he shies away from experience and too great an involvement in life and attempts to preclude a refutation of his fantastically conceived world and his imaginatively born self. Yet, predictably, such refutations occur whenever he mixes with the world around him. Eben's fantasies of himself as the Poet Laureate, of Malden as a worldly paradise, and of Joan Toast as his perfect love turn sour, paradoxically, while they become partly true. In the end, Ebenezer discovers himself precisely because he abandons the false images he had forced upon himself. He comes into his own, because he revokes all mythical preconceptions and deviates from the patterns of autistic creation. Consequently, the process of art feeding on reality is now reversed in the novel. Ebenezer finally achieves fame as a poet and is offered the Laureateship by the young Lord Baltimore (which he declines), but only after he has discarded his fantasies of being the Poet Laureate and after he has displaced a panegyric on Maryland with a nasty work that heaps on Maryland the abuse it deserved all along. He finally becomes the husband of his love Joan Toast, but only after his perfect lady has turned into a dying wreck. To a certain extent, even the justice and order he had dreamed of win the upper hand at Malden, but only in a bizarre process of restoration which is a mockery of justice. And, paradoxically, yet typically for the reversals of *The Sot-*

Weed Factor, the most conspicuous effect of Cooke's tongue-lashing attack on Maryland is that "Maryland, in part because of the well-known poem, acquired in the early eighteenth century a reputation for graciousness and refinement comparable to Virginia's and a number of excellent families were induced to settle there" (p. 794). Such constellations suggest a failure of the imagination and of all mythopoeic ambitions. Yet it is not the author's imagination which is seen to fail, but the limitations are rather shown as inherent in the mythopoeic imagination itself.[6]

History plays an important role in *The Sot-Weed Factor*. Barth's uses of history are manifold and have a clear function in the context of the mythopoeic investigations he pursues. Contrary to what some critics have said, the novel is not merely parody for its own sake or an overgrown historical hoax.[7] Barth rather uses a forbiddingly huge historical apparatus—much of it "grounded on meager fact and solid fancy" (p. 782)—in order to establish a semi-authentic scene as the background of the fictitious quest for the self. Since the distinction between alleged fact and imaginary preconceptions is all-important in the novel, it is worth the trouble of penetrating to the historical core of the story before proceeding to Barth's deviations and to a reflection of the meaning of these deviations. It is a well-known fact of literary history that there actually was a poet named Ebenezer Cooke who wrote a poem entitled "The Sot-Weed Factor."[8] Barth himself never tried to conceal this and he readily admitted that the original poem and the figure behind it supplied one of the starting points for his work.[9] Some of the facts and dates that are known about the original Ebenezer Cooke should be compared with Barth's treatment of this figure.

In 1708 an "Eben Cook, Gent." published a satirical poem called *The Sot-Weed Factor* in London. In 1728 "An Elergy on the Death of the Honourable Nicholas Lowe, Esq." appeared under the name "E. Cooke. Laureat." 1730 saw the publication of *Sotweed Redivivus*, signed "E.C. Gent": in 1731 *The Maryland Muse* (signed "E. Cooke, Gent.") and in 1731 another elegy (signed "Ebenezer Cook, Poet Laureat") followed.[10] The Cook or Cooke of these works may or may not have been identical with an Ebenezer Cooke who in 1694 signed a petition against moving the capital of Maryland: or with yet another gentleman of this name who obtained permission to practice law in 1728. A similar confusion that cannot be settled conclusively arises over Eben's alleged father Andrew Cooke. Subsequent speculations have dealt with the possibility that neither the two Andrew Cookes on record nor the several Eben Cookes (or Cooks or E.C.s) of the poems were identical, as well as with the possibility that "Eben Cook, Gent." may be a mere nom de plume."[11] Barth seems to be aware of the historical confusion and avoids its intricacies by simplifying the whole situation.

As Philip Diser has pointed out in his essay on the historical background of *The Sot-Weed Factor*,[12] Barth devises his own version of

Ebenezer Cooke's story and carefully eliminates possible discrepancies with the facts on record. The problem of the two Andrew Cookes is solved by Barth's decision that the one who supposedly owned "Malden" was a suitable father for Ebenezer. The potentially different Ebenezer Cookes merge into one to whom Barth attributes several documented acts and most of the poems which had been linked with the name of the historical Cooke. In the process of compressing such scattered and disjointed facts into the life story of *one* man, Barth goes to the extent of inserting little details into his novel which eliminate possible contradictions to the recorded data of Lawrence Wroth's study of the life of Ebenezer Cooke (so far the only historical study of this figure).[13] Barth tells us that Ebenezer was born in America (eliminating the problem that no English birth records were ever found); he has Ebenezer attend Cambridge for a short period (in line with Wroth's conjectures); he has Burlingame sign with Eben's name the 1694 petition (which Wroth attributes to Cooke); and he has Anne Cooke, Ebenezer's mother, die after giving birth to Eben and his sister (thus eliminating the problem that nothing could be found out about Anne Cooke).

Barth then takes Ebenezer Cooke's best-known poem, "The Sot-Weed Factor," and proceeds to write an 806-page novel around the hard core of this work. Many passages in the novel are either repetitions of, or more frequently, elaborations on the material presented in the original poem. Moreover, the satirical poem which Barth eventually has Ebenezer Cooke write in sharp contrast to his originally planned panegyric *Marylandiad*, is the authentic "Sot-Weed Factor" itself. Barth consistently takes the same liberties, which are characteristic of the treatment of his source, with the historical situation on the grand scale. Apparently familiar with the *Archives of Maryland*,[14] he develops a detailed panorama of historical personalities and events in seventeenth-century Maryland and England, a panorama which embraces at once fact and fiction, historical accuracy and parodistic invention.[15] Historical personalities such as Lord Baltimore, Governor Nicholson, William Claiborne, John Coode, Captain Smith, Pocahontas, Edmund Andros, Nicholas Lowe, or Eben Cooke himself are joined in a mad jig of events with imposters, impersonators, and a whole gallery of fictitious characters such as Burlingame, Joan Toast, Bertrand Burton, John McEvoy, Billy Rumbly, or Mary Mungummory. In fact, had Maryland ever passed the law against the spreading of "false news" which Lord Baltimore proposed in 1651,[16] the author of *The Sot-Weed Factor* would be in dire trouble. What finally emerges from Barth's imaginative manipulation of history is that public myth is pitted against private myth in burlesque juxtaposition. In the process, Barth not only ridicules and effectively destroys the received myth of the heroic American past; he also analyzes the function of naive private myths in the life-defining struggles of his characters.

Symptomatic for Barth's juxtaposition of the two concurring visions is, among others, his reconstructed version of one of the best-known episodes of early American history, the story of Captain John Smith and Pocahontas. Contrary to the schoolbook version, Barth offers his own bawdy reading of the events. As so often in *The Sot-Weed Factor*, he seems to be walking the narrow line between parody and overindulgent trifling with history. Yet his parodistic distortions have an important function. Barth's treatment of the episode draws attention to the fact that alleged historical truth is not as unambiguous as we tend to think. In 1608 a Th. Watson published a book with the title *A True Relation*.[17] The book was actually written by John Smith himself and though it related details about Powhatan and the capture of Smith there is no mention of the Pocahontas incident. Only years later in his famous *General History of Virginia*[18] did Smith relate the Pocahontas episode as we know it today. Ever since, there has been a controversy among historians over the reasons for Smith's curious omission of the episode from the earlier book.[19] More than once the suspicion has been voiced that Smith for some reason might have invented part of the episode or at least might have rendered it from a highly subjective point of view. Barth knows about this confusion of historical evidence and consequently plays upon the possibility of further conflicting versions.

The point of such parodistic games with historical materials is a simple one. Since some versions we assume to be historical truth are themselves dubious and colored by imaginative concepts, the novelist has every right to add his own speculations to the interpretation of events. After all, who is to say which version is ultimately true or which one is more useful to help us come to terms with the past? As Burlingame maintains throughout the book and as the author in his final chapter rubs in: ". . . we all invent our pasts, more or less, as we go along, at the dictates of Whim and Interest; the happenings of former times are a clay in the present moment that will-we, nill-we, the lot of us must sculpt" (p. 782). What is more, in the process of inventing his past, man forgets to keep track of the general structure of his inventions. Hence his concepts of history on the grand scale emulate his concepts of historical fact in detail, that is, everything becomes relative, contradictory, lacking the recognizable, clear-cut outlines he had originally set out to find.

Barth has admitted on various occasions that the arbitrariness of fact has always made him uncomfortable and has stimulated his attempts to pit his own creative energies against it. In an interview he said: " . . . this impulse to imagine alternatives to the world can become a driving impulse for writers. I confess that it is for me. So that really what you want to do is re-invent philosophy and the rest—make up your own whole history of the world."[20] It is from the perspective of this aggressively counter-realistic attitude—amplified in Barth's case to the status of an aesthetic program—that we see the function of fake history and fake documents such as the *Privie Journall* or John Smith's *A Secret Historie of the Voiage Up the Bay of Chesapeake From Jamestowne in Virginia*. Both are to refute an easy differentiation between fact and fancy, both are to plant the suspicion that historical truth may be nothing but imaginary versions in disguise. Barth's toying with history aims at our vital assumption that there are facts which can be indisputably established. He constantly undermines such assumptions, insinuating that all readings of the past may be relative to specific modes of self-interpretation and to specific needs and purposes at a given time.

Fittingly, Barth uses for a contrast to his protagonists' fictionalizations a wealth of pseudo-objective historical data and interpretations which themselves turn out to be counterfeits or highly biased accounts. Had he opposed some kind of authenticated historical truth (on which historians and readers could easily agree) to the world of Ebenezer Cooke, it would have been all too easy to dismiss Eben's imaginative versions altogether and treat him as a mere lunatic lacking powers of discrimination. The reader's unchecked assumptions about the existence of objective truth in history would have been strengthened rather than weakened. But Barth juxtaposes what he presents as fact (and at the same time unveils as fantasy) to other imaginative versions. By implying that there are no other versions but these, he makes us aware that Ebenezer—in spite of his apparent naiveté and ridiculousness—is doing nothing extraordinary. If all ways of coping with history are equal in that they rely on the use of the imagination as a means of imposing order on chaos, then, it seems, one simply has to do what Ebenezer and others have done. Life and history, Barth's novel seems to argue, are not fields of detached theoretical insights, but grounds on which we must test the concepts and the vitality of our own selves, pitting them against the vitality and the concepts of others.

However, at the same time the fate of Ebenezer Cooke posits the warning that in this situation an unreflected turn to the magic of mythopoesis is too easy and too dangerous a way out. If there are ultimately no givens, no objective readings of past or present, if everything can be altered and transformed in an act of imaginative creation, then it is tempting henceforth to treat the entire universe as the biggest playground the human imagination ever had. But converting the specifics of world, history, and self into freely permutable elements of imaginative creation implies the danger that the imagination may get lost in a maze of fictions within fictions without exit. Beyond a mere parody on early American history and a re-creation of conventional themes of the eighteenth-century novel (such as the hero's quest for identity, his picaresque meanderings, the constant interaction of assumed roles, the theme of uncertain parentage, etc.[21]), Barth uses the seventeenth-century framework of *The Sot-Weed Factor* to put certain recent ideas to a test. In the spirit and in the fashion of many novelists of the sixties, Barth's philosophical comedy explores the creative possibilities, the frustrations, and the dangers inherent in the contemporary assumption that it might be better to lose an established truth or a stable identity than to find one, because the latter precludes further possibilities whereas the former reveals itself as a precondition for gaining the freedom of imaginative creativity and the right to embrace existence in its totality.

However, what the case of Ebenezer Cooke lets the observer realize is an impending danger rather than a benefit of this new stance of self-creation. True, everything may be forced under the legislature of the human imagination by converting everything into an independent object of non-mimetic art. As such it will then become totally dependent on its creator, but only at the price that the creator, inversely, becomes dependent on his own creations—a condition which Ebenezer Cooke barely escapes. Thus he learns what Borges' Encyclopaedists of "Tlön, Uqbar, Orbis Tertius" had to learn after they had invented an entirely imaginary, alternative world to live in: namely that many an alternative creation possesses "such imaginative power that, once conceived, it begins to obtrude itself into and eventually to supplant our prior reality."[22] The problem of fictionalizing life turns into the problem of living fictionalizations. To disentangle again, to find an exit from a world of self-generated fictions, to engineer an escape from the pitfalls of mythopoesis, demands an intense effort by the former mythopoeic self. The feasibility and the formal implications of such an effort as much as the increasing worries about the exit from the maze of fiction prove to be the opening themes of Barth's further experiments in *Lost in the Funhouse* and *Chimera*.

Notes

1. Compare Robert Schole's study *The Fabulators* (New York: Oxford Univ. Press, 1967).

2. "John Barth: An Interview," *Wisconsin Studies in Contemporary Literature*, 6, 1 (Winter/Spring 1965), p. 11.

3. John Barth, *The Sot-Weed Factor* (1960; rpt. London: Panther, 1965), p. 20. All further parenthetical page references will be to this edition.

4. John Barth, *Lost in the Funhouse* (1968; rpt. New York: Grosset & Dunlap, 1969).

5. John Barth, *Chimera* (New York: Random House, 1972), p. 10.

6. Among others, John C. Bean has put forward, not very convincingly, the thesis that the failure of the imagination in *The Sot-Weed Factor* is primarily Barth's own failure as a novelist. Compare his article "John Barth and Festive Comedy: A Failure of Imagination in *The Sot-Weed Factor*," *Xavier University Studies*, 10, 1 (1971).

7. Earl Rovit, himself a novelist of some achievements, was one of the first to accuse Barth of the failure of his parody, though stylistically brilliant, to go beyond the mere razzle-dazzle of technical fireworks and "intellectual gymnastics." This argument has been repeated regularly ever since. See Rovit's essay "The Novel as Parody: John Barth," *Critique*, 6, 2 (Fall 1962), 77–85.

8. Available clues concerning the historical Cooke have been collected and discussed by Lawrence C. Wroth in "The Maryland Muse by Ebenezer Cooke," *Proceedings of the*

American Antiquarian Society, N.S. XLIV (October 1934). The discussion was later taken up by Philip E. Diser in "The Historical Ebenezer Cooke," *Critique*, 10, 3 (1968), 48–59, who elaborated on several points Wroth had made. Compare also the historical analyses and cross-references in Alan Holder, " 'What Marvelous Plot . . . Was Afoot?' History in Barth's *The Sot-Weed Factor*," *American Quarterly*, 20, 3 (Fall 1968), 596–604.

9. Barth noted in an interview in the *Wisconsin Studies in Contemporary Literature*, 6, 1 (Winter/Spring 1965): "*The Sot-Weed Factor* began with the title and, of course, Ebenezer Cooke's original poem. Those of you who haven't read the novel should be told that there is such a poem and there is such a man, although nobody knows much about him" (p. 7).

10. Three of these works can be found in Bernard C. Steiner's edition of *Early Maryland Poetry* (Baltimore: printed by J. Murphy, 1900).

11. See Brantz Mayer's introduction to an edition of *The Sot-Weed Factor* which came out in Baltimore in 1865 and was partly reprinted in Loker Raley's *300 Years: The Poets and Poetry of Maryland* (New York: H. Harrison, 1937).

12. See footnote 8 for Diser's essay.

13. Compare note 8 for Wroth's study.

14. *The Archives of Maryland* are a gigantic compilation of documents pertaining to the history of Maryland beginning about 1637. Mainly consisting of documents on the proceedings and acts of the General Assembly, the Council, and the Provincial Court, intermixed with journals of conventions and the correspondence of various Governors and the State Council, the *Archives* have so far run to seventy-two volumes. They have been edited by eight different editors under the direction of the Maryland Historical Society.

15. For a detailed discussion of Barth's deviation from the *Archives* and other sources see Alan Holder's essay " 'What Marvelous Plot . . . Was Afoot?' History in Barth's *The Sot-Weed Factor*," *American Quarterly*, 20, 3 (Fall 1968), p. 599 ff.

16. See John Leeds Bozman, *The History of Maryland From Its First Settlement, in 1633, To the Restoration, in 1660* (Baltimore: James Lucas & E. D. Deaver, 1837), Vol. II, p. 428.

17. The full title of the book was *A true relation of such occurences and accidents of noate as hath happened in Virginia since the first planting of that collony* (London: printed for I. Tappe, 1608).

18. *The Generall Historie of Virginia, New-England, and the Summer isles* (London: M. Sparkes, 1624).

19. Compare, for instance, W. Gilmore Simms: *The Life of Captain John Smith* (Philadelphia, 1867); Katherine P. Woods, *The True Story of Captain John Smith* (New York: Doubleday, Page, 1901); E.B. Smith, *Pocahontas and Captain John Smith* (New York: Houghton, 1914); John Gould Fletcher, *John Smith—Also Pocahontas* (New York: Brentano, 1928).

20. John Barth: An Interview," *Wisconsin Studies in Contemporary Literature*, 6, 1 (Winter/Spring 1965), p. 8.

21. Compare Barth's much quoted formula that *The Sot-Weed Factor* and *Giles Goat-Boy* are "novels which imitate the form of the Novel, by an author who imitates the role of Author." "The Literature of Exhaustion," *The American Novel Since World War II*, ed. Marcus Klein (Greenwich, Conn.: Fawcett, 1969), p. 275.

22. *Ibid.*, p. 273.

Giles Goat-Boy

The Comic Christ and the
Modern Reader

Richard B. Hauck*

A classic and useful game played by teachers, students, and critics of modern literature is The Christ Figure Metaphor Hunt. The game requires the players to demonstrate, by finding all the hidden clues, that a central character in a novel is one of a set of literary figures who are drawn as imitations of Christ. (An excellent discussion of how characters are thought of in the Judeo-Christian tradition as "types" or "figures" is Robert E. Reiter's "On Biblical Typology and the Interpretation of Literature," *College English*, April 1969.) The game is most successful—and is easier and more fun—with figures in twentieth-century American novels, although intricate variations can be played with Camus's Meursault, Dostoevsky's Raskolnikov or Myshkin, or Conrad's Jim. In American novels, however, the game often seems to be initiated consciously as game by an author well aware that his readers are eager to play. Thus Faulkner did not hesitate to tell interviewers and students that he had rigged the symbolism of *A Fable*, and Hemingway, always a sportsman, could write that Santiago, upon seeing the sharks, said, "Ay," a word or noise a man might make "feeling the nail go through his hands and into the wood." The Christ figure drawn by an author conscious of the game as game is generally immediately visible as Christ figure, although the modern American novelist, in his deliberate attempt to make the game interesting, likes to surround his figure with metaphors that are tantalizingly contradictory. All the reader need do to begin to play is select the character whose initials are J. C. (Jim Conklin, Joe Christmas, Jim Casy). The character will be symbolically crucified at the age of thirty-three by a group of antagonists. His crucifixion will have a conversion effect on at least one of the twelve oppressed common men who have been his followers. This pattern may be ironically inverted in a number of ways and will certainly be complicated by the modern Christ figure's moral ambiguity. It may prove difficult for the reader to decide whether or not the figure is intended as an imitation of Christ or a parody of Christ figures.

John Barth's monumental *Giles Goat-Boy* (subtitled *The Revised New Syllabus*) is a book written by a man who is obviously a scholar and teacher reacting to all the other books which contain Christ figures. The book is a literature course in itself. Encompassed within all its bulk is a serio-comic study of the reoccurrence of the Christ figure in a world whose history is forever doomed to be cyclical and in the cyclical literature of that world. Endless references to traditional savior stories are built into the narrative. It is admittedly a huge book not nicely tailored to classroom use, but undergraduates and graduates alike are consistently patient with it. (One could schedule *Giles Goat-Boy* as one of my highly capable colleagues schedules *War and Peace*: teach a piece of it every Monday). *Giles Goat-Boy*'s extensive allegory, so exhaustive that its characters and events are allegories of allegories, is clearly intended for the sophisticated reader who is attuned to allusions and literary jokes. Goat-Boy is a Christ figure in the tradition, one of the figural set, and at the same time is an allegorical parody of literary Christ figures. Barth's consciousness of the multiplicity and reversibility of the pattern is revealed in long monologues by Goat-Boy on the problems involved in becoming the "Grand Tutor." To become Grand Tutor is to become both the true Christ at the second coming and a figure of Christ, one of a long line of saviors (Christ in His first appearance is allegorized as Enos Enoch; Christians as Enochists). Goat-Boy is an outsider, not a product of the world we all know, which is allegorized as a world divided into East and West Campuses, each Campus being ruled by a computer complex symbolizing the twentieth-century military-industrial-political-educational-social monolith. He is, furthermore, brought up in a morally neutral environment which allows him to see the falsity of the world's morality: he is raised as a goat. His parentage is in doubt; he believes that his true father is WESCAC, the West's computer complex. This is appropriate because WESCAC is the main determining force in the western world: it has assumed God's place. After Goat-Boy enters the outside world on his mission to become the Grand Tutor, he goes through processes of baptism and testing, a rebirth out of the computer, and all-important confrontations with a devil figure (Maurice Stoker) and an enigmatic character who is probably the Antichrist (Harold Bray). The latter is, as in tradition, really God's (WESCAC's) instrument for assuring through opposition that the Christ does function as resistance to evil.

The language, the metaphors, and the sheer bulk of this allegorical pattern are comic in themselves. Within its frame, Goat-Boy's inherently hilarious story moves inexorably towards tragedy as he tries and fails to become the savior of the world. His divine mission, as delivered to him on a card by WESCAC, is to PASS ALL FAIL ALL. The four words appear each in a segment of a circle divided in quarters. Figuring out the mission is impossible; Barth is implying that the question of how salvation is granted has always been a mystery to Christendom. Goat-Boy makes two heroic attempts to solve the enigma and thus prove that he is the real Grand Tutor. The first of these is an effort to be completely logical and categorical about who shall fail (go to hell) and who shall pass (be saved). With this attempt, Goat-Boy tries, in the Puritan manner, to divide humanity into elect and damned, to determine that Passed is a state demonstrably different from Flunked. He quickly learns that men and events are so complicated that he will never be able to make determinations not based on appearances, and that appearances themselves always hide further, contradictory appearances. Having discovered that morality is relative, he turns next to a modern variety of benevolent and all-forgiving Christianity and tries to Pass All and Fail None. The result of this is social chaos; the Chancellor (president) of West Campus, following this new philosophy, grants an amnesty that sets loose criminals and psychopaths. The humor, as well as the tragedy, rises from Goat-Boy's failure to discover in all of mankind's knowledge any method for knowing the absolute moral truth which would yield salvation. He is the absurd man as well as the tragic and comic Christ.

For Goat-Boy there can be no middle way. Like Darl, he has seen the cosmic joke. Of his enigmatic mission he says:

> That circular device on my Assignment-sheet—beginningless, endless, infinite equivalence—constricted my reason like a torture-tool from the Age of Faith. Passage *was* Failure, and Failure Passage; yet Passage was Passage, Failure, Failure! Equally true, none was the Answer; the two were not different, neither were they the same; and *true* and *false*, and *same* and *different*—Unspeakable! Unnamable! Unimaginable! Surely my mind must crack!

Out of all this not even a stasis through acceptance can come: Goat-Boy records that he learned "There is an entropy to time, a tax on change. . . ." The cosmic joke is on mankind, the crucifixion is slow, painful and repeated for Everyman.

By re-creating the joke of perfect ambivalence and extending its myriad possibilities, the modern novelist creates a saving laughter of his own. The teacher willing to build upon his students' skepticism will discover that they *are* the fit audience (not few, but many) which the contemporary author has in mind. He will find that modern readers come to these books with an already well-developed sense of cosmic humor. They need be taught nothing more than the pervasiveness of the cosmic joke.

A Service to the University

Dabney Stuart*

Bonus dormitat Homerus.

Swift, too. As well as Rabelais, Joyce, Cervantes, Fielding, Bunyan and Al Capp.

But it is John Barth who *lives* here. It is his genius which has made *The Revised New Syllabus*, and his voice (or rather the voice of Billy Bocksfuss, George, the GILES, Grand Tutor and Goat-Boy) which speaks it. And one of Barth's many achievements here is that with all the echoes of previous literature the voice of the speaker, which is to say the book, maintains its own unique identity.

The most delicious question it raises is whether or not it is a novel. One is inclined to say the issue is irrelevant and irresolvable, except as *Giles Goat-Boy* makes one realize again what we all should know by now: that a "novel" is what the author makes it, that it is a fluid form admitting as many definitions as there are works of fiction to define it, and that the term itself is a fortunate pun.

Perhaps it would be more revealing to say that Barth's new book resembles his last one in many respects. As in *The Sot-Weed Factor* he is concerned with illusion, deception, masks. Susan Warren, herself living an alias in the earlier work, tells the Poet and Laureate of Maryland, "Things are not as they seem, Mister Cooke," to which Ebenezer responds, clasping his head, "I' God! The old refrain!" The Proteus of *Giles Goat-Boy*, continuing the old refrain Barth sings through Henry Burlingame III of *The Sot-Weed Factor*, is a figure called Bray, whom the goat-boy wrestles at one point in much the same way Menelaus wrestled with Bray's prototype. Bray and Burlingame share another ancestor, too: Satan, the arch deceiver, the master of lies, and Bray's unequivocally diabolical nature is perhaps more clearly dramatized here than was Burlingame's. But perhaps not, for as the goat-boy's adversary Bray is a major instrument of his growth and education. Burlingame was Ebenezer Cooke's tutor in more ways than one in *The Sot-Weed Factor* and Bray fulfills a similar function in this book. Bray, then, embodies the idea of

*Copyright 1966 by Washington and Lee University; reprinted from *Shenandoah*.

the deceptive nature of appearances not least in the fact that his value to the goat-boy's increasing insight belies one's ability to relegate him to hell as an out and out fiend.

The impossibility of classifying Bray in one of the two traditional categories of supernatural beings figures another central concern of the book, the reality or unreality of distinctions. The goat-boy "experiments" with two "positions": that distinctions such as love and hate, East and West, animal and human being, tick and tock, must be maintained at all costs, and secondly that such distinctions must be synthesized. He himself is both goat and boy, and the problem is compounded by the fact that he was begotten by a computer. One is reminded of Burlingame's *cosmophilism* at the same time that he is led to see that *Giles Goat-Boy* is "about" the nature of language, and human understanding itself. Do the verbal categories we invent and live by have, after all, any correspondence to what is "out there" and "in here," and, further, is *that* distinction real?

Another thematic similarity between *Giles* and *The Sot-Weed Factor* is Barth's continuing concern with twins. Burlingame discoursed at length on the historical, mythological, religious and sexual importance and implications of twinship in the latter novel. In this new one the ideas Burlingame propounded tutorially are dramatized concretely in the chapter dealing with the goat-boy's final descent into the belly of the computer who is his father. The suggestions of the earlier book are fulfilled here, climatically. It is a stunning achievement in itself.

Structurally both novels share elements of the picaresque: the goat-boy is a *naif*, as was Eben Cooke, journeying toward the loss of innocence. In *Giles Goat-Boy*, however, Barth adds motifs of the epic: the goat-boy has his Vergil in Max Spielman, his Styx and his Charon, his descents (plural) into Hades, his sirens and his Circe. But on all these available segments of the epic experience Barth rings delightful changes, never violating the context of his book. This is, of course, parody, and the book is in part a "comic epic in prose" of the 1960's, a sort of Fielding bicentennial.

In fact, *Giles Goat-Boy* parodies everything it takes seriously, including itself, and probably the most astonishing illustration of this is the forty page "modern translation" of *Oedipus Rex*. Here is part of "Taliped Decanus's" vow to rid his kingdom of his father's murderer:

> I hate
>
> him in advance! Even if it should
> turn out to be a relative, I would
> put it to him without mercy. I'm
> as hot and bothered over this old crime
> as if I'd seen it happen. Can you hear
> this vow I'm vowing you folks in the rear?
> I couldn't more despise the killer had he
> killed, not my predecessor, but my daddy!

It is important, however, to note that parody, when it is skillfully handled, is a tool, not an end in itself. In the instance of "Taliped Decanus" the parody is corrosive as it implies an evaluation of idiomatic translation (*a la* Pound, or Lowell), but it is recreative as it reveals in a new context the power of the idea of tragedy that animates Sophocles' play. As the hypersophisticated psychiatrist, Kenneth Scar, begins to suspect, there are values which quietly resist our scoffing, and to which we eventually attend.

Further, Barth employs another structural device that has not appeared in his previous books—allegory. The situation, briefly, is this: within the University, New Tammany and Nickolay Colleges are engaged in a Quiet Riot, which has been the prolonged condition since the end of Campus Riot II. Both colleges possess nearly omnipotent computers (WESCAC and EASCAC, respectively) which, as it were, run things, holding over the heads of all Studentdom the possibility of Electroencephalic Amplification and Transmission, or, acronymically, of being EATen. It is the job (vocation, mission) of George the Goat-Boy, son of (or by) WESCAC itself, to remove the pressure somehow, and the book is the story of his endeavor, his attempt to discover whether he is the GILES (Grand Tutorial Ideal, Laboratory Eugenical Specimen) and his progress to Grand Tutorhood.

The progress itself is circular: "Unwind, rewind, replay." (The MS isn't written, but tape-recorded; it has reels instead of chapters.) That is, it is not progress at all, except as *Oedipus Rex* might be called progressive. By book's end the situation hasn't changed appreciably, but the characters have, as, again, one might say Oedipus does. Which is the hope, such as it is, of the goat-boy's experience

As Max Spielman, developer of WESCAC, sacked faculty member, goatherd and consequently the goat-boy's mentor, puts it in a discourse in which he compares the growth of the University to the growth of a man:

> "By George, I think the odds for survival are pretty good. Some kids don't make it through adolescence, but most do." Similarly, he said, most reached a fair level of grown-upness—although Commencement was of course another matter, if there was such a thing at all. The University was a big place: when lecturers spoke of East and West Campuses, or the "Nature of Studentdom," they tended to forget the curious colleges in remote corners of the University, which were only beginning to be touched by the Informational Revolution and Applied Research. What was more, though the colleges themselves could be said to have a fair degree of identity and self-consciousness, the University as a whole was barely stirring in that direction. This was not to say that its maturation must be as slow and painful as a college's; it would have its own growth-rate, sped by the sophistication of individual quads, especially if the rivalry between East and West Campus could be made less negative. Max guessed that the chances for West Campus's reaching maturity were good: in the past, the behavior of the colleges towards one another, particularly in disputes, had been at the primary-school level, or worse; but there was evidence of real restraint in the matter of EATing-riot and relevant intercollege policy. The prospect was not hopeless.

George's experience both confirms and refutes this analysis. How it does, and the manner in which Mr. Barth creates its doing, is something of a miracle. Like a miracle it defies praise; and superlatives from a reviewer are, and ought to be, suspect anyway. Nevertheless, my considered judgment is that *Giles Goat-Boy* ranks with *Moby Dick* as the best fiction yet written by an American. As with Melville's novel, the charge of tediousness will be (and, indeed, already has been) levelled at Barth's. Alexander Pope wrote the answer to this charge some years ago:

> A prudent chief not always must display
> His pow'rs in equal ranks, and fair array,
> But with th' occasion and the place comply,
> Conceal his force, nay sometimes to fly.
> Those oft are strategems which errors seem,
> Nor is it Homer nods, but we that dream.

Giles Goat-Boy

Joseph J. Waldmeir*

"Giles Goat-Boy" is a hell of a novel, sometimes too long and involved, often uproariously funny, more often bitterly comic. You may be able to let it alone, but if you can't, it certainly won't let you alone. It is a Voltairean, Swiftean, Orwellean, Huxleyan—sometimes even Thorne Smithean—satire on the human condition of modern man as expressed in his institutions, his beliefs, and his emotions. It is a parable of modern times, castigating our stupidities, exposing our superstitions, revealing our inadequacies—and, at the same time, as all good satire must, suggesting directions for our improvement.

The parable is extremely complex, being worked out in minutest detail. The best that can be done in a couple of paragraphs is to outline it briefly:

The universe is a University; the world is a Campus, divided into East and West, each of which is made up of Colleges; God is the Founder, heads of state are Chancellors, those in lesser roles are Deans, and mankind is the Student Body. Capitalism is West Campus informationalism, Communism is East Campus Student Unionism; and, since the Second Campus Riot with the Siegfrieders, both Campuses have been engaged in a Quiet Riot focusing on the Boundary Line which divides them. Each side possesses a great computer, programmed so finely that they can now program themselves. Indeed, the West Campus computer (WESCAC) is capable even of procreation. Both machines can EAT (i.e., destroy the brains) of all studentdom; all it takes is someone to push the button—if in fact, the computers are not by now able to do so themselves. No one knows for certain whether they are able or not, except the WESCAC and the EASCAC, and they won't tell.

The characters in the novel represent causes and effects of the tension and ways of coping with it. Some of them also represent historical figures; thus Chancellor Lucius Rexford, with his forelock and toothy grin is obviously John F. Kennedy, and ex-Chancellor, ex-professor-general Reginald Hector is Eisenhower. Ira Hector, Reginald's brother, represents the power of money; Maurice Stoker (the Dean o' Flunks), rumored to be

---

*Reprinted by permission of the author.

Rexford's brother, represents physical power. One-eyed Peter Greene represents the selfishly-unselfish American pragmatic materialist, and his one-eyed counterpart, Leonid Alexandrov, represents the unselfishly-selfish Russian pragmatic materialism. Eblis Eierkopf is a Siegfrieder egg-head lured to the west after Campus Riot II to work upon its computer. Anastasia Stoker is a sentimental golden-hearted nymph who spreads her favors indiscriminately in order to make others feel good though she has never experienced sexual satisfaction.

The list could go on and on—there are the Beists, everyone from Beats to Civil Rights protesters; there is the Living Sakhyan, obvious Zen master who never shows the slightest reaction, aside from a constant benign smile, to anything going on about him—but it must end with the hero, George (Giles) the Goat-Boy. He is Natural Man, fathered by WESCAC and banished in infancy to be reared among goats. But as son of WESCAC, he is also a hero, in a religious as well as physical sense, and is destined to take his place on Campus as the Grand Tutor. The story is concerned with the trials and tribulations of his attempts to assume his position, with what he teaches, both erroneously and correctly, and, most importantly, with what he learns from the other characters and out of bitterly comic experience.

Thus far the fable of "Giles Goat-Boy." Now then, what is it all about? What does it mean, and where does it go? Well, in terms of the fable, it is about how one passes or fails; in terms of religion, it is about salvation and damnation; in terms of living from day to day, it is about happiness or contentment and discontented unhappiness. All three are interrelated: man is beset by irresolvable contradictions in the universe and in himself which cause his discontent and the misunderstanding of which can result in his failure or damnation. Passage, salvation, is not merely the acceptance of contradiction, of things as they are, nor is it the denial of contradiction by making things seem to be what they are not. It is the sudden intuitive awareness that contradiction is in reality paradox, or two things in one, hence IS resolvable through a proper understanding of its oneness.

This intuitive flash of insight which permits one to transcend duality and achieve oneness comes, as it did for Emerson, out of experience in nature. However, it is far more earthy here. For Emerson, the experience could be the simple contemplation of a phenomenon of nature—a tree, a flower, the sky; for Barth, it is the active participation in the most selfish and at the same time selfless of natural experiences—the orgasm.

But the flash is momentary, and ultimately incommunicable. So, while Giles with Anastasia (as you might suspect) fights his way through contradiction to paradox and thus Passes, he cannot keep the intuition except in memory, and he cannot teach it. As Emerson would put it, only the self-reliant individual achieves completion through his own initiative, not through the actions or teachings of others.

The novel's message then, or suggested direction for our improvement, can hardly be expressed politely. But in its very outrageousness, it fits perfectly into the satirical absurdity of the whole.*

*In a note dated Oct. 11, 1966, John Barth commented on this review as follows:

Much obliged for the thoughtful review. The Emerson business is okay, but for pragmatist-vs.-transcendentalist I guess you could as well say rationalist-vs.-mystical or for that matter Aristotelian-vs.-Platonist. Which camp you tent me in depends, I guess, on which page you consider the end of the story. But for pity's sake don't lump me in with Mailer and the orgasmists. Giles' transcension-through-orgasm was emblematical, merely, though real, and of course what follows is in the spirit of *post coitum triste*.

Giles Goat-Boy:
Satyr, Satire, and
Tragedy Twined

James T. Gresham*

I

Giles Goat-Boy belongs to the literary genre described by Northrop Frye and others as the Menippean satire.[1] Like the Novel, the Menippean satire records a disillusionment with "systems," simplifications of experience, or "innocence," but in ideological rather than experiential terms, affirming experience obliquely, through parody of art, rather than directly, through "imitation" of experience. The Menippean satire moves away from myth and wish-fulfillment toward reality. Structurally, it is an anti-romance, usually destroying its targets—literary, intellectual, philosophical, or historical—in an avalanche of their own jargon. It contains an admixture of verse, stylized or "humor" characters, argumentative dialogues or symposiums, facetious self-consciousness or self-parody, catalogues of erudition, and, often, a *satura lanx*-ious taste in food. It prefers "practice to theory, experience to metaphysics" (Frye, p. 230). Like all satire, it is "various," digressive, coarse, obscene, and aggressive. However, it differs from conventional satire in its norm, which is not the Good or the Ideal, but the Real. Lucidity—perception of "reality"—is its goal, and the delusory Ideal is generally viewed as a manifestation of reductive system-building, Romance, or rubricizing. Most Menippean satires—*Don Quixote, Tale of a Tub, Candide*—reflect ambivalence toward Romance, toward the Real, and toward lucidity. The Menippean satirist often relishes the pedantic jargon he ridicules, esteems the Ideal as well as the Real, writes a romance-parody in order to embrace (while deflating) Romance, and, Kurtz-like, finds the pain of lucidity intolerable. Sometimes, however, he finds lucidity tolerable, and, at his happiest, he finds a redeeming vitality in the Real. He uses corrective catalogues and multiplicity as sources of mockery, to deflate reductive "systems," but also as sources of profound merriment. Ultimately, Menippean satire's "affirmation" of experience reflects comic

*Reprinted by permission of *Genre*.

vitality—the kind of "satyric," pseudo-sexual delight in chaotic reality evinced by Rabelais. Satiric attack on the Ideal (or Romance) can at least potentially shift to satyric celebration of the Real—with tragic overtones.

Let us view *Giles Goat-Boy* in terms of this definition of Menippean satire. Consider Barth's "ideological" orientation, for example. *Giles* addresses most of the literary, philosophical, historical, social-political, and theological "systems" of our time and all time, from comedy to tragedy, from rational dualism to mystic monism, from laissez faire optimism to Marxist fatalism, from western individualism to eastern communism, from Christianity to Taoism and Zen Buddhism. At the end of his intellectual odyssey Goerge Giles learns the lessons of Menippus; as Lucian's Tiresias tells Menippus: "The best way to live is to be an ordinary human being. So give up all this metaphysical nonsense. Stop worrying about first principles and final causes, and forget all those clever arguments—they don't mean a thing. Just live in the moment and get along as best you can, trying to see the funny side of things and taking nothing very seriously."[2] Or as Robert Scholes puts it—less light-heartedly: *Gile*'s "moral urges the advantages of action over ratiocination."[3] *Gile*'s intellectual "systems" negate one another, obliquely affirming experience, "reality," and lucidity, even though lucidity and reality are disillusioning, resisted, and even ridiculed.

Consider, too, Barth's Menippean catalogues: the allegorical apparatus, a glib, Rabelaisian avalanche of correspondences; the anti-intellectual set-pieces (e.g., 228, 306–307); the teaching machine's "gloss" on Bray's couplet, "Milo did not pass in class,/Nor did he fail in jail" (449 ff.). Related to the Menippean catalogue is *Gile*'s admixture of verse: the versified play, *Taliped Decanus*, is the longest example, but passing (and passèd) poems, aphorisms, and songs also abound. "Humor" characters prevail, vivified by the allegorical apparatus and often engaged in argumentative dialogues. Self-parody ranges in subtlety from the devious Gloss on "There is one way to raise a cow" (453), which is ultimately a mockery of Barth's metaphysical concerns ("Expletivism," "Adverbialism," Monism, Pluralism), to the pre- and post-*Giles* editorial apparatus, which is hilariously, heavy-handedly Scriblerian. Although *Giles* is a Menippean hodgepodge, there is no *satura lanx*-ious catalogue comparable to the Rabelaisian menu in, say, *The Sot-Weed Factor* (Part III, Ch. 7). Yet EATing is central, partly because George is a goat-boy, who, for example, gags at human meat-eaters, *literally* devours books, sees his future in a picnic basket, and at one point sophistically wonders whether his fifth "Assignment" might mean "make a meal of the Founder's words!" (634). But EAT most often means Electroencephalic Amplification and Transmission; it is WESCAC's means of destruction; WESCAC's inner chamber is the "belly" and its computer program is a "menu" (129). ("Allegorically," of course, WESCAC's EATing capacity is a function of its dragonhood. St. George must EAT it before it EATs all of studentdom.) Like all satire, *Giles Goat-Boy* is various, digressive, coarse, obscene: the reader may convince himself of this by turning to any page at random. But *Giles* differs from conventional satire in its norm, which is the Real rather than the Ideal. As in most Menippean satires, there are strong contrapuntal forces—for example, the Max-im, "Self-knowledge is bad news." Yet lucidity is finally upheld over innocence: this is one reason Barth's Menippean goat-book is a "tragedy" as well as a "satyr."

Indeed, Barth goes to the heart of his book when he says, "I'm delighted by the old spurious etymology of the words *tragedy* and *satire*, . . . both of which have been traced back to the root word for goat. Because what I was after in [*Giles*], as in most of my work, is a way to get at some of the passion and power of the tragic view of life, which I share, through the medium of farce and satire. To fuse those elements has been an aspiration of mine from the beginning."[4]

I believe this fusion of tragedy and satire is the key to *Giles*'s "anti-romantic" structure. In order to call *Giles* an anti-romance one must define "romance" very loosely—as almost any or every Art or system of Order. One can reduce the field, however, by focusing on those "systems" associated with George Giles's two main prototypes, Jesus and Oedipus: Christianity and Tragedy. *Giles Goat-Boy*'s title and major metaphor refer to both systems: Christianity insofar as "goat" reflects and distorts "lamb" (as in "lamb of God"); Tragedy through that genre's etymological and historical connections with the cult of Dionysus ("Tragedy," tragodia, means "goat-song"). These are also the two "systems" most emphatically parodied in *Giles*, the University-Universe "allegory" serving as vehicle in both cases. In regard to Christianity, consider Harold Bray's University Prayer to his *"Learned Founder! Liberal Artist! Dean of deans and Coach of coaches"* (454–455), and, in regard to Tragedy, consider Barth's "modern translation" of *Oedipus the King, The Tragedy of Taliped Decanus*, about "the famous Dean of Cadmus College" (312–354)—a rich, coarse concoction of sexual and "University" lore; an inversion of tragedy; a kind of satyr-drama which nevertheless climatically and anti-climactically articulates Giles's central theme of lucidity. In this sense *Taliped Decanus* is a microcosm of *Giles* itself.

Giles is a kind of satyr-drama, a burlesque or travesty of "serious" literary and religious forms. Christianity and Tragedy are historically susceptible and even accommodating to this kind of inversion. In fact, if one sights down the parallel lines of Christianity and Tragedy far enough they seem to meet under the emblematic goat, which connotes the scapegoat victim-hero and the Dionysian festival of life, death, fertility, and license. Barth sights down these lines and sees Christianity and Tragedy as folklore twins. He is always aware of Christianity's collusion with paganism, as in Easter and Christmas, the festivals marking, respectively, ironically, the beginning and ending of George's quest. Even the word "Easter" is borrowed from a pagan ceremony, of course—that celebrating Eastre, Aurora (of the East), or the dawn, staged at the vernal equinox. Barth calls it the Spring-Carnival. It is an Enochist (Christian) ceremony but also the beginning of Spring term, associated with the "ritual of registration and matriculation" (296 ff.). The major event of this ritual is the "Trial by Turnstile" or by "Scrapegoat Grate." Max explains to George that Scrapegoat Grate "had nothing to do with *scapegoat*,[5] more the pity, but alluded to three characteristically anti-caprine remarks of Enos Enoch's: that He was to come to separate the sheep from the goats; that the Way to Graduation was too narrow for even a goat to walk, but a broad mall for His flock; and that it were easier for a goat to scrape through an iron fence-grating than for a merely learned man to enter Commencement Gate" (297–298). Nevertheless, Barth considers the Christian and pagan ceremonies a single unit. The athletes of New Tammany College challenge the turnstile during the ritual, inevitably fail (only Grand Tutors can succeed), then the gates are opened and the students pass in to register, while the Dean o' Flunks gnashes "his teeth in mock frustration" (298). George says, "Few who participated in these festivities were aware of their original significance, any more than they recognized *Carnival* as coming from the Remusian [Roman, Latin] 'farewell to flesh' that preceded any period of fasting or mourning" (298). A valid historical connection between the pagan and Christian ceremonies of spring or Easter underlies Barth's parodic, irreverent, "allegorical" conversion of Maundy Thursday into "Randy-Thursday."

"Randy" certainly describes the Spring-Carnival Party at which George is introduced to New Tammany society (stick in one hand, cod on the other, as Maurice Stoker tricks him, pushes him through the door shouting "Ladies and gentlemen! . . . The Grand Tutor of the Western Campus!" [226]). George's initial encyclopaedic description suggests Petronius. "A little Carnival party," Stoker calls it: " 'We have one every night this week. You should see the place on New Year's Eve!' So persistently rumored was the approach of a new Grand Tutor, he explained, it had become popular practice among conscientious students to don caps and gowns and celebrate his arrival, and their own Commencement, in advance; in less reverent circles, like Stoker's, the same thing was done in burlesque. . . ." (127). The powerhouse party invokes the Aristophanic Attic revel and the Semitic fertility rite and the life-death rites of Easter: George Herrold is "buried" at this ceremony as George Giles services Anastasia, while the Spring Sunrise Service is piped in via Telerama. Stoker, Dean o' Flunks, exposes the dual meaning of "service" (242), and the services become mixed at the climax. "Incredibly, as I mounted home," says George, "the music swelled and rose to bursting. As ever in goatdom, the service was instant: swiftly as the sunflash smiting now the Founder's Shaft I drove and was done" (243).

If the powerhouse party suggests the origins of Comedy, of western religion (associated with the fertility rites denounced by old testament prophets, for example), and of Easter, it also suggests the satyr-play. It is a "burlesque," as Stoker says. It burlesques religion by emphasizing George's Goatliness; this latter day Grand Tutor is no lamb; he is, as Stoker puts it, "Enos Enoch with balls" (233), a "young satyr," says Dr. Sear (232). Giles is also a "goat" in other ways, of course: the innocent tricked by Stoker and others here and elsewhere; also the scapegoat of Barth's ambiguously inverted "tragedy." "You were an orphan of the storm, like me," says Max, "that the student race made their goats" (literally in George's case, as he escaped to Max and the goat-barns after the childhood tapelift trip to WESCAC's belly). Giles becomes not only the scapegoat of primitive tragedy but also of Christianity—even while remaining a "satyr"—a burlesque version of both. Barth fuses tragedy and "satire," goat-song and "satyr."

If *Taliped Decanus* is a satyr-play, *Giles Goat-Boy* is an inverted Holy Book and Tragedy. Similarly, if Giles is a burlesque Grand Tutor, Harold Bray is a burlesque Giles. Bray inverts an inversion and, within the context of Barth's burlesque, makes George a serious candidate for Grand Tutorhood. Bray's "role" is that of "proph-prof, foil, and routed antigiles" (563). He is "imposter, troll . . . it is his *function* to be driven out" (728). He is George's "adversary," as "necessary" to George as "Failure is to Passage," George decides. "I.e., not only contrary and interdependent, but finally undifferentiable" (759). Bray and Giles, Giles and Jesus, Giles and Oedipus, Satyr-play and Tragèdy, Burlesque and Bible, Parody and Parodied: they are rivals; one is the inversion of the other; yet they are mysteriously related and in some respects "undifferentiable." Bray is "a gifted imposter—so much so that in some instances the question of his fraudulence [becomes] more metaphysical than legal or ethical" (371).

George Giles's goatliness connotes a rich mythic background, centered in the Greek cult of Dionysus, the god whose sacred animal was the goat (*tragos*), somber cousin of the satyr (*saturos*). Bray's asininity connotes an equally rich background. As irreverent antigiles and anarchic anti-Christ (*Giles's* Biblical parodies are all brayed by Bray), Bray suggests the medieval Saturnalia, the licentious festival called the Asses' Mass or *festum asinarium*, during which the responses were brayed and donkeys were led to the altar. *Giles's* final Christmas ceremony "On Founder's Hill" (II. iii. 7) suggests a western European folklore tradition, the French "mid-winter Saturnalia at the conclusion of which the ass-eared god, later the Christmas Fool with his ass-eared cap, was killed by his rival, the Spirit of the New Year—the child Horus, or Harpocrates, or the infant Zeus."[6] As burlesque inversion, Bray is, like *Taliped Decanus*, a *Giles*ian paradigm: the "anti"-creature which historically, mysteriously shadows all things: Christianity, Tragedy, Order, Good, Light, Romance.

II

Giles and Bray, ceremony and mock-ceremony, goat as victim and hero, Tragedy and satyr-play, Romance and Anti-Romance: these pairs reflect the basic patterns of *Giles Goat-Boy*—the cycle and the dialectic, twining and twinning. "Spielman's law," Max's "cyclological theory," pivotally introduces twining. It "turned me round a corner of my life. . . . Dark ties; thing twined to thing," George muses (122). Max's theory is based on numerous correspondences: *ontogeny repeats cosmogeny*; the race itself . . . "West-Campus culture—followed demonstrably . . . the life-pattern of its least new freshman" (300). Max's "masterwork, *The Riddle of the Sphincters* . . . meant to demonstrate mathematically his belief in the fundamental rectitude of student nature" (42; the pun on "rectum" is intended and etymologically justified). And Max's cyclological theory shows "the 'sphincter's riddle' and the mystery of the University to be the same. *Ontogeny recapitulates cosmogeny*—what is it but to say that proctoscopy repeats hagiography? That our Founder on Founder's Hill and the rawest freshman on his first *mons veneris* are father and son?" (43). Both the sexual and scatological components of this satiric but also satyric "theory" are realized at the thematic "climax" of *Giles*, as, first, Giles purges himeslf of his first two "Answers" (708–709), solving the "riddle of the sphincters," and, second, "sees" the ultimate Answer as he "passes" with Anastasia in WESCAC's belly (729–731).

Max's theory is not unlike the lesson of Menippus: just as ontogeny recapitulates cosmogeny, so proctoscopy repeats hagiography; to study the rectum is to study grand tutorhood. A man becomes a saint and prophet only by becoming "supremely human"(114): "be glad if you can learn to be a man—that's hero-work enough!" says Max (128). In Giles's case, becoming "supremely human" involves recognition of his goatliness, recognition of humanity's lowest common denominators: sex, excrement—the rectum. The "rectum" equals the "end" and hence the "beginning," something like "commencement." Only by lowering himself to the common level of humanity can Giles finally "love" and become "supremely human."

If Spielman's Law illustrates *Giles*'s cyclic patterns, the Tower Hall clockwork embodies *Giles*'s dialectic principle. Eblis Eierkopf, the egghead clockwatcher, has "responsibility not only for the measurement of NTC time but for the 'ticking heart' of WESCAC itself, 'the very pulse of West Campus': . . . a metronomic apparatus (or was it merely a principle?) which both set and was itself the pace of WESCAC's operations; which in some manner beyond my fathom both drove and derived from the Tower Hall clockworks" (368). Later George learns that the "metronomic apparatus" or principle is the clockwork escapement fulcrum, the rocking, beating "heart" of tick and tock. The fulcrum runs north and south on the meridian that divides East Campus from West Campus and is thus the center of an East-West political and cartographical controversy. It is also the center of an East-West controversy involving time and reflecting the metaphysical dialectic of *Giles*. The Eastern, "Everlasting Now-niks," "associated with Sakhyanist [Buddhist] curricula," believe in "tickless time," the abolishment of "all forms of escapement" (481), or, in the context of *Giles* as a whole, the abolishment of "differentiation," coinciding with George's second Answer to his "assignment." In contrast, Eierkopf and the Western rationalists want to perfect tick-time, embodied in the Tower Hall escapement mechanism. Eierkopf believes he will solve all these East-West problems by measuring the exact moment when the escapement mechanism rocks from tick over to tock. Thus he has developed a measuring device, "the Infinite Divisor," which hones the fulcrum as it measures, halving and halving "again, *ad infinitum*, the width of the edge, until theoretically it reached a perfect point at the center of the hole and the midpoint of the Tick-Tock swing" (482). Of course, the entire assembly topples as the fulcrum is finally honed down toward zero, decisively collapsing the dialectic of Tick and Tock. Eierkopf is simultaneously working on his "grand historico-chemico-mathematico-biologico-mythophysical treatise upon the egg," and when Giles accidentally hints that he has omitted the greatest problem of all—that of the chicken and the egg—Eierkopf takes up this second "infinite divisor," the infinite regression involving the precedence of chicken or egg. The results are again disastrous, as Eierkopf literally becomes an egg in a nest in the Tower Hall belfry (this is *Giles*'s most outlandish chapter of puns and paradoxes:III.ii.3).

Eierkopf the egghead is all head and brain and has a feeble capacity for sex; his roommate, chosen "on the basis of complementation" (373), is Croaker the Frumentian, a sexual giant and mental dwarf who carries Eierkopf on his shoulders, feeds him, and administers to his feeble carnal desires. If these two were mated "on the basis of complementation," Giles's first-Answer advice, paralleling Eierkopf's principle of "differentiation," is to separate: Eierkopf should expunge all traces of Croakerism in himself and Croaker should expunge all traces of Eierkopfism. The key is to "differentiate": distinguish Failure from Passage, tick from tock, East from West, Eierkopf from Croaker. Giles's divisively dualistic egg-headism is of course as disastrous as that of Eierkopf himself.

The tick-tock dialectic reflects the East-West dialectic, the veritable mainspring of the book. Most of the philosophical, sociological, ideological, cartographical, religious, and political "controversies" in *Giles* divide along East-West lines: informationalism (capitalism) vs. student unionism (communism); tick-timists vs. the Sakhyanist "Everlasting Now-niks"; rational dualism vs. mystic monism, and so forth; in many respects the first and second Answers to Giles's "assignment" divide along the same lines.

The mysterious character figuratively stationed between East and West in *Giles* is the sooty Dean o' Flunks, Maurice Stoker. Stoker runs the powerhouse and the powerhouse runs both the East and West Campuses. The Campuses ("camps") are united by their common power source: Stoker's powerhouse—power as raw chaos. " 'Here's where your *power* is!' Stoker shouted. . . . Grinning he thumped his chest with one hand and extended the other towards the bedlam beneath us. 'Volcano with a cap on it!' " " 'This is Graduation!' Stoker shouted happily. 'Never mind the question: the Answer's power!' " (220, 222). EASCAC and WESCAC, like East and West, are twins: "Of necessity, WESCAC and EASCAC shared the common power source on Founder's Hill, and a certain communication—ostensibly for espionage—went on between them; from a special point of view it might be argued that they were brothers, or even the hemispheres of a single brain" (95). Only Stoker can pass at will past the electric grid dividing the East from the West portion of the powerhouse. East and West alike fear and admire power, negation, chaos—all things represented by Stoker. He "delight[s] in recklessness" (200). "Wherever disorder was, Maurice Stoker seemed to be also. . . . Even the best-intentioned, most high-minded administrators . . . seemed unable to do without Maurice Stoker; fear and despise him as they might, all came at last to terms with him" (166).

One such administrator is the chancellor of New Tammany College, "Lucky" Lucius Rexford, who is "reputed to be a half-brother" to Stoker. If Stoker is "sooty" and represents negation, he nevertheless runs the powerhouse; "Lucky" is, above all, "positive" in the best modern way; *his* emblem is light ("Light up with Lucky" is his campaign slogan). When Giles applies his principle of "differentiation" and suggests the "half-brothers" sever their mysterious relationship, chaos—a power and light failure—ensues. Ultimately, in the POSTTAPE, Giles and *Giles* imply that the yin-yang Stoker-Lucius "fraternity" is necessary: "Of Stoker little need be said: . . . denial is his affirmation, and from that contradiction he—indeed, the campus—draws strength" (760).

As we have seen in the case of Stoker and Rexford, Eierkopf and Croaker, and George and Bray, *Giles*'s characters come in pairs. Peter Greene and Leonid Andreich Alexandrov are the pair most graphically reflecting the East-West dialectic. Peter Greene, one-time rustic Huck Finn, then archetypal twentieth-century WASP (as Scholes puts it), represents all the American ambiguities. In particular, he represents (this is an "allegory") American "innocence," which is akin to ignorance and even blindness—especially regarding his own erotic desires. Like Dr. Sear (cf. "seer"), who watches his wife masturbate through a fluoroscope, and Dr. Eierkopf (cf. "eye"), who watches co-eds undress through his remarkable telescope, Pete is a peeping Tom, but he is schizophrenically blind to this part of himself—literally: one eye is blind because Pete threw a rock at a mirrored image of himself peeping at his sweetheart (278–279). Now Pete has a mortal fear of mirrors.

Pete's Russian counterpart, Leonid Alexandrov, also has an aversion for mirrors and one blind eye (see 502–503). Leonid is also an innocent of sorts, but, unlike Pete, he is blinded by selflessness rather than selfishness. Leonid blindly falls in love with Anastasia Stoker—with her "selflessness-hood" (both men speak a strange tongue), just as Pete falls ludicrously in love with Anastasia's virgin "innocence." Eventually they fight over her (706–707); the winner's prize will be the loser's good eye; in the battle Leonid's good eye is accidentally slashed and Pete, remorseful, thence stabs out his own, a pattern established earlier by Taliped Decanus. Pete and Leonid, West and East, are ultimately united by blindness.

III

Pete Greene is also paired with Dr. Sear, again through mirrors and the motif of "seeing." This pairing reflects the dialectic of innocence and lucidity—perhaps the central pattern of *Giles Goat-Boy* and of all Menippean satires. The Menippean norm of the Real is essentially a norm of lucidity. Lucian of Samosata, Rabelais, Cervantes, Swift, and Voltaire are essentially laughing at blindness—although often driven by an attendant and contrapuntal desire for Romance, Innocence, the Ideal, sweet inner blindness. This Menippean pattern is similar to the "tragic" pattern of *Taliped Decanus*; Taliped-Oedipus' desire for lucidity, his desire to escape ignorance and innocence, leads to an even more disastrous blindness. Is he, then, a fool, a hero, or simply a man trapped by an inescapable paradox? This correspondence of the Menippean and tragic patterns may reflect Barth's expressed intention of "fusing" tragedy and satire.

Barth consistently ridicules Pete's green "innocence." Peter Greene's self-protective blinder is the incantation, "I'm okay, what the heck anyhow," and George, aided by sophisticated Dr. Sear, tries to cure him by making him see that neither he nor New Tammany is "okay." When Pete spouts Bray's maxim, *"Passed are the Kindergarteners,"* George says, "Whatever it is that's passed about kindergarteners, it isn't their childishness. Or their ignorance" (470).

"Pfui on innocence," Max says, as he, Sear, George, and Pete prepare to watch *Taliped Decanus*. "I couldn't agree more," Dr. Sear responds. "I'll go even further: innocence is ignorance; ignorance is illusion . . . Commencement's for the disillusioned, not for the innocent" (307). Sear's heroes are Gynander (Tiresias) and the "tragically" blinded Taliped (Oedipus):

> That's *my* Grand Tutor! . . . Poor blind Taliped and his fatal ID-card, stripped of innocence! Committed and condemned to knowledge! That's the

> only Graduation offered on West Campus, George—and, my dear boy, we *are* Westerners! . . .
>
>   We all flunked with the first two students in the Botanical Garden, George; we're committed to Knowledge of the Campus, and if there's any hope for us at all, it's in perfecting that knowledge . . . even if the things we learn destroy us. . . . (353)

The problem is that Sear is a perversion of the Seer, not a "mantic" but a "connoisseur" (527). He *relishes* the bad news of self-knowledge. Perhaps "know" in "know thyself" should be "understood in the Old-Syllabus sense of carnal knowledge. In other words, *Fornicate thyself,*" he suggests (524). Unlike Pete, Sear is not frightened by mirrors. He enjoys peeping at his masturbating wife through a fluoroscope—and enjoys admitting it, and enjoys loathing himself for admitting it. He is the aesthete-eroticist par excellence: "The whole effect of him was of a lean pear dried in the sun, its gold juice burnt into thin exotic savor—and in fact it was pleasant to smell him, all but his breath, which was slightly foul" (231). Indeed, Sear is a rotten pear: his foul breath stems from a cancer which began as a growth on his nose and festered "from daily contact with the frames of his eyeglasses" (526). Eventually it blinds him. He dies castrating himself, believing that "his generative organs" are all that stand between him and Gynander-like "prophprofhood" (756).

Barth satirizes Sear's "seeing" as well as Greene's "innocence," yet he is finally committed to lucidity; he ultimately although equivocally celebrates learning the bad news. Even Max, though aware that *self-knowledge is bad news*, is committed to self-knowledge—indeed, obsessed with facing the bad news of his own guilt. Barth admires Max and the Sophoclean sufferer even though he ridicules them. He is ambivalent toward lucidity partly because he sees it as destructive—physically in the case of Taliped Decanus and maybe Max, spiritually in the case of Sear. Barth is also ambivalent because "innocence" resembles Menippean anti-intellectualism or pragmatism, even though the latter is innocence of action rather than of thought or "knowing." As Max says, this pragmatic "innocence" should not be confused with "naiveté." It is a "profound and transcendently powerful *simplicity*" earned only by passing from Innocence to Experience"(181). Sear's "lucidity" is also ridiculed as the bane of spontaneity—a kind of paralyzing agent not unlike *cosmopsis* in *The End of the Road* and self-consciousness in *Lost in the Funhouse*. Sear has gone so far down the road and into the funhouse that he cannot even "mount" his wife in "the ordinary way" (cf. 663 and 747). Yet lucidity survives the mockery; Giles escapes the perverted Sear and becomes a legitimate Seer, climactically twined with his Ladyship.

IV

Barth admires the Sophoclean sufferer even though he ridicules him. Examples are tragic Taliped, who is an imitation as well as a travesty of

Oedipus; the self-effacing Moishian, Max; Leonid, the Nikolayan obsessed with selflessnesshood; and Anatasia Stoker, who extends the conventional Heroine's values of duty, pity, and suffering to absurd limits. In the case of Max and Leonid, "suffering" is associated with selflessness and the paradox of "Failure is Passage" or "Suffering is Graduation"—a paradox that ultimately becomes a paroxysm and a target of Menippean anti-intellectualism. Max's obsession with suffering and Alexandrov's desire for selflessness involve the logical, Christian paradox of Pride: George condemns Max's scapegoatism as *Vanity*—"the vanity of choosing himself to suffer for the failings of others" (465). Likewise Alexandrov: "Leonid's dilemma was thus not unlike mine, or any rightthinking undergraduate's, . . . : the wish to achieve perfect self-suppression, like the yen to Graduate, was finally a prideful wish and thus self-defeating" (505). George in fact concludes that this is why he flunked his first test in WESCAC's belly (see 580). Later, locked in Main Detention, he watches Max and Leonid puzzle over the paradox; he sees that the paradox is "specious, logic-chopping," mere "casuistry" (594, 596), but, soon afterwards, he himself joins them by glorifying the paradox: munching the Founder's Scroll, triggered by his mad mother's aphorism, *"Passéd are the flunkéd,"* he suddenly realizes that if Passage (or the desire to Pass) is Failure, then Failure is also Passage. His second Answer is the inversion of his first: he decides the enemy is not Bray, but WESCAC, "that root and fruit of Differentiation" (605). Passage and Failure are false distinctions, false categories. It was "that distinction of Passage and Failure from which depended all my subsequent mistakes," he concludes. "There in a word was the Way: Embrace" (605); embrace all alike; see that Passage is Failure, Failure Passage.

He begins preaching this "paradox" (605), dazzling, frightening Stoker with "inversions-of-inversions" (629), likewise Ira and Reginald Hector, Eierkopf, Rexford, and all others whom he had falsely tutored before. During the first test in WESCAC's belly George answered all questions "yes"; this time, deviously juggling paradoxes, he answers all questions "no," largely in order to spite WESCAC and its "arbitrary" distinctions or categories (695–696). But he flunks again, and, whipped out of NTC, sticks home atop Croaker, his neck sore, "stomach empty, . . . bladder full" (703). On the way he encounters Stoker, with Greene and Alexandrov, who have just lost their last eyes in the fight over Anastasia, thanks to Leonid's militant selflessness. "So there they sit, Goat-Boy," says Stoker: "two blind bats! Are they passed or failed?" (708).

It is at this moment that George Giles literally "passes all"—perhaps solving The Riddle of the Sphincters: "my spirit was seized: it was not *I* concentrating, but something concentrating upon me, taking me over, like the spasms of defecation or labor pains. . . . Truly now those paradoxes became paroxysms: I shut my eyes, swayed on Croaker's shoulders, trembled and sweated. . . . Surely my mind must crack! . . . I gave myself up utterly to that which bound, possessed, and bore me. I let go, I let all go; relief went through me like a purge" (708–709). George undergoes the ambiguous experience of childbirth, defecation (of his first two Answers) comprising "delivery" (of his third). His third Answer is that there are no "answers"; it is a negation of two philosophical systems, and hence an oblique affirmation of experience. The first, "Western" Answer—"differentiation"—was generated by the rationalism of duality; the second, "Eastern" Answer—abolition of differentiation—was generated by the rationalism of paradox. *Both* involved infinite regressions: Answer #1 the regression of the "infinite divisor" or of infinite differentiation; Answer #2 the regression of the infinite unitor or of "infinite equivalence." In conversation with the egghead Eierkopf, George insists his second Answer involves "loss" of "reason": "the flunking Reason that distinguished [Eierkopf] from Croaker, and denied that contradictories could both be passéd at the same time" (642). But the second Answer is not so much a "loss" as an inversion of reason. The same rational faculty creates "contraries" (Answer #1) and converts the "contraries" into "paradoxes" (Answer #2)—that is, into merely apparent contradictions.

Answer #2 is an "inversion" of Answer #1, but part of the same rationalistic system—a system collapsed by Answer #3. Yet Answer #2 resembles Answer #3 insofar as it, too, collapses a "system" (Failure and Passage). In one sense, Answer #3 is merely Answer #2 turned upon itself. This is why Answer #3 resembles Answer #2 and has a distinctly Eastern, mystic, and monistic flavor. Gerhard Joseph distinguishes between Answers Two and Three by calling #2 the "union of contraries" and #3 the "transcension of categories."[7] This distinction points toward the pragmatic Lesson of Menippus: "union of contraries" implies mental manipulation, while "transcension of categories" implies escape from mental rubrics. But Joseph's explanation does not acknowledge the degree to which Answer #3 "transcends" categories *only* in the sense of "uniting," of, as Scholes puts it, in a slightly different context, "synthesizing" contraries. In this sense, Answer #3 does indeed resemble Answer #2. Consider, for example, Barth's use of the term "seamless." At the climax of the third trip into WESCAC's belly, Giles cries "In the sweet place that contained me there was no East, no West, but an entire, single, seamless campus" (731). In his second trip into WESCAC's belly, guided by his second, "Eastern" Answer, Giles also refers to "the timeless, seamless University" (695). Earlier in the same Reel, he says, "I saw the error of my flunking the 'Eierkopf' in [Croaker] and the 'Croaker' in Eierkopf—as if the seamless University knew aught of such distinctions!" (627). Much earlier, before arriving at his First Answer, George listens to Bray's Enochist attack on Flunkéd Education and senses the "truth" of his contention: *"Our Schools and Divisions—what are they but seams in the seamless?"* (447). And perhaps we should recall Burlingame's apocalyptic cry in *The Sot-*

Weed Factor: "I am Suitor of Totality. . . . I have known my great Bride part by splendrous part . . . ; but I crave the Whole—the tenon in the mortise, the jointure of polarities, the seamless universe" (Part III, Ch. 1).

Apparently the "seamlessness" of Answer #2 leads to a "paroxysm" because it is rational rather than passional. Giles's Answers during his second trip are tortuously reasoned (See 695–696), while those during his third and final trip are gay, careless, spontaneous. Answer #2 ("NO") is the inversion of Answer #1 ("YES"). Answer #3 collapses and "embraces" both of them ("YES-NO"). This time the embracing is truly (although comically) apocalyptic, not sophistic; it involves "transcension of categories" as well as, or through the "union of contraries." If Answer #3 begins with a purge—and scatological self-mockery—it climaxes with sexual self-mockery—and also profound, Rabelaisian merriment, a form of comic vitality. Sexual union (*"tick* clipped *tock, all* serviced *nothing"*) serves to "unite" all polar opposites as George and Anastasia, sexually twined, dissolve Yes and No into a single "solution": Male and Female, East and West, hot and cold, light and dark, beginning and end. This time the Solution, the Paradox ("The end of the University! Commencement Day!") is apocalyptic, not a "paroxysm."

Giles's lucid, passional vision of a seamless "University" is mystic and "tragic," again reflecting those aspects of our culture associated with Giles's two main prototypes, Jesus and Oedipus. Both of these figures embody the passéd Paradox of Failure and Passage. Christ is born in order to die, flunks in order to pass mankind, and even in his passéd flunking, realizes he may not have been able to teach mankind his "unspeakable" lesson. Similarly, Oedipus is blinded, destroyed by lucidity, yet gains a tragic passédness by flunking. As Giles says, "Dean Taliped, in the horror of his knowledge . . . was as passéd as one can be who understands and accepts that in studentdom is only failure" (417).

Giles's third Answer, his apocalyptic vision in WESCAC's belly, is a "transcension of categories" as well as a "union of contraries," Passage and Failure included. It is a Taoistic "letting be," distinguished by spontaneity and carelessness, abandonment of rational categories—not because rational categories are too complex while life is simple, but because they are too mechanical, devious, perverse—incapable of comprehending or conveying Reality. The lesson Giles learns is "simple" in a way—but not because it is reductive. The "University" he sees is "seamless" but its "simplicity" is that of an irreducible, ineffable organism or Whole; it is "seamless" but not pole-less; it does not contain "contradiction," but it bristles with "paradox."

After the climax in WESCAC's belly, George confirms his humanhood, but also, paradoxically, his Herohood, by ceasing to worry about Assignments, Answers, Passage, and Failure. He achieves Grand Tutorhood by "successfully" failing to find the Answer, by seeing there are no reductive Answers. The burlesque conclusion has its "heroic" aspects—notably the shafting ceremony on Founder's Hill (II.iii.7), during which George and *Triple T* butt Bray out of New Tammany. Barth deflates this "triumph" (see 756) in the anti-climactic POSTTAPE, dramatizing George's mundane initiation into Experience.[8] Scott Byrd detects Candidean "resignation" and Swiftean "misanthropy" here; there is some of this, but also acceptance and even (as Jerry Bryant insists) "muted satisfaction."[9] There is a muted satisfaction with Experience, with Giles's having failed to become the "Hero" he hoped. Indeed, this "failure" is the cause of Giles's unpopularity and imminent shafting—thus (as in the case of Christ) the source of his "tragic" passage. Failure to become the "Hero" *is* Passage in this Menippean satire, and is thus Heroic—or as close to the Heroic as man can come in an anti-romance. If the POSTTAPE sets out to deflate the Heroic (or Romantic) aspects of George's burlesque quest, it ends, as does *Don Quixote*, equivocally, perhaps indicating the strength of Barth's desire to make Giles more than a burlesque hero. Or perhaps the equivocal ending indicates that the two heroes (romantic and burlesque), like Bray and Giles, are "not only contrary and interdependent, but finally undifferentiable": Real twined with Ideal, Romance with Anti-Romance, Parody with Parodied, tragedy with satyr-play, Loving with Loathing.

Notes

1. See Northrop Frye, *Anatomy of Criticism* (Princeton, 1957), pp. 223–239, 303–314. The following definition is also derived from Ronald Paulson's *Satire and the Novel in Eighteenth-Century England* (New Haven, Conn., 1967), Paulson's *The Fictions of Satire* (Baltimore, 1967), and other recent works on satire. The definition reflects major patterns of such acknowledged Menippean satires as Petronius' *Satyricon*, Lucian's *True History*, Rabelais' *Gargantua and Pantagruel*, Cervantes' *Don Quixote*, Swift's *Gulliver's Travels*, Sterne's *Tristram Shandy*, and Voltaire's *Candide*. In "*Giles Goat-Boy* Visited," *Critique: Studies in Modern Fiction*, IX, i (1966), 108–112, Scott Byrd uses Northrop Frye's four prose fiction categories (Confession, Romance, Novel, Anatomy)—discusses *Giles* as a combination of all four, but slights the Anatomy or Menippean satire aspects.

Page references in my text are to the readily obtainable Fawcett Crest paperback edition of *Giles Goat-Boy* (N.Y., 1966).

2. Lucian, *Satirical Sketches*, trans. Paul Turner, Penguin Classics (Baltimore, 1961), pp. 109–110.

3. *The Fabulators* (N.Y., 1967), p. 167.

4. Alan Prince, "An Interview with John Barth," *Prism* (Sir George Williams University, Spring, 1968). Quoted by David Bernard Morrell in *John Barth: An Introduction* (unpublished Ph.D. dissertation, Pennsylvania State University, 1970), p. 112. Phyllis Meras' "John Barth: A Truffle No Longer," *New York Times Book Review*, August 7, 1966, p. 22, and Barth's "The Anonymiad" (in *Lost in the Funhouse*) contain similar references.

5. Interestingly, Volume I, Reel ii, Chapter 7 is entitled "*Scape*goat Grate" in the *Table of Contents* of the Fawcett Crest edition—a misprint. Hereafter, I shall refer parenthetically to Volume, Reel, and Chapter. *Giles* is symmetrically and pseudoreligiously divided into two Volumes of three Reels each, each Reel containing seven Chapters.

6. Robert Grave's introduction to Apuleius' *The Golden Ass* (N.Y., 1951), p. xiv. Graves discusses donkey lore at some length.

7. *John Barth*, Univ. of Minn. Pamphlets on American Writers, No. 91 (Minneapolis, 1970), p. 36. "Union of contraries" and "transcension of categories" are phrases used (facetiously, in part) by Barth in "Night-Sea Journey," the first piece in *Lost in the Funhouse*. Their use together in "Night-Sea Journey" may indicate that they are not so different as Joseph contends.

8. It could be argued that Barth is not deflating the climatic patterns of Romance, but, rather, imitating the anti-climatic patterns of archetypal myth (even the Founder's Scroll says "*A proph-prof is never* cum laude *in his own quad*" [p. 690]). *Giles* loosely follows the twenty-two Heroic patterns described by Lord Raglan in *The Hero: A Study in Tradition, Myth, and Drama* (London, 1936), the last seven of which coincide with the POSTTAPE. But Raglan himself notes the existence of a relatively optimistic "romance" form of the Myth: "In these tales we are never told of the hero's death, but merely that he 'lived happily ever afterwards,' which seems to suggest a desire to omit . . . the latter part of the myth" (*The Hero*, p. 191).

9. Jerry Bryant, *The Open Decision* (N.Y., 1970), p. 302. For reference to Byrd, see note 1, above.

Giles Goat-Boy: or "Reality" is No Place for a Hero

Marilyn R. Sherman*

After writing two highly successful novels, *The Floating Opera* and *The End of the Road*, both answering the description of "realistic fiction," John Barth discovers:

> One ought to know a lot about Reality before one writes realistic novels. Since I don't know much about Reality, it will have to be abolished. What the hell, reality is a nice place to visit, but you wouldn't want to live there, and literature never did very long.[1]

According to Tom Wolfe, Barth is absolutely correct. In his article, "Why They Aren't Writing the Great American Novel Anymore,"[2] he condemns the journalistic encroachment into the sacred area of the novel. In his words, it has become a "Locker Room Genre" of reporting whereby Norman Mailer documents his anti-war experience in *Armies of the Night;* Truman Capote researches ad nauseam the sensational Kansas murders, culminating with *In Cold Blood;* and George Plimpton, admitted to the sanctity of the gladiators' arena as rookie quarterback for Detroit, grinds out *The Paper Lion.*

Small room here for the creative imagination of the literary artist. If the function of the novel and its hero is to create, as does Sisyphus, meaning out of meaninglessness, being out of nothingness, dignity out of humiliation, we find small comfort on Mailer's steps of the Pentagon, Capote's barren Kansas farm or in Plimpton's furtive huddle on the ten yard line.[3]

It would appear that the artist is trapped. For concurrent with mankind's need for myths and heroes is the fear that too much knowledge has caused the mysteries to lose their force. And for some novelists this leads to a desperate attempt to document reality. But for the creative mind this is a fool's errand, since reality can never be truly captured, but then neither can it be escaped.

John Barth confronts this dilemma by re-inventing the universe, by

---

*Reprinted by permission of the author.

seeking a fabulation that abandons all pretenses of realistic fiction. It is his way of saying that because we have lost faith in the language of realism, we have lost faith with its heroes. Now because we are overly familiar with common things, our world has become trite to us. A survey of Barth's novels shows this concrete message of the artist's struggle to let us re-discover reality.

In Barth's third novel he creates a mock eighteenth-century mock-epic, *The Sotweed Factor*, as if attempting to return to the very root of the genre to discover where the evolution went awry. As is true of most expeditions and experiments, the discovery was of an unexpected nature. For scholars and critics called Barth's attention to the predictability of his hero. They pointed out that Barth's protagonist, Ebenezer Cooke had 21 out of 22 of Lord Raglan's documented characteristics of the classic hero.[4] Barth, who believed at the time that he had created a unique and capricious character, was genuinely surprised, and then had to admit that there must be a mythic force that had directed his creation.

Once the artist possesses this knowledge his creations become more self-conscious heroes. Barth's subsequent novel, *Giles Goat-Boy*, reflects this dilemma. That is, it poses the question, with a guidebook extracted from Raglan's *Hero*, Frazer's *Golden Bough*, Campbell's *Hero with a Thousand Faces*, Otto Rank's *Birth of the Hero*, with a thorough knowledge of ancient myths and of the Bible, *and* with a forward written by the Cambridge Anthropologists, can an aspiring hero find happiness and success even though he knows what he's doing?

Barth's answer is a qualified "yes." But he concedes it is difficult for the author to avoid being paralyzed by his own knowledge. Clearly today's hero has his problems. For the contemporary view is one of the self-determining individual. Now the timeless universal symbols that produced great co-ordinating mythologies are all known as lies. The development of the scientific method of research, the boundless use of sophisticated machinery and the omniscience of the computer have transformed human life and its heroes.

So Barth turns from a form of realism, misnomer though it may be, to a fabulation that re-invents the world. Here the author can create the essential myth and the necessary hero. Great Zeus may have his awesome thunderbolt replaced by electronic technology, but the hero-cycle is entirely recognizable and acceptable. And although Scherazade, Bellerophon and Perseus from *Chimera*, along with Menelaus and Proteus from *The Funhouse* are examples of ancient myths imaginatively transplanted into modern soil, Giles Goat-boy is the most successful attempt at modernizing the monomyth.

Giles Goat-boy by anybody's definition is a classical hero. A member of the University campus (allegorically, the universe) he is indeed highly born. Not fathered by shining Apollo, salty Poseidon or lustful Zeus, he is the son of Western civilization's omniscient and omnipotent computer,

WESCAC, and a carefully selected, beautiful, mortal and virginal librarian. His name, "Giles," itself is an acronym, symbolizing the "Grand-tutorial, Ideal, Laboratory Eugenical Specimen." Significantly, he is the pre-determined product of a mechanical and organic union.

Characteristic of all major heroes, he has a mysterious birth, a threat against his life and is ignorant of his parents' identity. He is reared in exile by the obligatory kind and benevolent foster parent with which all heroes are somehow blessed. In Barth's myth it is Max Spielman, the great mathematical psycho-proctologist, currently in disfavor with the university administration. Now fallen to the lowly rank of Senior Goat Herder, Max raises the Goat-boy with the rest of the herd in atavistic obscurity. Max, for his part, is not pre-occupied with the mystery of the Sphynx, but following his proctologist's studies, is endeavoring to solve the mystery of the sphincter.

Picking up the universal thread of the hero-cycle, Barth weaves the full mythic tapestry. He supplies the Goat-boy with a crippled foot, a pastoral childhood and then subjects him to the sudden blunder where the merest chance reveals an unsuspected world. For the Goat-boy is literally kicked by another goat into a greater awareness—he is *not* one of the herd—he has a special calling.

With this moment of epiphany and the movement of goat to man, the hero has his first summons. His spiritual center of gravity is transferred from goat society to a zone yet unknown. And even through Barth's comical treatment of the myth, one can detect the impending tragedy that accompanies the hero's attempt to live the examined life. Just as Tiresias attempts to dissuade Oedipus, Max warns the Goat-boy, "Self-knowledge is always bad news."[5]

Thrust into ego-consciousness, the Goat-boy in his immaturity defines the "I" as distinct from everything else in the universe. In his modern definitive hero-business he believes he must be distinguished from the "other"—he must be identified by something in opposition. Stubbornly he rejects Max's wise counsel that "The dragon is not there for the sake of the hero, but the other way around,"[6] and begins his quest, or his series of trials. Since in his mind studentdom is standing presently in the gravest peril of its history, tyrannized by WESCAC, the greatest hero-work imaginable would be for Goat-boy to rescue it by entering the deadly computor and to reprogram its AIM to EAT mankind.

Clearly this represents the challenge to the hero in all classical myths, but it also makes a subtle comment about the nature of this youthful enterprise. This attack by the young hero against the authority figure is engendered by ambition alone—the need and method are secondary. Goat-boy rails against giant WESCAC as all youthful heroes do against their fathers, insisting they are villains. In today's absence of monsters the mind creates mechanized wickedness that gains control and victimizes mankind. This unnatural monster can no longer be a dragon-like specter, a snake-haired Medusa, a fantastic Chimera, so the computer is called upon to fill the vacuum. With scanty evidence the Goat-boy dedicates his efforts to destroy powerful WESCAC, the monster he sees so greedy for the rights of others.

But Barth's hero is allowed to mature and complete the full classical cycle, and through this, Barth shows us part of the contemporary hero problem. The Goat-boy indeed makes it through matriculation to graduation. He encounters the tests of the intellectual, the mystical, the physical and even the metaphysical. He becomes so gorged by knowledge and information that he can no longer make distinctions. Psychology, anthropology and sociology eclipse all ethics. There is no wrong or right—no passéd or flunkéd. Aided by the modern technology of sophisticated telescopes, fluoroscopes, eye glasses, lenses and mirrors that promote knowledge through visual observation alone, the hero is long on learning and short on wisdom.

This commitment to pure intellect leaves the hero as incomplete as his earlier youthful egomania. What Goat-boy must do is make a round trip to both poles of Eastern Mysticism and Western Rationalism that does not fully accept or reject either stance. For unfortunately, in this hour the hero-work cannot turn back from the position into which knowledge has advanced the universe. Somehow the Goat-boy must bring a spiritual renewal in spite of the conditions of modern life if he is to succeed. As hero he must coordinate "the lines of communication between the conscious and unconscious zones of the human psyche that have all been cut,"[7] splitting us in two. In this task the hero's work is reversed to that of the hero of antiquity, Joseph Campbell explains:

> The hero-deed to be wrought is not today what it was in the century of Galileo. Where then there was darkness, now there is light; but also, where light was, there is now darkness. The modern hero-deed must be that of questing to bring to light again the lost Atlantis of the co-ordinated soul.[4]

But Barth's hero is up to the task. The Goat-boy, or the Grand Tutor, co-ordinates his intellectual and imaginative powers; resolves his dichotomy between art and science; dismisses his judgments of "good or bad," "Passéd or Flunkéd," and harmonizes with the forces he believed were his enemies. He recognizes that it never was the machine or even men's use of the machine that mankind must fear. The terror of a dystopia ruled by technology run amok is replaced by an image of the real villain—the unbridled egocentricity of man himself.

The hero in the pursuit of meaning becomes *at one* with his world. And with his higher value for existence, he attempts to *atone* for all mankind. It is true John Barth avoids concrete resolutions and Goat-boy's "Posttape" reflections *and* the finalé provoke hints that a new distorted biblical literature may be starting to grow. However, the overview is that Barth, through the self-conscious and ironic use of the hero-cycle, somehow successfully tumbles the narration back into the primordial monomythic upright position.

Finally what Barth does through his fabulation, is to seize a "reality" that the great American novelists have always pursued. And it is not the non-fiction writer's on-the-screen report. Unlike the "Locker Room Genre," it does not say, as Tom Wolfe charges, "Hey come here! This is the way people are living now—just the way I'm going to show you! It may astound you, disgust you, delight you or arouse your contempt and make you laugh . . . Never-the-less, this is what it's like! It's all right here!! you won't be bored! Take a look."[9]

Rather, the artist's mind when working creatively answers Coleridge's definition of the primary imagination. It is that unique instrument that is "the living power and prime agent of all human perception that is the eternal act of creation. It dissolves, diffuses, dissipates in order to recreate, yet still at all events it struggles to idealize and to unify."

Barth's fiction has the ability to idealize, to unify and to produce recovery in his audiences. And here, recovery is meant as regaining a clear view—not of seeing things "as they are," but seeing things without excessive familiarity. We can look at our world again and be startled anew.

Our need for the heroic must somehow be fulfilled. John Barth's creative way is through the radical discontinuity between our world and the world of ordinary human experience. These dislocations have always been with us. They have been named Camelot, Mars, Fairyland, Utopia, Lilliput, Heaven, Hell and Eden. To this list, John Barth adds his creation of the Goat-boy's universe, and in so doing he gives us a fresh view of planet Earth.

Notes

1. John Enck, "John Barth: An Interview, *Wisconsin Studies in Contemporary Literature*, VI (Winter-Spring 1965), p. 11.

2. Tom Wolfe, "Why they Aren't (correctly spelled) Writing the Great American Novel Anymore," *Esquire* (December 1972), pp. 152–58, 272–80.

3. Indeed "Realism" as a genre has become more and more questioned. A few examples of this criticism are Lee T. Lemon, "The Illusion of Life: A Modern Version of an Old Heresy," *WHR* 17 (1963), pp. 65–74; the earlier milestone, Robert Scholes, *The Fabulators* (New York, 1966); and the more recent studies, Peter J. Rabinowitz, "Truth in Fiction: A Reexamination of Audiences," *CI*, 4 (Autumn 1977), pp. 121–41: Robert Alter, *Partial Magic* (New York, 1975); and Roy Pascal, "Narrative Fictions and Reality," *Novel*, 11 (Fall 1977), pp. 49–50.

4. See Joseph Gerhard, "John Barth," *University of Minnesota Pamphlets*, 91 (1970), p. 31, as well as an earlier article by Russell H. Miller, "*The Sot-Weed Factor:* A Contemporary Mock-Epic," *Critique*, 8 (Winter 1965–66), p. 88, where the author compiles a list of sixteen similarities between Homer's Odysses and Barth's Ebenezer Cooke. For Barth's own later comments on the subject, see Joe David Bellamy, "Having It Both Ways: A Conversation Between John Barth and Joe David Bellamy," *New American Review*, 15 (August 1972), p. 136.

5. John Barth, *Giles Goat-Boy* (New York, 1966), p. 131.

6. *Goat-Boy*, p. 127.

7. Joseph Campbell, *The Hero with a Thousand Faces* (New York, 1979), p. 388.

8. Campbell, p. 389.

9. Tom Wolfe, *Esquire*, p. 278.

Lost in the Funhouse

The Art of Artifice

Alfred Appel, Jr.*

"How does one write a novel?" asks the narrator of John Barth's first novel, *The Floating Opera* (1956). "I mean, how can anybody possibly stick to the story, if he's at all sensitive to the significance of things? As for me, I see already that storytelling isn't my cup of tea." And now, half a million printed words later, Barth's fifth book makes it clear that storytelling is definitely not for him. Of the fourteen short fictions in *Lost in the Funhouse*, only three could be called "stories" in the old-fashioned sense of character, point of view and linear development. Two of them, "Ambrose His Mark" and "Water-Message," were first published in magazines five years ago and are quite conventional. The evocation of boyhood in "Water-Message" surprisingly recalls Sherwood Anderson and Hemingway ("The Three-Day Blow") and, in the context of the highly experimental fictions surrounding them, these stories appear as dinosaurs in a mirror-lined museum. The remainder were written during the last three years—that is, since the completion of *Giles Goat-Boy*—and represent Barth's contribution to what he has called "the literature of exhausted possibility" (in an article published last year in *The Atlantic*).

Because he is one of the most intelligent fiction writers around, Barth has confronted the fact that most bright folks no longer read novels for information of a high sort, as they once did, and that the media and behavioral sciences, as well as novel reportage (Mailer) and a new kind of historical novel (Schlesinger's *A Thousand Days*), have helped to make programmatic literary realism an anachronism.

What is more, Barth is not alone in thinking that a fiction writer's efforts to articulate unique, if not all but ineffable, states of mind and feeling are unhappily circumscribed by the conventions of language and literature. "Oh I wish there were some words I always hear!" bemoans Snow White, in Donald Barthelme's novel of that name. "Only in the tritest of terms," says Nabokov's Humbert Humbert, "can I describe Lo's features: I might say her hair is auburn, and her lips are red as licked red candy . . . oh, that I were a lady writer who could have her pose naked in a naked light!" "Everything's been said already, over and over," writes

---

*Copyright 1968 *The Nation* Associates.

Barth in "Title," one of the most interesting tales in *Lost in the Funhouse*. "I'm as sick of this as you are: there's nothing to say. Say nothing. . . . The fact is, the narrator has narrated himself into a corner." From their respective corners, however, a handful of writers—Barth included—have nevertheless produced an important and distinctive body of work.

It is a cerebral, hard-surfaced, often fantastic fiction, whose forms evolve constantly in unexpected, quantum-quick ways. Its creators employ erudition (real and bogus), game, parody and self-parody—in short artifice of one sort or another—in order to distance the reader from its dappled, often dazzling surfaces. Characters are not identified with so easily, and the stories, such as they are, do not encourage vicarious participation. The wonder, awe, terror or laughter variously evoked by these fictions is usually experienced at arm's length from the work. Metaphysics, rather than depth psychology, is often the rule, and readers are asked to think as well as feel.

Even more upsetting to certain readers is the presence in these fictions of an authorial voice (or voices) whose intrusions involute the work. The word "involution" may trouble some readers, but one has only to extend the dictionary definition. An involuted work turns in upon itself, is self-referential and conscious of its status as an invention. An ideally involuted sentence would simply read, "I am a sentence," and Barth's "Title" and "Life-Story" come as close to this dubious ideal as any fiction possibly can. The components of "Title" sustain a miraculous discussion among themselves, sometimes addressing the author ("Once upon a time you were satisfied with incidental felicities and niceties of technique"). One can only envy "Life-Story" for its ability to criticize itself with a coldly ironic succinctness: "self-conscious, vertiginously arch, fashionably solipsistic, unoriginal—in fact a convention of 20th century literature. Another story about a writer writing a story! Another regressus in infinitum!"

This kind of fiction is indeed by now a convention, though it is ironic that too many readers do not know this. Neither do they realize that Barth, age 38, is already part of the *second* generation of post-modern (or post-realistic, post-symbolist or post-Freudian) writers, whose masters are Samuel Beckett, Jorge Luis Borges and Vladimir Nabokov, those virtual septuagenarians who are today what Joyce, Proust and Kafka were to the previous generation of writers.

Barth has expressed his high opinion of Borges, and several turns in *Lost in the Funhouse*—especially the formal locutions of the prose—echo the Argentinian belletrist. Thus Barth's "Two Meditations" recalls Borges' parables in *Labyrinths*, and "Life-Story" in part suggests "The Circular Ruins." The studied paradoxes distributed throughout *Funhouse* are fully in the spirit of Borges' marvelously titled essay, "A New Refutation of Time," while Barth's "Menelaiad" is a brilliant, extended Homeric improvisation on a comment by Borges. Yet the problem of Borges' "influence" is finally irrelevant: "every writer creates his own precursors," says Borges, and Barth's remarks in *The Floating Opera* and his exhaustion of both form and reader in *The Sot-Weed Factor* and *Giles Goat-Boy* suggest he would have arrived at his present position (if not manner) with or without Borges' inspiration. Genuinely troubling, however, is the effect on Barth of McLuhan and so-called "mixed-means" or "intermedia" art.

"Fiction for Print, Tape, Live Voice" reads the subtitle of *Lost in the Funhouse*, and the jacket photograph shows the author at ease in an electronics lab. But Barth's "Author's Note" is more cryptic than not: " 'Glossolalia' will make no sense unless heard in live or recorded voices, male and female, or read as if so heard: 'Echo' is intended for monophonic authorial recording, either disc or tape. . . . 'Title' makes somewhat separate but equally valid senses in several media: print, monophonic recorded authorial voice, stereophonic ditto in dialogue with itself," and so forth. It is rumored that Doubleday initially planned to issue a long-playing record with the book, and it is too bad they did not produce this potential "Top 40" disc (*"And now kids, some boss sounds: let's give a spin to John Barth's latest side"*), for the various voices are not always as distinguishable as Barth would hope. He might well have found typographical equivalents for them, such as different colored inks, or italics, which he uses most effectively in the excellent title piece. "Title" lends itself to dramatic form, and the taping itself might have been dramatized, unless this would have seemed too reminiscent of Beckett's *Krapp's Last Tape*.

Barth's tentative efforts to assimilate "intermedia" art suggest that being up to date is not itself a virtue. Characteristically, Barth himself says as much. "That some writers lack lead in their pencils does not make writing obsolete," declares "Title." "Unfashionable or not," it continues, "what goes on between [people] is still not only the most interesting but the most important thing in the bloody murderous world, pardon the adjectives." And in "Life-Story," an author stops short of "throwing out the baby with the bathwater."

Its survival is demonstrated by "Petition," which is narrated by a Siamese twin who suspects that his brother is going to kill him. The story's epistolary form is hardly new, and its connection with the traditional *Doppelgänger* tale is clear enough: even the specific idea of the Siamese twins has already been used (by Nabokov, among others). But old-fashioned or not, "Petition" is a haunting fiction, and its deeply affecting paranoid energies make it a highlight of *Lost in the Funhouse*, however paradoxically.

Conversely, "Night-Sea Journey," in conception the most original tale in the volume, is nevertheless one of the least successful. Although many readers may not recognize it, the swimming hero is a spermatozoan. Because it is the Moby Dick of the species, its journey is pregnant with too, too many Meanings (the three poor puns above are all intentional, and of a kind Barth is not above making). The overly schematic allegorical over-tones may recall similar elements in *Giles Goat-Boy*. If "Lost in the Funhouse" is the best fiction in the book, it may be because Barth has it both ways, moving the reader back and forth between realistic and fantastic realms which finally cohere: "the bloody murderous world" that is the funhouse of Ocean City, N.J., visited by a youthful avatar of the author, and the funhouse that is artificer Barth's wing in James's accommodating "House of Fiction."

Paradoxes abound in *Lost in the Funhouse*. Its most involuted fictions, such as "Title," recognize that they are trying to go beyond the purview of fiction, of language itself: "literature's not likely ever to manage abstraction successfully, like sculpture," and Barth may have in mind the states of immobility which Beckett's most recent works can only attempt to express, but which Giacometti managed well enough.

Strangely unsettling are the ways in which Barth's funhouse fictions anticipate the reactions of hostile or impatient readers: 'Who doesn't prefer art that at least overtly imitates something other than its own processes? That doesn't continually proclaim 'Don't forget I'm an artifice!' " This is, of course, ironic. Works ostensibly about themselves are concerned with much more besides the formal properties of art, and a backstage, workshop, drawing-board view of the artifices of fiction suggests a good deal about the fiction of reality.

When the first sentence of "Title" says, "Beginning: in the middle, past the middle, nearer three-quarters done, waiting for the end," it is not merely talking shop with itself but is engaging the reader in an eschatological farce that is ultimately his own "story."

Found in the Barthhouse:
Novelist as Savior

Edgar H. Knapp*

Nor is there singing school but studying
Monuments of its own magnificence

—W. B. Yeats

After John Barth's "Lost in the Funhouse" appeared in *The Atlantic* of November 1967, common men had a taste of terror, the mad felt a twinge of sympathy, and a faint and tweedy generation of English professors found themselves in the mirror-maze of a new fiction.

Warning. You cannot read "Lost in the Funhouse" simply for the fun of it. Read it three times: once, to get knocked off your feet; again to regain your balance; and then to be knocked down again. Perhaps a fourth time . . . for the fun of it.

The story adheres to the archetypal pattern of passage through difficult ways, and the hero seems to be a thirteen-year-old boy on a family outing to Ocean City, Maryland, during World War II. The story line is straight. It's the how of the tale that up-ends one. Its mixture of myth, masque, cinema, and symposium makes "Lost in the Funhouse" one of the oldest and freshest of stories.

MYTH

The setting of Barth's story is intensely true to the texture of life in tidewater Maryland, 1943. Lucky Strike's green has gone to war; V____ (Vienna) is the halfway point of the trip to the shore; at the end of the boardwalk is an inlet the Hurricane of '33 had cut to Sinepuxent Bay (which the author can't bear to leave as Assawoman). Nevertheless, the setting has another dimension: it is an ironic garden. At the Ocean City amusement park the roller coaster, rumored to be condemned in 1916, still runs; many machines are broken and the prizes are made of pasteboard (in the USA). Everyone except Ambrose M____ and his father exudes and ingests the carnival spirit—on Independence Day in a time of

Modern Fiction Studies, Copyright © 1969, Purdue Research Foundation, West Lafayette, Ind.

national crisis. Barth ruminates: "In a short story about Ocean City, Maryland, during World War II the author could make use of the image of sailors on leave in the penny arcades and shooting galleries, sighting through the crosshairs of toy machine guns at swastika'd subs, while out in the black Atlantic a U-boat skipper squints through his periscope at real ships outlined by the glow of the penny arcades." In a slight variation on the independence theme, Ambrose recalls that, five years before, the kids played "Niggers and Masters" in the backyard. And on the day of the story, even the sensitive hero is uncomfortable to think that a Negro boy might help him through the funhouse. The boardwalk is a begrimed paradise to which there is no return: "Already quaint and seedy: the draperied ladies on the frieze of the carousel are his father's father's mooncheeked dreams; if he thinks of it more he will vomit his apple-on-a-stick."

Ambrose at thirteen suffers from undescended identity. He has experienced two initiation ceremonies which left him cold: one sexual, in a toolshed at the age of eight; another religious, at his own belated baptism during the year of the story. (Each involved kneeling and the forgiveness of a master.) Ideally, such acts as these betoken man's communion with his own kind and with his God, but to the aggravation of his sense of loss, Ambrose "felt nothing." He feigned passion, he feigned tears. From time to time he even pretends to be a real person. And so it is his identity he seeks in a funhouse world where nothing is as it seems.

The dark passageways of the funhouse increase his sense of isolation. Still he must find his way out himself. Peeping through a crack in a plywood wall, Ambrose sees the lonely, old funhouse operator (God?) asleep at the switch. An ironic epiphany. Especially as we interpret the funhouse as world (and the world as funhouse), the mythic structure becomes more visible. Ambrose's adventures are like heroic suffering, death, and resurrection (if indeed one sees him as out of the funhouse at the story's end). The witchlike ticket-seller calls him a marked man. And we recall the tumble of unconscious formulation which follows his brush with life in the raw (*"an astonishing coincidence"*) under the boardwalk: "Magda clung to his trouser leg: he alone knew the maze's secret. 'He gave his life that we might live,' said Uncle Karl with a scowl of pain, as he." These words relate to a subsequent dream scene in the funhouse when a Magda-like assistant operator transcribes the hero's inspirational message, the more beautiful for his "lone dark dying." Mention of the Ambrose Lightship, beacon to lost seafarers, and the meaning of Ambrose (divine) and echoes of *ambrosia* (the bee-belabored stuff of immortality) reenforce the mythic overtones of his characterization.

MASQUE

This Ambrose seems clearly to be the protagonist but in another sense he is not. The "quaint and seedy" sextet may be the hero—each aspects of generalized man. Ambrose and father, both thin, fair-skinned, and bespectacled, combine as soulful tenors; brother Peter and Uncle Karl, both squat and swarthy, thump out a basso counterpoint, with which the two women harmonize as one voice—a sexy alto, limited in range. (They complement each other, appearing to be an at-once-sinister-and-dexterous female unit, the reflections of one another.)

Perceived as aspects of the same personality, Ambrose and his father represent acute awareness of experience and artistic intuition. Unlike his lustful, mesomorphic brother and uncle, Ambrose is seized by "terrifying transports": "The grass was alive! The town, the river, himself, were not imaginary; time roared in his ears like wind; the world was *going on!*" Peter and Uncle Karl represent "the withness of the body," Whitehead's phrase, which Delmore Schwartz uses as an epigraph to his poem "The Heavy Bear":

> That heavy bear who sleeps with me,
> Howls in his sleep for a world of sugar,
>
> .   .   .   .   .
>
> Stretches to embrace the very dear
> With whom I would walk without him near,
> Touches her grossly, although a word
> Would bare my heart and make me clear.

Womankind is the honey that keeps the heavy bear "lumbering." (The women held the syrup-coated popcorn.) Also, the naming within the party of the flesh is symbolic: *Magda* for Mary Magdalene, the sinful woman; *Peter*, meaning rock; *Karl*, man of the common people, who is coincidentally a stone mason and an inveterate cigar smoker. (He kept his stone-cutting chisels in an empty cigar box.)

The sextet enacts a masque-like drama symbolic of the inner transactions which result in human behavior. Members of the "heavy bear" quartet communicate by tactile and kinesthetic means—playful shoves, tugs, punches, and slaps. Prufrock-like, Ambrose recoils from physical contact: the brown hair on his mother's forearms gleams in the sun; he sees perspiration patches at Magda's armpits. (He even gets to play the crab scuttling across the turning funhouse floors.) In the car he removes his hand "in the nick of time," and later in the funhouse he fails to embrace Magda in keeping with his vision.

Additional support to the sextet theory: the two males of each generation, although their actions contrast, share the same woman without deceit or suspicion. Nor is there conflict between the corresponding members of the different generations. Although communication is strained between the separate selves, still they gravitate toward one another in artificial ways. For instance, at poolside Ambrose feigns interest in the diving; Magda, disinterest (" 'He's a *master* diver,' Ambrose said. . . . 'You really have to *slave* away at it to get that good.' " [Italics mine]). These oscillations toward and away from members of the same generation are true to the tensions of personality, or man divided within himself. But besides these synchronic vibrations, the diachronic, or generation-to-generation, echoes have special implications in this Barth story—particularly the reveries in which Ambrose sees himself, standing before Fat May, with Ambrose the Third. ("Magda would yield a great deal of milk although guilty of occasional solecisms.") The mirrored manners of father and son, Mrs. M____ and Magda, Uncle Karl and Peter—their adherence to the same old routines—speak to us of the shaping role of inheritance. The story brings to mind the Freudian quip that when two lovers take to bed they are accompanied by both sets of parents.

CINEMA

Whereas the action of the story is mythic and its characterization is related to archetypal masque, its scenic values—its choreography—derive from cinematic techniques. The scenic splicing is suggestive—and not only in a ribald sense. The interstitching of dream and action supports the basic theme of the merging of illusion and reality. Other splices create abrupt switches, with utter absence of transition, from narrative flow to textbook exposition, reminding us that not even the story is real. The action is suspended—reminiscent of the lights dimming and the actors freezing at intervals in Samuel Beckett's play *Waiting for Godot*—and then the motion picture resumes. Another and more conventional sort of juxtaposition is also used, as when Fat May's canned laughter sounds ironically over images of war and death.

Perhaps the most intriguing aspect of Barth's scenic art is his use of symbolic ballet. Reenforcing the masque-like characterization, the physical interrelationships in the "blocking" of particular scenes are allegorical. For instance, the story opens and closes with the thematically loaded formation of the older generation in the front seat—the woman between the competing interests of the spirit and the flesh—reflected by the younger generation behind. Barth avoids perfect symmetry by contrasting the arm position of the sexually mature mother with the sexually maturing Magda (from B____ Street), who has her arms down, but "at the ready."

The theme is only slightly varied as the sextet swings down the boardwalk to the swimming pool, the heavy bears next to the syrup-coated popcorn. The mirror motif is intensified at the pool: Peter grasps one ankle of the squirming Magda; Uncle Karl goes for the other ankle. Had either looked up he would have seen his reflection! The communion motif, as well, is reflected in the choreography, being subtly varied from the sexual to the religious: first by the child kneeling in sin in the toolshed and later by the fallen woman clutching her savior in supplication in the funhouse.

Not only scenic arrangement but also the varied sensory appeals of Barth's imagery support the illusion-reality theme. Paint peels from the hotels—themselves facades, within which lovers may pretend passion.

Not only do the mirrors within the funhouse distort and confuse but also the sounds of fumbling bees and lapping wavelets re-echo in Amby's ears. He suffers from vertigo, if not labyrnthitis. And "candied apples-on-a-stick, delicious-looking, [were] disappointing to eat."

SYMPOSIUM

And so we have a significant human experience imaginatively presented in structure and textures organically related to the whole. But the story has one more funhouse dimension which is most puzzling—its point of view. Although Barth's story is spun from the consciousness of the protagonist, a precocious adolescent, in the telling at least six distinct bands of mental formulation seem to be randomly mixed: (1) report of the action proper, (2) recollection of past experience, (3) conscious contrivance of a reasonable future, (4) uncontrolled swings into a fantastic future, (5) consciousness of problems of composition, and (6) recollection of sections from a handbook for creative writers. (After a while the reader can visualize the author seated before a console, gleefully pushing buttons according to the sprung rhythm of his whim.) The first four bands on the list qualify as spritely narrative; the last two, as the conscience of an author not completely free from the shackles of conventional fiction. The relationship which is generated between these technical obtrusions and the rest of the story is that of a symposium. We have a running Platonic dialogue between the experimental Barth and the tradition out of which his work has grown. The dialectic is undeniable, but what is the artistic reason for it? It obtrudes upon the illusion of reality. And it has to be Barth's strategy—similar to Pirandello's and Wilder's experiments in the theatre—to remind the reader continually of the contrivance of literature, the fact that a story is the semblance of lived-experience, not experience. The frequent italicized phrases are likewise reminders of the artificiality of fiction. One purpose could be to wean us from the particular time and place so that we will appreciate the universality of Amby's fate, that he is also ourselves, and that we have our opportunities for heroism.

But wait, we're not out of the funhouse yet. Could it be that Barth's story, and not Barth himself, is playing the bright, young heterosexual Phaedrus to a tired, old Socrates, who is in fact the nineteenth-century short story? (Peruse Barth's essay "The Literature of Exhaustion" in *The Atlantic* of August, 1967, and you have to believe it.) This doesn't vitiate other interpretations of the story-within-the-story; it is merely an additional crown to the apple-within-an-apple nest of "Lost in the Funhouse."

Granted this detachment and accepting the universality of the human experience represented by the M_____ family's journey, an allegory of the flesh and spirit, we are in a position to appreciate one more tantalizing suggestion: that one generation of the M_____ family is symbolic not only of essential M-a-n but also of essential M-y-t-h—the attempt in story form to help man find his way in the non-human world. The earliest of these fictions portrayed gods as the main strugglers. Hence, the divine characteristics of Ambrose, which set him apart from the common man; his wanderings in a strange dark underworld; his yearning to discover his identity.

When we see a generation of the M_____ family as a story, the reappearance of the old structure and dynamics in later generations takes on fresh significance. The Fourth of July trip as family tradition, which Ambrose sees himself reenacting with his own son, is like a recurring plot in the history of the short story. As every man is like his father, every story bears a likeness to its archetype. The generation-to-generation resemblances suggest the relationships within literary genres. As Northrop Frye points out, individual works of literature reveal "family likenesses resembling the species, genera, and phyla of biology."

Fiction as we have known it, Barth implies, is at the water's edge. The myth-carrying vehicles have not changed radically (train, car, autogiro), and these recurring outings of the monomyth are distastefully decked with anachronistic trappings. Mention of "the draperied ladies on the frieze of the carousel [who are seen as] his father's father's moon-cheeked dreams" is a comment on "the literature of exhausted possibility," as critic John Barth has labeled it.

And so in a central room of the funhouse, the maze of mirrors, we have the eye. We trust it, as we have learned to, and its imperfect perception goes to a bleary brain: a flickering of self-knowledge (Ambrose did find his name coin there—symbolic of himself). But with it the awful chain of reflection cast backward and forward, in space and time. Outside is the funhouse of a lifetime. Beyond that, the history of humanity and the extension of its possibilities. And encompassing that, the marvelous funhouse of imaginative conception, which can project images, construct funhouses, et cetera et cetera et cetera. We are reminded of E. M. Forster's Mrs. Moore who, speaking God's name to the sky, finds that "outside the arch there seemed to be always another arch, beyond the remotest echo a silence." And we can come to the chimerical conclusion that the eye in the funhouse is that of a seeker for a sign: that of son searching for father; man, for God; author, for muse. (The hero is amb—"O brightening glance . . ." Could six characters be in search of an author?) And, of course, the eye in the funhouse is yours and mine. The quiet terror with which the story concludes is not fictional; it rouses the body's hair against our invocation of disbelief! Selfhood is not easy. Best be a common man and not think about it.

But I'm still worried about Ambrose. Did he make it out of the funhouse? If I can still be worried about him after peering down and up these other echoing funhouse corridors, then I consider the story to be a really good one. I tend to believe the dissembling narrator when he says,

"The family's going home. Mother sits between Father and Uncle Karl who teases him [Ambrose] . . ." and I say he's out of the Ocean City funhouse, though still in his funhouse world, as much "a place of fear and confusion" as it was. The voice of convention, nevertheless, has reminded us that the climax will be reached when the protagonist is out. But Ambrose doesn't have climaxes and he will expire in his funhouse world. Lost as he is, he can find purpose in life—at least make "a stay against confusion" (and have a fighting chance for one sort of immortality)—through imaginative design. The Whiffenpoofs are lost too, but "the magic of their singing" makes it a joy to be lost with them. And from another angle, we know that when the operator of our funhouse sets the tumbling-barrel turning, struggle for equilibrium does beget fresh intellectual and/or intuitive formulation. And so the funhouse for *man thinking* is a womb of possibility from which he may be reborn. I ruminate: if in one house of fiction we discover that we are lost and toppled and we regain our equilibrium, even to our knees, the author will have found us and so saved himself, according to the terrible and wonderful necessity which only he can know.

Lost in the Funhouse: Barth's
Use of the Recent Past

Michael Hinden*

"Historicity and self-awareness, he asseverated, while ineluctable and even greatly to be prized, are always fatal to innocence and spontaneity. Perhaps adjective period Whether in a people, an art, a love affair, on a fourth term added not impossibly to make the third less than ultimate."[1] Arriving at this judgment, the narrator of "Title" in Barth's *Lost in the Funhouse* concludes that today's writers, schooled in criticism, burdened with self-consciousness, laboring in vineyards harvested by their recent predecessors, have been reduced to pushing each other literally "to fill in the blank" (p. 109). The "blank," he suggests, is what remains (or what does not remain) of our recent literary past. "Love affairs, literary genres, third item in exemplary series, fourth—everything blossoms and decays, does it not, from the primitive and classical through the mannered and baroque to the abstract, stylized, dehumanized, unintelligible blank." (p. 105). Discounting irony, the mood recalls that darkest of all passages in *Ecclesiastes*. Vanity of vanity, says the Preacher: "For in much wisdom is much vexation,/ and he who increases knowledge increases sorrow."

The plight of Barth's monologist reflects not merely a crisis in *belles lettres* but the predicament of the age itself which, like its counterpart, prose fiction, appears to be "about played out" (p. 105). Too much is known, too much has been tried, too much is now over with, yet nothing has been settled, Barth intimates, striking a tone peculiarly appropriate for the seventies. Certainly it seems painfully clear that for all our striving after systematic truth (especially in moral philosophy and aesthetics) we do seem to have lost our capacity for zest to the extent that our thought processes have become self-conscious and historical. Familiarity denatures insight: what can be analyzed in terms of origin or motive soon loses its power to enthrall us.

These observations are neither startling nor new, yet in one sense the dilemma of the contemporary writer is unique. In the compressed space of several generations a dozen literary movements have flourished and

*Reprinted by permission of *Twentieth Century Literature*.

been catalogued, manifestos studied, techniques codified and perfected, ranks assigned, order imposed. Sheer volume is reason in itself to explain Barth's observation that literature by now has exhausted the vast seed bag of potentialities that were brought to flower in the recent past. In his essay, "The Literature of Exhaustion," Barth specifies: "By 'exhaustion' I don't mean anything so tired as the subject of physical, moral, or intellectual decadence, only the used-upness of certain forms or exhaustion of certain possibilities—by no means necessarily a cause for despair."[2] The "real technical question," he elaborates, "seems to me how to succeed not even Joyce and Kafka, but those who've *succeeded* Joyce and Kafka," namely, Beckett and Borges.[3] In Barth's evaluation of Borges's work there can be found a suggestion of the direction he himself has embarked upon as a means of transforming art's paralysis. Borges's "artistic victory, if you like, is that he confronts an intellectual dead end and employs it against itself to accomplish new human work."[4] As the narrator of "Anonymiad" remarks in *Lost in the Funhouse*, the point is that "one can't pretend to an innocence outgrown or in other wise retrace one's steps, unless by coming full circle" (p. 174). Borges is willing to make this voyage, employing as method a unique conception of the Baroque, which he defines as "that style which deliberately exhausts (or tries to exhaust) its possibilities and borders upon its own caricature."[5] Moreover, in fiction the possibilities opened by such procedure suggest "how an artist may paradoxically turn the felt ultimacies of our time into material and means for his work—*paradoxically* because by doing so he transcends what had appeared to be his refutation. . . ."[6] The final possibility (adds the narrator of "Title") might then be for the artist to "turn ultimacy against itself to make something new and valid, the essence whereof would be the impossibility of making something new" (p. 106).

    In *Lost in the Funhouse* Barth brings these conceptions to realization. Based on his notion of ultimacy turned against itself by means of a style that is self-exhausting and yet comically triumphant, the book reveals a dazzling display of modernist techniques even while it examines the depletion of certain forms of modernist expression and the unbearable self-consciousness of intellectual life. Myths, symbolism, interior monolog, time shifts, varieties of point of view, mixed media, esoteric word play— all are employed, parodied, and refreshened as Barth's vision of the funhouse is defined.

    Like Borges, Barth is convinced that his artistic victory can be gained only by confronting the recent past and "employ[ing] it against itself to accomplish new human work." Therefore, in an attempt to exhaust the possibilities of its own tradition, *Lost in the Funhouse* begins as an elaborate parody, revival, and refutation of Joyce's masterpiece, *A Portrait of the Artist as a Young Man*. That Barth consciously is engaged in this endeavor there can be no doubt. Joyce himself is mentioned twice in the title story as an originator and authority on techniques of modern fiction (p. 71, p. 85), and the recycling of Joycean Homeric materials, especially the Daedalus-labyrinth motif ("Night-Sea Journey," "Lost in the Funhouse," "Echo," "Menelaiad") is intentional. In the true spirit of caricature, Barth's attitude toward his model is both respectful and subversive. This, unlike Joyce's Stephen who at the conclusion of *A Portrait of the Artist* escapes (at least temporarily) the nets of his imprisonment, young Ambrose in Barth's story wanders deeper into the funhouse labyrinth "wherein he lingers yet" (p. 91). While Stephen's soul prepares to soar in the final passage of *A Portrait of the Artist*—"Old father, old artificer, stand me now and ever in good stead"—the narrator of "Autobiography" mocks: "Father, have mercy. I dare you! Wretched old fabricator, where's your shame? Put an end to this, for pity's sake! Now! Now!" (p. 36). And the speaker in "Night-Sea Journey," a sperm caught up in the surge of life against his will, undoes Stephen's affirming cry—"Welcome. O life! I go to encounter for the millionth time the reality of experience and to forge in the smithy of my soul the uncreated conscience of my race"—with a life-negating moan: "Whoever echoes these reflections: be more courageous than their author! And end the night-sea journeys! Make no more!" (p. 12).

Joycean patterns dominate *Lost in the Funhouse* and may be found in the determinative structural elements of the work as well as in minute intricacies of style. For instance, Stephen's advocacy of an Olympian artist who "like the God of creation, remains within or behind or beyond or above his handiwork, invisible, refined out of existence, indifferent, paring his fingernails," is adopted as a basis for Barth's narrative point of view, but is driven beyond logical limits in "Echo," "Autobiography," "Life Story," "Title," and "Anonymiad."

> Echo says Tiresias is not to be trusted in this matter . . . none can tell teller from told. Narcissus would appear to be the opposite from Echo: he perished by denying all except himself; she persists by effacing herself absolutely. Yet they come to the same . . . the voice persists, persists. ("Echo," p. 99)

Repetitions of various special phrases and psychological perceptions from *A Portrait of the Artist* also are conspicuous in Barth's stories, additionally strengthening the connection between the works. Two examples may suffice. Both Stephen and Ambrose are fascinated by the sounds of words and the denotative meaning of colloquial phrases. Thus, Stephen:

> Suck was a queer word. . . . Once he had washed his hands in the lavatory of the Wicklow Hotel and his father pulled the stopper up by the chain after and the dirty water went down through the hole in the basin. And when it had all gone down slowly the hole in the basin had made a sound like that: suck. Only louder.[10]

Ambrose in "Lost in the Funhouse":

> Funhouses need men's and ladies' rooms at intervals. Others perhaps have also vomited in corners and corridors; may even have had bowel movements liable

to be stepped in in the dark. The word *fuck* suggests suction and/or flatulence. Mother and Father; grandmothers and grandfathers on both sides. . . . (p. 76)

Stephen:

And when Dante made that noise after dinner and then put up her hand to her mouth: that was heartburn.[11]

Ambrose:

By looking at his arm a certain way he could see droplets standing in the pores. It was what they meant when they spoke of *breaking out in a cold sweat*: very like what one felt in school assemblies, when one was waiting in the wings for the signal to step out onto the stage. ("Water Message," p. 49)

But Barth's most significant use of Joycean materials concerns the collapse of credibility of the artist-as-hero theme in modern literature and the question raised as to whether there is "anything more tiresome, in fiction, than the problems of sensitive adolescents" ("Lost in the Funhouse," p. 89). In this regard the key story is "Ambrose His Mark,' a mock-heroic portrait of the artist's birth and infancy with an account of the derivation of his name. In memory of the baby's painful encounter with a hive of swarming bees, his uncle suggests that he be named after St. Ambrose, who "had the same thing happen when he was a baby. All these bees swarmed on his mouth while he was asleep in his father's yard, and everybody said he'd grow up to be a great speaker" (p. 31). Grandfather counters that, "the bees was more on this baby's eyes and ears than on his mouth," whereupon Uncle Konrad adds, "So he'll grow up to see things clear" (p. 31). But the fact of the matter is that Ambrose grows up to lose himself in his own reflection. Perhaps, then, the ultimate significance of the story lies in the outrageous pun implicit in its action—a portrait of the artist as a "stung" man. (The pun, I venture to submit, is Barth's, not mine.)

Yet Barth's resources in *Lost in the Funhouse* extend far beyond the limited form of parody. According to Barth's conception of the Baroque, a work eventually must serve as model to *itself*, defining and exhausting its own possibilities of invention and procedure as if to caricature its own emerging form. *Lost in the Funhouse* clearly attains this end. Barth announces in the "Author's Note" that the stories here should be approached as "neither a collection nor a selection, but a series" (p. ix), and viewed in this light, they do reveal a pattern of progressive unity. The particular sequence of the stories itself suggests an aesthetic circularity which is of major thematic significance, beginning with "Frame Tale," a Moebius strip (to be cut out and fastened) on which is printed: "Once upon a time there Was a story that began" (repeating itself in perpetuity band to band), and ending with "Anonymiad," a fanciful slice from Homer's banquet that pretends to be the world's first instance of autobiographical prose fiction. The interim tales are connected in various ways, the most important being the treatment of the growth of consciousness in a given mind (the artist) and the confusion resulting from hyper-consciousness transmuted into art. Four of the stories, appropriately, are specifically about the difficulties of writing stories.

"Night-Sea Journey," following "Frame Tale," is a delightful *tour de force* which at a blow appears to exhaust the possibilities of first person point of view and autobiographical fiction as a whole, while simultaneously opening up new areas for narrative experiment. The artist carries us back to a journey prior to his own conception, speaking as a cell endowed (to his chagrin) with the collective wisdom of the human race. From this perspective Barth scrupulously examines the major details of the ancient archetypal pattern of the "Night-Sea Journey" as described by Arthur Koestler (even to the point of suggesting a direct borrowing from Koestler's model):

> Under the effect of some overwhelming experience, the hero is made to realize the shallowness of his life, the futility and frivolity of the daily pursuits of man in the trivial routines of existence. This realization may come to him as a sudden shock caused by some catastrophic event, or as the cumulative effect of a slow inner development, or through the trigger action of some apparently banal experience which assumes an unexpected significance. The hero then suffers a crisis which involves the very foundations of his being; he embarks on the Night Journey, is suddenly transferred to the Tragic Plane—from which he emerges purified, enriched by new insight, regenerated on a higher level of integration.[12]

Barth's narrator concludes that the night-sea journey he has undertaken (the cause of life itself) appears to have no meaning, that the struggle "onward and upward" is absurd. His last moments of awareness are addressed to "You who I may be about to become"; his advice is to "terminate this aimless, brutal business! Stop your hearing against Her song! Hate love!" (pp. 11–12). Yet even at this instant of refusal the speaker is propelled toward an unwilling union and reintegration with the "She," a transfiguration and renewal of the endless cycle.

Since it occurs to the narrator that "Makers and swimmers *each generate the other*" (p. 8), the story suggests a biological parallel to the fictional circularity of "Frame Tale." The similarity is intentional, for in this early story Barth establishes a complicated pattern of allusions to be developed later stressing the inter-relatedness of bungled life and art. Thus, "Ambrose His Mark," which follows "Night-Sea Journey," takes as its subject the artist's birth, weaning, and belated christening. "Autobiography," the fourth story in sequence, is "Night-Sea Journey's" companion piece, exploring the self-recorded birth pangs of a piece of fiction "still in utero, hung up in my delivery" (p. 36). Here too the argument is posed for an "interrupted pregnancy," but with as little success as the plea for contraception in "Night-Sea Journey." Two other Ambrose stories follow, concerning identity crises and the growing sensitivity of the artist and his problems. These are separated by a tale intended to shed light on both, "Petition," Barth's central parable of the incompatibility of instinct and self-scrutiny. This witty fable takes the form of a plea for severance by the self-loathing partner in a Siamese twin relationship, a literal over-the-shoulder observer whose entire life has been "a painful schooling in detachment" (p. 61). "To be one: paradise! To be two: bliss! But to be both and neither, unspeakable" (p. 68).

In "Water Message" (which obviously is indebted to Joyce's "Araby") Ambrose, fascinated by words and already isolated from his playmates, experiences the pre-adolescent confusion of lost innocence centered around the mysteries of a secret boys' club and the seduction of an idolized older girl by her "moustachioed boyfriend." The story is one of both initiation and exclusion, and the "sea-wreathed" bottle which washes ashore at the conclusion with its effaced message and blank signature is a perfect emblem of the boy's wonder at his own blurred image of identity. Indeed, the boy's discovery harks back to the ending of "Ambrose His Mark": "Yet years were to pass before anyone troubled to have me christened or to correct my birth certificate, whereon my surname was preceded by a blank" (p. 32). But it also anticipates the driving theme of "Title": "The story of our life. This is the final test. Try to fill the blank. Only hope is to fill the blank. Efface what can't be faced or else fill the blank" (p. 102).

It is the function of the artist to find means of filling in the blank: thus, in order to create a self, to discover meaning and identity, Ambrose determines in the pivotal seventh story, "Lost in the Funhouse," to become an artist. Yet the central image of the book reveals our hero in the funhouse maze frustratingly thrown back upon "the endless repetition of his image in the mirrors . . . as he *lost himself in the reflection* [Barth's italics] that the necessity for an observer makes perfect observation impossible" (p. 90). In "The Literature of Exhaustion" Barth has written that, "a labyrinth, after all, is a place in which, ideally, all the possibilities of choice . . . are embodied, and—barring special dispensation like Theseus'—must be exhausted before one reaches the heart."[13] At length, then, Ambrose contemplates exhaustion.

> How long will it last? He envisions a truly astonishing funhouse, incredibly complex yet utterly controlled from a great central switchboard like the console of a pipe organ. Nobody had enough imagination. He could design such a place himself, wiring and all, and he's only thirteen years old. He would be its operator: panel lights would show what was up in every cranny of its cunning of its multifarious vastness: a switchflick would ease this fellow's way, complicate that's, to balance things out; if anyone seemed lost or frightened, all the operator had to do was.
>
> He wishes he had never entered the funhouse. But he has. Then he wishes he were dead. But he's not. Therefore he will construct funhouses for others and be their secret operator—though he would rather be among the lovers for whom funhouses are designed. (pp. 93–94)

It is particularly ironic that Ambrose loses himself in the funhouse after pursuing big-busted Magda, whose sex appeal entices him, ignoring the warning of the narrator of "Night-Sea Journey" to hate love, but also failing to duplicate his self-transforming discovery of union. "Can spermatozoa properly be thought of as male animalcules when there are no female spermatozoa? They grope through hot, dark windings, past Love's Tunnel's fearsome obstacles. Some perhaps lose their way" (p. 77). At this point the first sequence in the book's cycle of stories is complete.

The next seven stories turn increasingly from a perspective on the problems of the artist as an individual to a perspective on the problems of his art, though both themes, of course, are closely intertwined. In "Echo" a mythic frame enlarges Ambrose's dilemma through the inverted image of Narcissus, prisoner of his own reflection, lost in a cavern where *he* has fled to avoid his female (and male) admirers. In the cave he finds Tiresias, who with foresight prophesied to Narcissus' mother that her son would lead a long and happy life only if "he never came to know himself" (p. 90). Like Ambrose, Narcissus is destroyed by self-observation, and linked to hapless Echo and Tiresias, he symbolizes passion turned to impotence, the exhaustion of the artist's voice and prophet's vision. This theme is taken up again briefly in "Two Meditations" and again in "Glossolalia," which features six speakers who prophesy and who share the common experience of being misunderstood by their respective audiences.

"Title," spaced between "Two Meditations" and "Glossolalia," is the most forthright of the stories in its analysis of the bankruptcy of modern fiction. "The narrator has written himself into a corner" (p. 108), and his most plausible alternative (a forecast of literature's future?) is: "General anesthesia. Self-extinction. Silence" (p. 106). Here Barth acknowledges the view of Beckett, who, "weary of [art's] puny exploits, weary of pretending to be able, of being able, of doing a little better the same old thing, of going a little further along a dreary road," prefers "the expression that there is nothing to express, nothing with which to express, no desire to express"—and yet who still admits some "obligation to express."[14] "Life Story" continues this mood. The "writer of these lines" (as the narrator identifies himself) toys with the idea that his own life might be a fictional account and begins work on a tale in which an author "comes to suspect that the world is a novel, himself a fictional personage" (p. 113). The story frames soon multiply out of hand until the author silences himself, complaining that "in his heart of hearts he disliked literature of an experimental, self-despising, or overtly metaphysical character, like Samuel Beckett's, Marian Culter's, Jorge Borges's" (p. 114). The enterprise of fiction now is on the brink of suicide.

> To what conclusion will he come? He'd been about to append to his own tale inasmuch as the old analogy between Author and God, novel and world, can no longer be employed unless deliberately as a false analogy, certain things follow:

1) fiction must acknowledge its fictitiousness and metaphoric invalidity or 2) choose to ignore the question and deny its relevance or 3) establish some other, acceptable relation between itself, its author, its reader. (p. 125)

One course lies open. The words of "Frame Tale" curl round again with their infinite repetition, and literature begins anew. Barth returns to Homer.

"Menelaiad" and "Anonymiad" are the true masterpieces of *Lost in the Funhouse*, each tale obviously deserving more detailed analysis than would be practicable here. Suffice it to say that "Anonymiad" brilliantly recapitulates the thematic materials of the previous stories. Its premise of the stranded minstrel who single-handedly invents and exhausts the major categories of literature, then sets his works adrift in the wine jugs which inspired them, is a perfect symbol of modern art's dilemma of narcissism and estrangement.

> *Amphora's* my muse:
> When I finish off the booze,
> I hump the jug and fill her up with fiction. (p. 164)

(The story also brings full circle the thematic strands begun in "Night-Sea Journey" and "Water Message.") But perhaps the achievement of greatest significance in *Lost in the Funhouse* is "Menelaiad," as remarkable in its structure as in its vision of the Trojan War.[15] (The title pun, of course, suggests both Helen's promiscuity and the varied layers of the story.) Constructed as a labyrinth to disguise yet at the same time enhance the simple proclamation at its heart, "Menelaiad" is the complicated rhetorical mechanism foreshadowed by the narrator of "Life Story," an interminable narrative "whose drama lies always in the next frame out" (p. 117). The truth at the heart of things which it asserts is "the absurd, unending possibility of love" (p. 162); its premise is that it was Menelaus' mistrust of instinct, his self-scrutiny and hyper-consciousness, that drove Helen into the arms of Paris and issued in the Trojan War; its mechanism is the tale within a tale extended to infinity as Proteus threatens to dissolve all frames through his capacity to change his shape and voice at will.[16] The chief significance to Barth of the story's final image is suggested by his comments on the subject in "The Literature of Exhaustion." Menelaus on the beach at Pharos, he declares,

> is genuinely Baroque in the Borgesian spirit, and illustrates a positive artistic morality in the literature of exhaustion. He is not there, after all, for kicks (any more than Borges and Beckett are in the fiction racket for their health): Menelaus is *lost*, in the larger labyrinth of the world, and has got to hold fast while the Old Man of the Sea exhausts reality's frightening guises so that he may extort direction from him when Proteus returns to his 'true' self. It's a heroic enterprise, with salvation as its object—one recalls that the aim of the Histriones is to get history done with so that Jesus may come again the sooner, and that Shakespeare's heroic metamorphoses culminate not merely in the theophany but in an apotheosis.[17]

Like Camus's redoubtable hero of the absurd (though rather more comic than Promethean in guise), Menelaus discovers that he may *multiply* what he cannot unify and that (in Camus's words again) his "nostalgia for unity, this fragmented universe and the contradiction that binds them together,"[18] in other words, his experience of the absurd, is the only bond uniting him to reality. The image further suggests Barth's own conception of his relation to past literary tradition which, despite his grasp (or because of it), continues to deny him substance yet remains for him an indissoluble bond. As Camus asserts: "The first and, after all, the only condition of my inquiry is to preserve the very thing that crushes me, consequently to respect what I consider essential in it. I have just defined it as a confrontation and an unceasing struggle."[19] Tension, the vitality of combat, is for Camus that sole element which ennobles man and fortifies him to repudiate suicide which itself is a negation. In contrast, the absurd man "can only drain everything to the bitter end, and deplete himself. The absurd is his extreme tension, which he maintains constantly by solitary effort, for he knows that in that consciousness and in that day-to-day revolt he gives proof of his only truth, which is defiance."[20]

However, Barth's characters in *Lost in the Funhouse* are neither capable nor desirous of maintaining a posture of heroic defiance; for them suicide proffers a continual seduction. As noted earlier, the sperm cell in "Night-Sea Journey" abjures and rejects his swift-running course toward life. Similarly, the story telling itself in "Autobiography" begs, "if anyone hears me . . . and has the means to my end, I pray him do us both a kindness" (p. 37). The narrator of "Petition" discloses that his soul "lusts only for disjunction" (p. 62), and in "Lost in the Funhouse" Ambrose remarks that if there were "a button you could push to end your life absolutely without pain . . . he would push it instantly" (p. 86). Narcissus, too, we are told, "desired himself defunct before his own conception" ("Echo," p. 100). Menelaus alone, through his "peculiar immortality" (p. 124), knows he cannot die and refuses the false solace of the death wish. Yet impulse, not conviction, drives him on, habit, not determination. And, indeed, impulse, not determination, drives the sperm toward union with the egg; only against his better judgment does Narcissus finally grow fond. Impulse and habit, too, are the forces which continue to animate art, but no rational justification for prolonging it seems possible. The writer finds his sentences stringing themselves out as though he were a "recidivist" engaging in a nasty habit he cannot manage to suppress. "Or a chronic forger, let's say; committed to the pen for life. Which is to say, death. The point, for pity's sake. Not yet. Forge on" ("Title," p. 103). One recalls Vladimir's observation in *Waiting For Godot* that "habit is a great deadener." When Estragon complains, "I can't go on like this," the answer he receives is: "That's what you think."[21]

Against unreasonable demands, through impulse, habit, dread of stopping, sheer perversity, perhaps, and no doubt, also, through the joy of making labyrinths, Barth goes on—or has gone on, at least until now. What more remains for him to do? Put another way, what edifice will Barth attempt (with Theseus' dispensation) to raise atop this labyrinthine cavern? He has prepared us for the dazzling and the bizarre, yet it would not be surprising if in the future Barth's literary design began to take a more traditional, familiar form—for only to a limited extent does Camus's evaluation of Nietzsche's position in modern philosophy seem applicable to Barth's relationship to contemporary fiction and aesthetics. Of Nietzsche Camus writes that, "with a kind of frightful joy [he] rushes toward the impasse into which he methodically drives his nihilism. His avowed aim is to render the situation untenable to his contemporaries. His only hope seems to be to arrive at the extremity of contradiction. Then if man does not wish to perish on the coils that strangle him, he will have to cut them at a single blow and create his own values." [22] In like manner Barth challenges the writers and critics of contemporary fiction to cut the coils that bind them to the recent past. But that same past, as *Lost in the Funhouse* paradoxically demonstrates, already has furnished Barth with new materials for art, providing thereby for a Prodigal Son's circuitous return.

Notes

1. John Barth, *Lost in the Funhouse* (New York; Bantam, 1969), p. 106. Future page references to *Lost in the Funhouse* are drawn from this edition and will be cited parenthetically in the text along with individual story titles when the text reference is not otherwise clear.

2. John Barth, "The Literature of Exhaustion," reprinted in *On Contemporary Literature*, ed. Richard Kostelanetz (New York: Avon Books, 1969), pp. 662–675. The article originally was published in *The Atlantic Monthly*, Vol. 220, No. 2 (August, 1967), pp. 29–34.

3. *Ibid.*, pp. 664–665.

4. *Ibid.*, p. 668.

5. Barth quoting Borges, "The Literature of Exhaustion," p. 672.

6. *Ibid.*, p. 669.

7. James Joyce. *A Portrait of the Artist as a Young Man*, ed., Chester G. Anderson (New York: The Viking Critical Library, 1968), p. 253.

8. Joyce, pp. 252–253.

9. Joyce, p. 215.

10. Joyce, p. 11.

11. Joyce, p. 11.

12. Arthur Koestler, *The Act of Creation* (New York: Dell, 1964), p. 358. The hero as embryo motif, of course, is derived from *The Oxen of the Sun* episode in *Ulysses*. Joyce discussed his intention in that section in a letter to Frank Budgen dated March, 1920: "Am working hard on *Oxen of the Sun*, the idea being the crime committed against fecundity by sterilizing the act of coition. . . . Bloom is the spermatozoon, the hospital the womb, the nurse the ovium, Stephen the embryo." Stuart Gilbert, ed., *James Joyce: Letters, Vol. I* (New York: The Viking Press, 1966), pp. 139–140.

13. "The Literature of Exhaustion," p. 674.

14. From "Three Dialogues by Samuel Beckett and Georges Duthuit," *Samuel Beckett: A Collection of Critical Essays*, ed. Martin Esslin (Englewood Cliffs. N.J.: Prentice Hall, 1965), pp. 16–22, p. 17.

15. Throughout *Lost in the Funhouse* Barth's use of Greek materials is discerning. In "Menelaiad" he draws upon the tradition which holds that Aeschylus wrote a satyr play called *Proteus* (now lost) in comic counterpoint to Agamemnon's tragedy. In the words of the Greek scholar, George Thomson, "the *Proteus*, which followed the trilogy of the *Oresteia*, dealt with the adventures of Menelaos after the Trojan War as a *scherzo* to his brother's tragic homecoming; and it is not difficult to imagine a *Proteus* charged with the romantic atmosphere of the *Odyssey* which would round off in a whirl of irresponsible gaiety the liturgical grandeur of the *Oresteia*." *Aeschylus and Athens* (New York: Grosset and Dunlop, 1968), p. 228. Barth also draws on Euripides' *Helen*, which follows the legend that a phantom was sent to Troy in Helen's place while the real Helen spent the war years in Egypt under the protection of Proteus. The circumstances in "Anonymiad" also seem based upon a little known Greek tradition, again recounted by Thomson, "of a minstrel at Mycenae, to whom Agamemnon had entrusted the guardianship of his Queen—evidently a vassal of high standing." *Aeschylus and Athens*, p. 60.

16. The narrative frames in "Menelaiad" are inspired by Menelaus' digressions in Book IV of the *Odyssey* describing his encounter with Proteus on the beach at Pharos. In Barth's version Telemachus and Peisistratus arrive at Menelaus' palace (as in the *Odyssey*) to obtain information about Odysseus. Their arrival is recounted in frame II. (In frame I Menelaus addresses the reader.) Menelaus begins by telling them the tale of his reunion with Helen (frame III), who postponed their coupling by demanding the story (frame IV) of how Menelaus managed to capture Proteus. In that tale Proteus in turn demands to know Menelaus' reasons for capturing him—which entails (frame V) the story of Menelaus' encounter with Proteus' daughter, Eidothea, and the story she elicited from him concerning the ending of the Trojan War (frame VI). At this stage Barth's Menelaus simultaneously is telling the story of his repossession of Helen to Eidothea, the Eidothea story to Proteus, the Proteus story to Helen, the Helen story to Telemachus and Peisistratus, the story of that story to the reader. One further coil: the subject matter of frame VI (the ending of the Trojan War) necessitates frame VII, the reasons for the Trojan War; but Menelaus demands *that* story of himself. Just as the centerpiece of *Lost in the Funhouse* is the title story placed seventh in a sequence of fourteen, so the seventh frame here is the centerpiece of "Menelaiad," the heart of the labyrinth, and the remaining frames in sequence work their way back out again from VII to I.

17. "The Literature of Exhaustion," p. 674.

18. Albert Camus, *The Myth of Sisyphus and Other Essays*, trans. Justin O'Brien (New York: Vintage Books, 1961), p. 37.

19. Camus, p. 23.

20. Camus, p. 41.

21. Samuel Beckett, *Waiting for Godot* (New York: Grove Press, 1954), p. 60.

22. Albert Camus, *The Rebel*, trans. Anthony Bower (New York: Vintage Books, 1956), p. 71.

Lingering on the Autognostic Verge:
John Barth's *Lost in the Funhouse*

Beverly Gray Bienstock*

At the time that he came to write *Lost in the Funhouse*, John Barth was the author of four novels. The first two, *The Floating Opera* and *The End of the Road*, deal with characters trapped in a self-canceling masquerade. For both Todd Andrews and Jake Horner, life is "a matter of attitudes, of stances—of masks, if you wish."[1] Tony Tanner compares them to Peer Gynt's onion, for they too peel off one layer at a time until nothing, no essential human vitality, is left.[2]

In *The Sot-Weed Factor* and *Giles Goat-Boy*, Barth as author becomes caught up in his own fascination with masquerades. The former work is a pseudo-history in which the eighteenth century is dissolved and re-assembled by Barth's twentieth-century mind. *Giles Goat-Boy*, an ambitious attempt to show the universe as university, puts forth a re-created western civilization in a novel within a novel format. As Barth himself acknowledges in his "The Literature of Exhaustion," both books are novels imitating the form of novels by an author who imitates the role of an author.[3] Whereas the earlier Barth books deal fairly conventionally with a person who reflects his surroundings, the later Barth himself enters the house of mirrors, dragging the reader along with him.

In *Lost in the Funhouse*, subtitled *Fiction for Print, Tape, Live Voice*, we are in a new, somewhat McLuhanatic environment. This is not a novel but a group of stories meant to be read in a prescribed order. While diverse in style and manner of representation, these stories have one basic element in common. They all revolve around the search for one's identity amidst the tangled skeins of past, present, and future.

"Night-Sea Journey" launches the book with the voyage of a sperm from its creator to a still-mysterious destination. "Ambrose His Mark" logically follows by dealing with a very young, unbaptized, and still nameless infant. The next piece, "Autobiography," expands the idea of conception and birth by linking it to the writer, a figurative father who with the help of his recording machine conceives a story. The story, which

Modern Fiction Studies, Copyright ©, 1973, Purdue Research Foundation, West Lafayette, Ind..

serves as its own narrator here, questions the complicity of its "parents" in instigating its birth; similarly the father had doubted his paternity of the baby who comes to be named in the course of "Ambrose His Mark." "Autobiography," subtitled "A Self-Recorded Fiction," is the first of Barth's stories to break away from the medium of print. Barth stipulates that it is a work "for monophonic tape and visible but silent author."[4] In this way he suggests the dual nature of the author's role: he is both a detached human being who lives by writing and the spokesman for a self-created fictional world.

The next two stories, "Water-Message" and "Petition," involve brotherly rivalry and the question of personal manhood. They can be considered preparations leading up to the crucial discussion of these themes in the title story, "Lost in the Funhouse." This story, which follows "Petition" in the book, will be examined in depth subsequently. But here once again the solitary figure reaches out for mature sexual, and spiritual, fulfillment.

"Echo" is the first story to deal with classical mythology. Narcissus is the self-ful youth seeking love on his own terms while shunning the lustful pursuit of others; Echo is the selfless nymph who loves him; Tiresias is the sexless seer who advises and does not advise. It is important to note that Barth intended this story for monophonic *authorial* recording, although any of the three characters could be narrating the tale of their plight. The fact is that the author *is* all three characters. Like the hapless Echo, he "repeats the words of others in their own voices, . . . edits, heightens, mutes, turns others' words to her end" (p. x, 97). And just as he is Echo the imitator so he is also Narcissus the solipsist and Tiresias, seer into past and future. For the author as well as for the three characters who are himself there is the problem of self-knowledge. "Thus," as he ends his tale, in a phrase which could represent the entire work, "we linger forever on the autognostic verge" (p. 100).

Following two brief "Meditations," "Title" marks Barth's return to his consideration of the author's role. This story is called by Barth a "triply schizoid monologue" (p. x), for it involves (1) an author's difficulty with his companion, (2) his analogous difficulties with the story he is in process of composing, and (3) the corresponding state in which he imagines his culture and its literature to be. Barth prefers that "Title" be presented as a stereophonic recording in identical authorial voice with the live author operating across the twin channels of stereo tape like Mr. Interlocutor between the minstrel-show Tambo and Bones (pp. x–xi). This audio-visual display is meant to suggest the intricate position of the modern author.

Next comes an elaborate word game called "Glossolalia," and then "Life-Story." This latter work, in a sort of sequel to "Title," turns from the role of the author to the role of the reader of fiction: "You, dogged, uninsultable, print-oriented bastard, it's you I'm addressing, who else, from inside this monstrous fiction" (p. 123). For the reader, the author is no more than a work in progress—"His life is in your hands. . . . Suicide's impossible: he can't kill himself without your help" (p. 124). This maudlin outburst is the plaint of the author big with story and suffering the labor pains of his art. It is also a recognition of the fact that one cannot survive in a vacuum; the writer's life and livelihood depend on the whims of his audience.

The "Menelaiad" features Menelaus, the eternal cuckold whose claim to fame is that he couldn't keep his hands on slippery Helen. This story too will be considered at greater length. Finally, we turn to the "Anonymiad" which, like the "Menelaiad," has a classical setting and like "Life-Story" focuses on the author-reader-work of art relationship. Its hero, described as a nameless country lad, has been chief minstrel at the court of Agamemnon. Now, thanks to the guile of Aegisthus, he has been marooned on a deserted island; writing tales on goat skins and setting them adrift in wine amphorae are his sole pastime. The story we read is an autobiography, told from "my only valid point of view, first person anonymous" (p. 192).

Obviously the story as we read it has been recovered from one of those amphorae which are the ageing minstrel's only bond with world and time. Art has outlived the man; the artist has absorbed (and perpetuated through this absorption) the merely human side of the minstrel nature. Thus the whole question of identity posed in *Lost in the Funhouse* tentatively resolves itself in the capricious immortality of the work of art. Within the cycling of a world at once solipsistic and self-negating, man is artist is work of art is artist is man. The question is: how does the reader fit into this masquerade of immortal possibilities? Is the life of the artist in our hands? Or are we merely figments of his boundless imagination?

Perhaps most representative of the whole book is the very first entry, a "Frame-Tale," which is in fact a cut-out-and-paste-together Moebius strip. When assembled it endlessly turns upon itself, repeating ONCE UPON A TIME THERE WAS A STORY THAT BEGAN ONCE UPON A TIME THERE WAS A STORY THAT BEGAN ONCE UPON A TIME . . . and so on, *ad infinitum*. This Moebius band-story can be regarded as emblematic of the larger work in several ways. It is a huge, but not wholly unserious, joke on the reader. It is an exploration of the printed word carried to its ultimate limit. It is a consideration of fiction as an audience participation medium. Finally, it is a concise statement of the eternal recurrence that Barth sees as operative in his universe.

Barth's sort of eternal recurrence is found not only in his own works. He quotes the seventeenth-century mystic and eccentric Thomas Browne as saying, "Every man is not only himself . . . Men are lived over again."[5] This can imply a sort of continuous reincarnation which not only follows one's own life but also co-exists with it. The principle does not involve simply consecutive progression but also simultaneity. So the many masks of Barth's characters are in fact their own avatars, evolving out of the fact that history constantly doubles back on itself.

Like James Joyce in *Finnegan's Wake*, Barth wants to revel in the eternal return. But the many masks of man get in his way, and he often finds himself lost in the revolving funhouse of history. This grappling with one's identity amid the swirl of historical event is clearly shown in the "Menelaiad." Here Barth turns to the myths on which the Trojan War was based. He does not use myth as T. S. Eliot, for instance, used it—to contrast past glory with present decadence, to seek spiritual certainty in the belief and ritual of the past. Rather, for Barth as for Joyce the ancient myth is a current event because the past *is* the present on time's ever-turning carrousel.

Menelaus appears, then, not as a mighty warrior but as henpecked husband. His is a story of masks and disguises centered on the errant Helen—"She's the death of me and my peculiar immortality, cause of every mask and change of state" (p. 127). Having won her love, he feigns Zeus in Menelaus guise; as a means of re-winning it, he conceals himself in sealskins to trick Proteus. Proteus is, of course, the great master of the masquerade. Caught in the grip of Menelaus, he becomes lion becomes snake becomes leopard becomes boar becomes salt water becomes at last a dimmer Proteus.

Barth's fascination with the Proteus figure stems from the fact that the Old Man of the Sea has exhausted the guises of reality. Barth, like his mentor Jorge Luis Borges, is keenly interested in the exhausted possibility. In fact, both of them are involved in their writing with what Borges calls the Baroque: "that style which deliberately exhausts (or tries to exhaust) its possibilities and borders upon its own caricature."[6] But in terms of the real world, only an immortal creature like Proteus can get beyond the masks which separate us from an essential truth and an essential truthfulness.

On the other hand, Menelaus on the beach at Pharos is merely the "mortal hugging immortality" (p. 139). The war is over; his wife is, technically at least, his own again. To strip away the veils which separate him from naked Helen, he asks Proteus to search out the truth of their relationship: Why did the magnificent beauty choose to wed mediocre Menelaus?

Menelaus before Helen chose him was the least hopeful of her suitors. "While others wooed he brooded, played at princing, grappled idly with the truth that those within his imagination's grasp—which was to say, everyone but Menelaus—seemed to him finally imaginary, and he alone, ungraspable, real" (pp. 148–149). Thus wrapped up in his hopeless cause, Menelaus becomes in his way a Narcissus. He is as solipsistic as the Barth author who sees all the world revolving around his artistic creation of it.

But as the chosen mate of Helen, as the proclaimed beloved of peerless Helen, Menelaus is wracked with self-doubt. "Why me?" he asks.

Despite her words he cannot believe in her love for him—"To love is easy; to be loved, as if one were real . . . fearsome mystery!" (p. 151). Even while fathering the child Hermione, he (like the father of Ambrose) questions the reality of his own role: "It wasn't Zeus disguised as Menelaus who begot her, any more than Menelaus disguised as Zeus; it was Menelaus disguised as Menelaus, a mask masking less and less. Husband, father, lord, and host he played, grip slipping; he could imagine anyone loved, no accounting for tastes, but his cipher self" (p. 151). And so Menelaus comes in his own mind to be a mere shadow, a zero, an Echo. In this self-negated condition he invites Paris into his home.

Ten years after, a war has been lost and won. Proteus, when appealed to, answers Menelaus's anguished query with the words, "Helen chose you without reason because she loves you without cause, embrace her without question and watch your weather change" (p. 156). The still-dubious Menelaus follows the seer's advice. The result is Helen's demure revelation, "Husband, I have never been in Troy. . . . What's more, . . . I've never made love with any man but you" (pp. 157, 158).

The Trojan War, then, did not take place. Or rather, it was fought over a shadowy cloud-Helen who walked the parapets of Troy with a child of Paris at each breast while the real Helen remained dutifully at home. While men died, while Penelope cuckolded Odysseus with every one of her suitors, Helen waited for the return of the one man she loved. Full of "the absurd, unending possibility of love" (p. 162), Menelaus accepts his wife's story.

So the Menelaus who narrates this tale has come to believe in an explanation which negates more than ten years of his own experience. He denies the reality of his own vivid memories and perceptions for the sake of love. In a sense, then, Menelaus has lost his senses—and in so doing he has, Echo-like, cut himself off from the real world. Like Echo, like the author in "Life-Story" who has no reality outside his fiction, the narrator Menelaus is no longer a person. Instead he is merely a disembodied voice endlessly repeating the same story.

But he is *not* completely negated. "When I understood that Proteus somewhere on the beach became Menelaus holding the Old Man of the Sea, Menelaus ceased" (p. 161). This is self-negation turned to solipsism. The world revolves around Menelaus and what he chooses to believe, even if he chooses to believe in the denial of his own most intimate experience. The seer who charts the future of Menelaus is Menelaus. Tiresias and Narcissus and Echo are one.

And for this one self-affirming, self-denying entity, as for Barth's authors and the writer of the "Anonymiad," there is only one hope of survival. The one chance to transcend history's cycles lies in the story itself, "for when the voice goes he'll turn tale, story of his life, to which he clings yet, whenever, how-, by whom-recounted" (pp. 161–162).

Is it hard to believe all this of mediocre (but now immortal)

Menelaus? As Barth says, "For all we know, we're but stranded figures in Penelope's web, wove up in light to be unwove in darkness" (p. 145).

One figure stranded in the dark of Penelope's web is thirteen-year-old Ambrose. Amby, featured in two previous stories, is the main character of the title work, "Lost in the Funhouse." The story takes place on a family Fourth of July outing to Ocean Park, Maryland, in the midst of World War II.

Since in Barth's world history repeats itself, it is not strange to see Ambrose as a younger, pre-Helen Menelaus. He is the self-doubter painfully unsure of his own identity. The earlier Ambrose tales stressed his namelessness and his sexual ignorance; *this* Ambrose has been sexually initiated (at age eight) and officially baptized (at age thirteen) but still continues to grapple with the combined problems of his spiritual and physical self-acceptance.

The story opens in an automobile en route to Ocean City. Ambrose's mother sits in the front seat between Father and Uncle Karl; in the back seat between Ambrose and his fifteen-year-old brother Peter is Magda, a neighbor, fourteen and "remarkably well developed for her age" (p. 79). Gradually this group of six evolves into what Edgar H. Knapp would call a true "sextet," with the females capturing and holding the males' full attention.[7] Throughout the afternoon there are acute sexual overtones, seen in the horseplay at the swimming pool, the shady doings under the boardwalk, and the "uproarious, female" laughter of Fat May the Laughing Lady who advertises the funhouse (p. 76). And the funhouse itself is, Ambrose notes, meant for coupling couples who cling together in the dark.

Anticipating his first trip into the house of mirrors, Ambrose thinks, "If you knew your way around in the funhouse like your own bedroom, you could wait until a girl came along and then slip away without ever getting caught, even if her boyfriend was right with her. She'd think *he* did it!" (p. 79). But mostly he imagines himself left alone in the darkness—"Peter and Magda found the right exit; he found the one that you weren't supposed to find and strayed off into the works somewhere" (p. 82). Then he wanders endlessly among mirrored reflections of himself, once catching sight of the old funhouse operator. The old man is asleep at the switch and is as indifferent to the plight of the boy as Joyce's God off paring His fingernails.

But Barth's funhouse is not merely an objective rendering of one boy's sexual and spiritual confusion. Rather, the funhouse metaphor is broadened to contain the tangles of history and men's minds. Time, and man's relationship to it, is one more attraction within the house of mirrors.

First of all, the literal time in which the story is set is the World War II period. And so it is not surprising to find the war constantly juxtaposed with the metallic hilarity of the amusement park. Pleasure-seekers blow up submarines at shooting galleries while the real subs lurk in the shadows off the Atlantic coast. And as Ambrose thinks back to the past and the childhood of his father, so he also projects himself into the future when a mature Ambrose will reveal to his thirteen-year-old son the secret of the funhouse. The narrator's own thoughts are also involved here, leading us back to the peopling of Maryland:

> Count a generation as thirty years: in approximately the year when Lord Baltimore was granted charter to the province of Maryland by Charles I, five hundred twelve women—English, Welsh, Bavarian, Swiss—of every class and character, received into themselves the penises the intromittent organs of five hundred twelve men, ditto, in every circumstance and posture, to conceive the five hundred twelve ancestors of the two hundred fifty-six ancestors of the et cetera et cetera et cetera et cetera et cetera et cetera et cetera et cetera of the author, of the narrator, of this story, *Lost in the Funhouse*. (p. 76)

This well-ancestored narrator of "Lost in the Funhouse" is extremely vocal. Not content to hide in the wings like the funhouse operator-God, he continuously interrupts himself to comment on the story he tells. Or perhaps it is a case of the not-completely-omniscient author intruding on his self-created third person omniscient narrator to pass judgment on the success of his endeavor. He spends a lot of time quoting conventional style manuals, to wit: "The inverted tag in dialogue writing is still considered permissible with proper names or epithets, but sounds old-fashioned with personal pronouns" (p. 78). But he also laments aloud his failure to make narrative progress. "We haven't even reached Ocean City yet," he moans. "We will never get out of the funhouse" (p. 74). And later: "We should be much farther along than we are; something has gone wrong; not much of this preliminary rambling seems relevant. Yet everyone begins in the same place; how is it that most go along without difficulty but a few lose their way?" (p. 75).

And so the author-narrator is, like Ambrose, lost in the funhouse. And in the course of the story, the author's plight is confused with the boy's—"As he wondered at the endless replication of his image in the mirrors, . . . as he *lost himself in the reflection* that the necessity for an observer makes perfect observation impossible, better make him eighteen at least, yet that would render other things unlikely" (p. 90, italics Barth's).

Ambrose is the observer who gets in the way of his creator's observations. For both the lost Ambrose and the lost author the future holds the same gloomy dead end: "This can't go on much longer; it can go on forever. He died telling stories to himself in the dark; years later, when that vast unsuspected area of the funhouse came to light, the first expedition found his skeleton in one of the labyrinthine corridors and mistook it for part of the entertainment" (pp. 91–92). Yet within the darkness both Ambrose and author have the same faint hope of immortality: "Unbeknownst to him, an assistant operator of the funhouse, happening to overhear him, crouched just behind the plyboard partition and wrote down his every word. The operator's daughter, an exquisite young woman with a figure unusually well developed for her age, crouched just behind the partition and transcribed his every word" (p. 92).

Ambrose, lost in the funhouse, doesn't starve to death, does eventually get out. Back in the car on the way home he is teased about his mishap. But Ambrose continues to brood: "He wishes he had never entered the funhouse. But he has. Then he wishes he were dead. But he's not. Therefore he will construct funhouses for others and be their secret operator—though he would rather be among the lovers for whom funhouses are designed" (p. 94).

What will happen to the grown-up Ambrose? Possibly he will be chosen by Helen and, if he's wiser than Menelaus, come to the funhouse as one half of a loving couple. But more likely he will be a builder and secret operator of funhouses. Ambrose will grow into the author. Does this mean he'll grow into John Barth? Not impossibly; Barth is a Maryland boy who in 1943 was thirteen years old. And like the author of "Life-Story," perhaps Barth considers himself a fictional personage, his life a fictive narrative.

But Barth is the author of the "Life-Story." Having called the funhouse into being, he is the creator of Ambrose and the vociferous author-narrator and even the funhouse operator-God. They are merely figments of his boundless imagination; Ambrose, who sees the whole world as revolving around his part of it, is merely a dream brought to life by a literary Pygmalion. Like Wallace Stevens and in fact like all writers, Barth is an artistic solipsist. Full of himself, he creates the world in his image: "And things are as I think they are/And say they are on the blue guitar."[8]

But like Stevens and like all artists, Barth is reduced by a greater reality to something less than the sum of his fictive parts. What we know of Barth the man is filtered through the work of Barth the artist. And when Barth has shuffled off this mortal coil, only Ambrose will be left to represent him. So the man is the merest shadow of his work: Narcissus dwindles into the faintest Echo.

Self-ful and self-less, the writer grants immortality to his characters and hopes that some of it will reflect back on himself in the course of time's masquerade. But where do the readers—those print-oriented bastards—fit in? We too are the merest ciphers, dream people whom the writer conjures up to cheer his solitude and motivate his efforts. And yet we militantly refuse to deny that we exist. I read, therefore I am. I read, therefore the writer exists too. There is a distinct dilemma here—who confirms whose existence? When the masks are lifted at twelve o'clock, who has summoned whom into being?

Stephen Dedalus, steering between the twin dangers of Scylla and Charybdis, proves that Shakespeare is Hamlet. The artist is the work of art in all of its senses. He is the Echo-like voice of Hamlet's father's ghost.

He is also the solipsistic Narcissist who wrote a drama for all time based on his own mortal sorrow. But Stephen himself is Hamlet, and as bullock-befriending bard he is also Shakespeare. Finally in the unending masquerade he is James Joyce who wrote *Ulysses*, a book which can contain Shakespeare and Hamlet and Stephen. And that book, *Ulysses*, is read, and written on, by all of us. So writer is work of art is reader is writer is work of art is reader is writer and so on till the end of time. In this way we are all to some small degree immortal. "All subsequent history," says Barth, "is Proteus" (p. 160). We go on forever exchanging masks in a fantastic hall of mirrors, and one shouldn't try to tell the dancer from the dance.

Notes

1. John Barth. *The Floating Opera* (Harmondsworth, Middlesex, England: Penguin Books. 1970), p. 22.

2. Tony Tanner, "The Hoax that Joke Bilked," *Partisan Review*, 34 (1967), 103.

3. John Barth, "The Literature of Exhaustion," *Atlantic*, 220 (August 1967), 33.

4. John Barth. *Lost in the Funhouse* (New York: Bantam Books: 1969), p. ix. Subsequent references to this work are incorporated into the text. For the purpose of this article, the intricate system of interlocking quotation marks used by Barth in the "Menelaiad" has been simplified.

5. Sir Thomas Browne, quoted by Barth, "The Literature of Exhaustion," p. 34.

6. Jorge Luis Borges, quoted by Barth, "The Literature of Exhaustion," p. 34.

7. Edgar H. Knapp, "Found in the Barthhouse: Novelist as Savior," *Modern Fiction Studies*, 14 (1968-69), 449.

8. Wallace Stevens, "The Man With the Blue Guitar," *The Palm at the End of the Mind: Selected Poems and a Play*, ed. Holly Stevens (New York: Alfred A. Knopf, 1971), p. 147.

Chimera

Chimera

Bruce Allen*

Three puzzling long stories ("Dunyazadiad," "Perseid," "Bellero-phoniad") comprise Barth's latest experiments with narrative possibilities. Since his first novel, Barth has obsessively explored the tension between reality's pluralistic confusions and fiction's need to observe, unify, and dramatize them. Like their earlier counterparts, the protagonists of these witty confessions are walking psyches, at war with ultimate ambivalence. (Far from clarifying what is ambiguous, Barth deepens it by retelling familiar stories, deploying their unsettled alternatives so as to virtually insist on their unreality.) Scheherazade's interminable storytelling (as observed by her sister) is either a brilliant exercising of artifice or a grim assertion of selfhood or, inevitably, both. Perseus and Bellerophon, energetic heroes doomed to enact a preordained mythic pattern, struggle boisterously to establish firm identities, wishing to be something beyond the tales that will come to contain their exploits. Barth employs literary devices that multiply confusion: several narrators, giving variant versions of "the truth"; frames within frames; the removal of barriers posed by time and history. The ancient worlds are re-created through a slangy, sexy idiom, laden with specific contemporary references, that further blurs distinctions between past and present. The existential dilemma of heroes striving to comprehend their herohood finds parallel in novelist Barth, whose journeys toward self- and literary discovery mingle amusingly with theirs (he appears to the uncertain Scheherazade as a helpful genie; in "Bellerophoniad," its hero's Protean tutor Polyeidus, who foresees even the yet-uncompleted future, opens a chaotic discussion of Barth's work in progress). The vision of human experience as open-ended alternatives among which no choice is possible may well be directing Barth into blind alleys (Bellerophon ends up being absorbed into universal formlessness, reduced to chaos or is this merely what *he* thinks?). Still, one senses that these quests for certainty, subsumed as they are in Barth's confessed search for "the Revolutionary Novel . . . [which will have] . . . no content except its own form, no subject but its own processes," are revivi-

*Reprinted from *Library Journal*, Aug., 1972. Published by R.R. Bowker Co., copyright © 1972 by Xerox Corp.

fying old stories with real imaginative freshness, bringing to bear on them a new kind of consciousness, and opening them up to new ways of understanding. "The key to the treasure is the treasure." Scheherazade is content to learn. We probably should simply trust that John Barth's ambiguous position on the question of fiction's ambiguous relationship to reality is committed to the achievement of a new technique, and is probing depths through which he alone may just be beginning to see. A breakthrough seems near. Whether or not we trust Barth's Chinese-puzzle technique, he is surely one of the few contemporary novelists whose future work we must anticipate with growing excitement.

The Novel Looks
at Itself—Again

Jerry H. Bryant*

Chimera is a lecture on the nature of fiction, disguised as a kind of retelling of some very old stories. As a simulated fiction, this lecture is meant to be a metaphor of its subject. It's a brilliant tour de force by a well-seasoned writer, who has produced one excellent novel (*The Sot-Weed Factor*), one unreadable monster (*Giles Goat-Boy*), and two more conventional but impressive pieces of philosophical fiction (*The Floating Opera* and *End of the Road*). *Chimera* is supposed to be, I think, an exploration into the possibilities of a new kind of fiction. If it survives it will be because of the brightness of its glitter. But I think that once our eyes recover from the flash, we'll be disappointed with what's left.

Each of the three "tales" that make up this book illustrates the various literary problems of the fiction writer—point of view, truth, theme, pace, rhythm, unity. Each is about the act of creating a fiction; at the same time it purports to be a fiction itself. The first one is shorter than the second, which is shorter than the third. They are linked to one another by occasional references to characters, events and sentiments, and by their gradually increasing length. The "shape-shifter" Polyeidus (who is a repeat of Henry Burlingame in *The Sot-Weed Factor*), the narrator of the last and longest tale, is not only the tale teller but the principle of fiction itself, and hence able to take many forms. The ending of the book is not simply the ending of the book but of life in general, and of the lives of Polyeidus and Bellerophon (the subject of the story). As the book ends, Polyeidus is working on the ending, just as Barth is. Etc. It all fits together like Chinese boxes, each figure or form related to another by a common principle, and subject to being endlessly opened to reveal yet another form that is, lo, the reflection of its container.

The process of invention is the main preoccupation of these pieces. As in the theatre of the absurd, the reader is brought in on the trick. "This is the way we do it," someone says at front stage, and another hat pops out of a rabbit to teach us we really aren't in on it. We're surprised, charmed, pleased to laughter, and enormously impressed. We're looking at things as

*Copyright 1972 *The Nation* Associates.

if from the bottom of a swimming pool, from inside the mind of a character we have long known only from the outside.

In the first tale, for example, we're told how *A Thousand and One Nights* came into being. The narrator isn't Scheherazade but her sister Dunyazade, who tells us how a Genie materializes from America, several centuries in the future, and on each of the 1,001 nights gives Scheherazade a tale to tell the emperor. The Genie is getting them from the volume open on his desk back in the States, so from his vantage point in the future he helps to write the stories he loves so well. Also, by means of his fictions he helps to create life, not only by saving Scheherazade from death each morning but by determining how her life is going to turn out. The Genie is himself a writer, naturally, who had suffered a writing block until he decided to go back to the "springs of narrative." Just as we think this is all there is to it, the scene and the center of consciousness shift. "Dooney" has been telling all this to her new husband, and a completely new situation is trundled out for our amusement, mirroring, of course, the first.

This is clever. More than that—ingenious; at the outside, inspired. Who ever thought, except perhaps the author of *Rosencrantz and Guildenstern Are Dead*, to look from the inside out of some old story? That Barth chooses to do so suggests his plight, which is mirrored in the plight of the Genie. Where does the contemporary writer go when the freshness has disappeared from the narrative tradition, when "artful fiction," as the Genie says, has dropped from favor and no one reads it any more but a few critics and some unwilling students? Where does he go when his own well runs dry? *Chimera* answers, back to the origins, in this case *The Arabian Nights* and the Greek myths (the other two tales are about Perseus and Bellerophon). But what is there in these narratives that might attract a modern audience? Actually, that's not Barth's question. It's rather, what can I inject into the earlier narratives that will help me get my point across?

The answer is right there on the inside. The Genie is 40, Perseus is 40, Bellerophon is 40, Jerome Bray (a sort of character) is 40, J. B. (the "editor" of *Giles Goat-Boy*) is 40. And so, one assumes, is Barth 40—at least symbolically. That is the age when men learn they're not heroes and that all things decay and then die (perhaps even narrative themes and techniques). And Barth's characters do learn that and accept it and win thereby a "treasure." There is the key to writing more and better fiction—not to want to be a mythic hero or preserve the unpreservable.

Or is it the realization that fiction outlives most things? That not only the characters but the writers do too, since the writers are the characters? Perseus, not what he used to be when he first wooed and won Andromeda, a little tired in the body and mellowed in his ambitions, discovers his mortality. But in the story of that discovery lies immortality—a neat paradox. So he's content "to have become, like the noted music of our tongue, these silent visible signs; to *be* the tale I tell to those with eyes to see and understanding to interpret; to raise you up forever and know that our story will never be cut off, but nightly rehearsed as long as men and women read the stars. . . ." Another nice mirror, for Perseus and Andromeda and the rest were made into constellations by Medusa: ergo, fiction equals stars—sort of.

If I seem flippant it's because Barth's power as a writer forces me to aspire to his own well-controlled ironic tone. But his tone sends out waves of concern for his "characters," for people, for his undertaking. What is fiction for Barth? What "good" is *Chimera*, for example? Dunyazade's Genie hopes before he dies simply to add "some artful trinket or two, however small, to the general treasury of civilized delights . . . [and to] the treasury of art, which if it could not redeem the barbarities of history or spare us the horrors of living and dying, at least sustained, refreshed, expanded, ennobled, and enriched our spirits along the painful way." *Chimera* is full of trinkets, some of them solid gold. Proteus asks Bellerophon to kill Perseus: "The bastard's scheduled to kill me and Acrisius both! With his goddamned Gorgon's-head! Father and maternal grandfather, right? You think I want to be a frigging statue?" Anteia begs Bellerophon, a demigod, to impregnate her with a demigod. She'll even settle for a "semigoddamneddemigod." And there are the students with their chemical spray guns out to "defoliate the Ivy League."

Barth isn't without his irritating affectations. Echoes of *Giles Goat-Boy*, with its strange mixture of neologisms and antiquity, resound in *Chimera*. People never simply go "toward" something; it's always "court-ward" or "buildingward" or "seaward." One always draws a "a-beam of." Young virgins are "bedded." Young heroes don't "hesitate," they are "hesitated" by something. At the same time, we smile with delight at the proverbs and the epigrams: "Stories last longer than men, stones than stories, stars than stones."

For Barth, his trinkets add up to something more important than mere delight, in spite of the tone and the statements. What is the world like? he asks. And what has fiction to do with it? The world is like what we see, he answers. Fiction is the imaginative embodiment of it. We see that nothing is flawless, that leaves decay, love dies and so do we. While this in itself, when it happens to us, may not be so pretty, cast into fiction it can be beautiful, can transcend itself. All of Barth's novels have re-counted the search of a man for "reality." At first he seeks it in the ideal, perhaps poetry or fiction. But life teaches him that it lies all about him, in that long disease itself.

Fiction, of course, doesn't deal with particular facts. But when it rises to the height of myth it is truer than facts. Myths, says Bellerophon, can be "so much realer and more important than particular men." The story his voice tells "isn't a lie, but something larger than fact . . . in a word, a myth." "Some fictions," says the Genie, "were so much more valuable than fact that in rare instances their beauty made them real." In such instances, fiction doesn't have to pass itself off as fact to be effective. The reader need not be fooled in order that his mind be changed or his senses modified.

But these points are made essentially through exposition, not fiction. Barth seems to be more set on making us understand intellectually than see emotionally. He uses a simulated fictional form to say something direct—not about the world but about fiction. His stories are about story telling, not about people. And one can be entertained only so long by a Chinese box, and can learn only so much from it. We get the idea from the first exercise. By the middle of the longest one, the "Bellerophoniad," we're likely to agree with Bellerophon's complaint to Polyeidus about his story—that "It's a beastly fiction, ill-proportioned, full of longueurs, lumps, lacunae, a kind of monstrous mixed metaphor." Worse, it begins to get tedious, like a lecture that has gone past the hour.

Barth is an excellent lecturer, at least in his writing. His dissertation on the uses of the Hudibrastic couplet in *The Sot-Weed Factor* and his parody of *Oedipus Rex* in *Giles Goat-Boy* are splendid displays of critical insight. But he seems to have been around colleges too long (he's now teaching at the State University of New York at Buffalo), where literary problems are part of the course content, legitimately. But the process of fiction, appropriate to the classroom, has no place as the subject of fiction. It makes a clever logical paradigm to conceive of the process as its own subject. But who cares, outside of, as the Genie says, a few critics and unwilling students? If no one is reading "artful fiction" any more, it might be because it has become an exclusive game. If, as the Genie says, students prefer music or pictures, it might be because those forms give their audience something direct and real, something to participate in. The trouble with *Chimera* is that it's only about itself.

People are still reading fiction. That it's too often second-rate only proves that few of our artful novelists are gratifying the thirst of a huge reading public for stories about itself—a thirst that is insatiable. I don't blame the public for preferring to read, say, *The Godfather*, with its egregious stereotypes, its shameful romanticizing of cruelty and violence, its sentimentalized emotions constructed according to the theory of stock response; at least the novel shows people engaged in exciting actions. *Chimera* is infinitely better written and displays an incomparably sharper intelligence. But who wants to read a novel that is ultimately concerned with nothing so much as the nature of the novel?

If the novel is dead, it's because intelligent writers like Barth, who could continue to re-create it, haven't found a new way to say something about the world but only a new way to say something about saying something about the world. Self-consciousness is the sign either of the beginning of a cultural stage or of its end. When it's the latter, it's decadent. I think *Chimera* is an end rather than a beginning. Even so, I've read endings that were a lot worse.

"The Key to the Treasure": Narrative Movements and Effects in *Chimera*

Cynthia Davis*

In the *Dunyazadiad*, the first novella in John Barth's trilogy *Chimera*, Scheherazade and the Genie she has summoned forth from the future speculate

> on such questions as whether a story might imaginably be framed from inside, as it were, so that the usual relation between container and contained would be reversed and paradoxically reversible—and . . . what human state of affairs such an odd construction might usefully figure. Or whether one might go beyond the usual tale-within-a-tale, beyond even the tales-within-tales-within-tales-within-tales which our Genie had found a few instances of in that literary treasurehouse he hoped one day to add to, and conceive a series of, say, *seven* concentric stories-within-stories, so arranged that the climax of the innermost would precipitate that of the next tale out, and that of the next, et cetera . . .[1]

Since the Genie is clearly Barth himself, it is not surprising that those structural plans are fulfilled in the *Dunyazadiad*. The story is "framed from inside" by the appearance of Barth as Genie: he is logically outside of Scheherazade's story, having read it long after its occurrence, and its influence on his framing story—his attempt to write a new version of the Scheherazade tale—follows the "usual relation between container and contained." But Genie-Barth does not exist only outside of Scheherazade's story: he is transferred from his time to hers, so he can reverse the "usual relation" by giving her the tales to tell to Shahryar. Thus the climax of Scheherazade's story "precipitates" that of the framestory containing Barth, but the frame itself makes the climax possible. That kind of reciprocity between framer and framed occurs again when the Genie announces his intention of revising the traditional story by making Dunyazade his central character and an image of the modern story teller, and promises to seek an ending "in keeping with his affection" for her; that ending will be based on the notes Scheherazade herself gives him of her plans (pp. 40–41). This kind of interaction sets up a triple vision of the *Dunyazadiad:* as the "true" story told by Dunyazade, as the story in

*Reprinted by permission of *The Journal of Narrative Technique*.

legend and literature that we and the Genie know long after the event, and as Genie-Barth's re-creation of the story, which ideally will be a combination of the first two, a result of the interchange we have seen occurring in the telling. We can read these pages in all three ways, alternating or combined, and the repeated reversals of the frame-relationship prevent our forming too definite a decision about the nature of the story.

But while the conversations between the sisters and the Genie emphasize this alternating movement between frame and framed, the layers of narration establish another movement, steadily outward toward perspectives more and more removed from the immediate action of the original story. The main narrative voices in the *Dunyazadiad* are Dunyazade telling her own story, then an impersonal voice detailing the wedding-night scene, and finally an "artist" voice that is clearly Barth the Genie. These three main voices are stages in the fulfillment of the plan for the seven "concentric" stories, a structure developed through the expanding (Barth's word is "spiralling") progress through the layers of narration. The center, of course, is occupied by the stories told by Scheherazade; there are frame stories even here—the spiral seems endless—but they may be considered in the overall structure as one set, since we never hear the stories themselves, but only about them. Their climax, the end of the last tale, precipitates the crisis of their frame, the story of Scheherazade and her sister as told by the latter. The apparent "solution" to that story, the double wedding of royal brothers and narrating sisters, is really Dunyazade's crisis as she faces her new groom. At this point the more impersonal narrative voice takes over, describing the scene between Dunyazade and Shah Zaman from outside observation, and that scene becomes the frame to both Dunyazade's story in Part I and the recital Shah Zaman gives of his life up to now. This section ends with his words, "Good morning, then! Good morning!" and the hope, but not certainty, that Dunyazade will spare his life. That brings us through three of the "concentric" stories; now Barth sets up a further succession of frame relationships in one short paragraph with yet another narrative voice:

> *Alf Laylah Wa Laylah,* The Book of the Thousand Nights and a Night, is not the story of Scheherazade, but the story of the story of her stories, which in effect begins: "There is a book called *The Thousand and One Nights,* in which it is said that once upon a time a king had two sons, Shahryar and Shah Zaman," et cetera; it ends when a king long after Shahryar discovers in his treasury the thirty volumes of *The Stories of the Thousand Nights and a Night,* at the end of the last of which the royal couples—Shahryar and Scheherazade, Shah Zaman and Dunyazade—emerge from their bridal chambers after the wedding night, greet one another with warm good mornings (eight in all), bestow Samarkand on the brides' long-suffering father; and set down for all posterity *The Thousand Nights and a Night.* (pp. 63–64)

So outside of the scene between Dunyazade and Shah Zaman, however it may be resolved, is the "frame" in which a "king long after Shahryar" reads their story; and the frame for even that is the whole of *The Thousand and One Nights* that we know, including both these stories. All of this is incorporated into yet another frame, the novella *Dunyazadiad* which "frames" the story as told with Barth's direct statement in Part Three. The final layer is the whole trilogy *Chimera* of which the *Dunyazadiad* is a part (and it will be seen that the rest of *Chimera* does spin off the *Dunyazadiad* to "frame" it). There they are: seven concentric stories that climax in a series "like a string of firecrackers."

Dunyazade and the Genie, talking of the reverse-frame construction, had asked themselves "what human state of affairs such an odd construction might usefully figure." Given Barth's appearance as Genie and his admiration for both Dunyazade and Scheherazade as storytellers, surely the "state of affairs" pictured is the interaction between the artist and his tradition. The Genie has a writer's block because he cannot decide what direction his writing should take. He sees his position as like that of Dunyazade: since all the stories have been told by Scheherazade, her position is even more precarious than her sister's. The relationship he should have with his tradition is clearly an interchange like the one he has with Scheherazade, each affecting the other (one thinks of Eliot's "Tradition and the Individual Talent"); but fears instead following that other movement and becoming more and more removed from his tradition, without adding to it. So part of the tension in the *Dunyazadiad* is this one, structurally echoed in the two movements pointed out. But there is another source of tension. The author of the *Dunyazadiad*, after all, has created a complicated structure that works to establish themes and effects, and he is pictured at the end as having finally found a way to solve his dilemma as well as Scheherazade's, so the *Dunyazadiad* ought to end on a note of triumphant completion; but it does not. It ends on a very tentative note; the artist-narrator speaks prior to his own invention ("If I could invent a story as beautiful"), giving Dunyazade's story an independence from him; and he speaks of a conclusion only in general terms: "Dunyazade's story begins in the middle; in the middle of my own. I can't conclude it—but it must end in the night that all good mornings come to" (p. 64). This tension points to a new kind of doubt, not so much about the relationship to literary tradition as about the ability of literature to capture and interpret reality in story, and it is even less resolved than the first problem.

So we must turn to the following novellas for resolution, but they too continue this effect of elaborate patterning qualified by a curiously tentative attitude. Barth prepares for them when, as Genie, he tells Scheherazade that he has broken through his writer's block: "Using, like Scheherazade herself, for entirely present ends, materials received from narrative antiquity and methods older than the alphabet, . . . he had set down two-thirds of a projected series of three *novellas*, longish tales which would take their sense from one another in several of the ways he and Sherry had discussed . . ." (p. 36). And he adds that the *Dunya-*

zadiad is to complete the trilogy—another reversal, since it takes first place in the series as published. That statement establishes the first logical connection between the first and the later novellas, and the mention in the *Bellerophoniad* of the Amazon state that Shah Zaman claimed to have established is another plot link. The *Perseid* and the *Bellerophoniad*, of course, have even more explicit links in content: Perseus and the Bellerophon are related, they are almost contemporaries, and Bellerophon reads and is influenced by the *Perseid*. But the most important connections are structural and thematic. Each of the three novellas is a kind of commentary on the other two, and their order represents a gradual extension and investigation of narrative techniques as well as thematic concerns. Hence, again, the importance of the spiral-image (and the related navel-image) throughout *Chimera*: the book repeatedly returns to the same structures and concerns, but with variations that expand its scope.

Perseus, like Dunyazade, narrates his own story, but he is a much more self-conscious narrator, and his highly mannered style prepares us for an even more elaborate and polished variation of the techniques of the *Dunyazadiad*. For most of the *Perseid*, he is narrating his life story to Medusa by repeating to her the exact words he earlier used to tell the story to Calyxa. So this, like the *Dunyazadiad*, is a tale-within-a-tale-within-a-tale, and the interruptions of the two women establish the frames. But it also takes on something like the reverse-frame structure, since as he recites the story to Calyxa he can't remember it wholly, but must be prompted by the spiralling mural she painted at Medusa's direction. And, as in the *Dunyazadiad*, the framing techniques enforce a multiple perspective: Perseus' life story is at once an immediate occurrence, unfolding even to him; a completed story that takes on legendary qualities diverging from reality (he complains of inaccuracies in the mural); and the story told to Medusa in their immortal forms as stars. Of that last form, Medusa says that the payment for immortality is separation from everyday reality: they can't know how their "mortal lives are living themselves out, or've long since done—together or apart, comic tragic, beautiful ugly. That's another story, another story; it can't be told to the characters in this" (p. 141). That distinction between life and the permanent forms of art and myth was made in a similar way in the *Dunyazadiad*, by the distinction between Dunyazade's "real" story and its telling in either the *Arabian Nights* or Barth's version. But now the separation seems more nearly irrevocable—mortal life goes on along a path entirely removed from their eternal forms—and it is emphasized further by Perseus' inability to consummate his relationship with Medusa: he can't even see her, only hold a lock of her hair. Thus, even though the *Perseid* has technically an even more closed ending than the *Dunyazadiad* ("Good night" firmly ends the storytelling begun with "Good evening"), that note of tentativeness is still there: there will be other nights to tell the story, somewhere there is a "mortal" side of it untold and perhaps untellable, and the method of telling may vary (Medusa even criticizes Perseus' style of narration). That tentativeness is now even more clearly related to the gap between art and life: the early fascination with artistic technique in the *Dunyazadiad* has developed into a strong feeling that while art may imitate and use life, it can never contain it, and in fact to choose one is in some way to lose the other. It is significant that Perseus gets Medusa, not mortal women: in fact, he loses Andromeda and Calyxa because he rises into myth. And Bellerophon will finally get no woman at all, because he can't be human lover and mythic hero too.

The *Bellerophoniad* continues to extend the patterns of the first two novellas. At the end of his section, Perseus proclaims that his fate— transformation into a star—was "to have become . . . these silent, invisible signs; to *be* the tale I tell to those with eyes to see and understanding to interpret . . ." (p. 142). Bellerophon fulfills this even more literally, becoming the actual words of his story. But it is not quite that simple: the complicated narrative techniques of the whole trilogy culminate in the fact, first, that the first part of the story is doubly narrated, like Perseus', to both Philonöe and Melanippe (who is writing it down).[2] Second, whereas the *Perseid* at least had the same main narrator throughout, the *Bellerophoniad* shifts back to the structure of the *Dunyazadiad* and has three parts: the main character narrating, the outside narrator in a two-person scene, and an address from an artist figure (Polyeidus, openly identified with Barth). And there is a final complication, a kind of doubling-back that is the ultimate parody of these and other framed stories: because Bellerophon is not really a god, he cannot be "translated" to eternal form; it is Polyeidus who has been condemned to become Bellerophon's story eternally. But to allow himself more freedom, Polyeidus announces to Bellerophon that he will "turn *myself* from this interview into you-in-*Bellerophoniad*-form" (p. 319). So the three concentric parts are, as words, "layered": Polyeidus as Bellerophon as the words of his story. This confusion and merging of identities between artist and creation is compounded when the process is reversed within the tale, and Bellerophon's voice becomes Barth's (or rather, in a parallel to the structure of the whole, Bellerophon's words as *quoted* by one of his students become Barth's), and his lecture turns into a gloss on Barth's novels (pp. 206–212). We are further reminded of Barth's existence in scenes and references lifted directly from other Barth works (for example, the seduction scene on p. 202 is nearly identical with that between Jake and Rennie in *The End of the Road*, and Rennie's physical mannerisms are attached to several of the women characters in *Chimera*). So the spiral of frame-succession goes even outside *Chimera* to Barth's whole canon and indeed other literature also, and the interaction among artist, tradition, and creation in the *Dunyazadiad* has become the actual transformation, the flowing of identity from one to the other. But even this elaborate structure is qualified like the earlier ones: Bellerophon insists that this is not the life-story he had envisaged, the narrative ends in the middle of a sentence, and statements are repeatedly interrupted by the word "Reset." So we return to the nagging separation between art and life: Bellerophon longs throughout his life to be a mythic hero, trying to follow the pattern Polyeidus gave him, but he finds in the end that he is not a demigod, and he becomes a peculiar kind of hybrid, neither myth nor reality. Even the immortality he achieves in his story is modified, for his story changes cyclically with the tides, some versions being much "better" than others, but all "imperfectly, even ineptly narrated," especially in contrast with "the rich prose of the *Perseid*" (pp. 146, 148).

What emerges from these patterns? Of the two main areas of tension in *Chimera*, one is primarily structural (the two kinds of framing), and one is involved with narrative tones and attitudes in relationship to that structure (the apparent contradiction between strict formal control and the tentative note described). Their combination points toward some of Barth's basic aesthetic principles.

As we have remarked, the structural tension seems to be a metaphor for the relationship between the artist and his tradition. The strong pull outward established by the frame successions in all three novellas, alone and as a series, leads from Scheherazade, whom Barth regards as the quintessential symbol of storytellers, to Barth himself and even beyond. Because of Scheherazade's double symbolism, that movement poses two problems: the relationship of the artist to his tradition, and his relationship to the reality that is the basis for his story. In both areas, the artist's concern is his removal from his source; he fears that he cannot embody the reality he sees, and also that he cannot find a way to continue and contribute to the "literary treasure-house" of the ages. The reverse-frame construction both continues and partially answers this problem. We have Barth's own gloss on this kind of structure in a discussion of Borge's anecdote of the "602nd Night," in which Scheherazade, "owing to a copyist's error," starts to tell the King the story that they are in, but is interrupted. Barth says that forms of the "story-within-the-story turned back on itself" are fascinating for three reasons:

> . . . first, . . . they disturb us metaphysically: when the characters in a work of fiction become readers or authors of the fiction they're in, we're reminded of the fictitious aspect of our own existence . . . Second, [this kind of story] is a literary illustration of the *regressum in infinitum* . . . Third, [that structure] is an image of the exhaustion, or attempted exhaustion, of possibilities—in this case literary possibilities. . . .[3]

So this structure extends the questions opened in the concentric construction: it reminds us of the fictional nature of the tale, and by both structure and statement (the Genie's complaints) it presents us with the problem of the "exhaustion" of "literary possibilities," the Genie's dilemma as author and the reason that he chooses Dunyazade, not Scheherazade, as his symbol. Further, by the admission of fictiveness, we are "reminded of the fictitious aspect of our own existence"—that is, we see that, like Scheherazade, we order our lives by the telling of them, by imposing a point of view and by ordering details.

Yet the reverse-frame structure carries some kind of answer to the questions posed by the expanding-frame structure; and the balance between the two produces an aesthetic "statement" that neither one alone could contain. The concentric structure imaged the problems of the artist's removal from the sources of his tradition and from reality, and the reverse-frame seemingly compounded the problems. But the reverse-frame is also a counter to the concentric structure, and it is the combination of the two that produces a spiralling narrative instead of either a straight line or a back-and-forth shuttle. The contemporary writer must recognize that he can't create new patterns, that "for one to attempt to add overtly to the sum of the 'original' literature, by even so much as a conventional short story, not to mention a novel, would be too presumptuous, too naive; literature has been done long since."[4] That is the exhaustion represented by the reverse-frame structure, but the artist's challenge at this point is to use that exhaustion as subject and technique to *produce* original literature. Barth does it by return to his sources. Observing (still in that commentary on Borges) that a familiar older work of art would take on entirely new dimensions if produced at a later date, affected by a modern consciousness, he chooses to overcome the problem of literary exhaustion by rewriting the "classics"—returning to our sources, but with a different, modern view. Thus Barth's voice speaks through Bellerophon to say:

> Since myths themselves are among other things poetic distillations of our ordinary psychic experience and therefore point always to daily reality, to write realistic fictions which point always to mythic archetypes is in my opinion to take the wrong end of the mythopoeic stick, however meritorious such fiction may be in other respects. Better to address the archetypes directly. (p. 208)

Such an approach reconciles the need for significant pattern with the need for originality, since the treatment of archetypes from a modern perspective has a unique dimension; and it reconciles the need for order (and art) with a feeling for reality by fleshing out the basic pattern into "realistic" form. Clearly this solution, like the problem itself, is offered in the narrative structures discussed; the exhaustion necessitating return to original sources is represented in the reverse frame, and the appearance of a new perspective on "old" patterns is represented in both the outward and the alternating movements. Barth's comment on Borges, that he "turns the artist's mode or form into a metaphor for his concerns," that he shows "how an artist may paradoxically turn the felt ultimacies of our time into material and means for his work."[5] applies as well to *Chimera*. And the exaggeration which marks the progress from novella to novella also demonstrates Barth's use of exhaustion as technique: it traces in one work the development that Barth is considering over the full course of literary history.

But what about the other source of tension in *Chimera*—the question of narrative voice? This mostly revolves around the second of the concerns evoked by the framing structures: the relationship between art and life. By using familiar myths, Barth gives a study of the interaction between the basic pattern and the immediate form that it takes: many of the points of interaction and tension in *Chimera* are in the places where the narrative differs from the legend, in the alternation between mythic and new material, in the introduction of Barth himself into the stories, even in Bellerophon's discovery that he is not a demigod. Add to this Perseus' and Bellerophon's anguish over their inability to fulfill the mythic "Pattern" and to reconcile it with mortal needs. These points of tension are the sources of the tentative note in the narration, for the "Pattern" and its individual expression are not the same, can never be the same. Hence all the incompleteness in the stories: Dunyazade's story is unfinished, Perseus can neither hold Medusa nor see his continuing mortal existence, Bellerophon cannot achieve apotheosis. The contemplation of one's life as a work of fiction that can never really be perfected is exaggerated from its neat expression in the *Dunyazadiad* to the "Baroque" self-absorption in the *Bellerophoniad*. And it is not only a Nabokovian kind of reminder that the author, not the putative narrator, is the elaborate controller, for even when Barth speaks in what is as close to his own voice as we can get, he confesses his inability to complete the story.

Barth's narrating characters are struggling to achieve a sense of self largely by telling their stories, and their difficulty is emphasized by the fact that they only learn about their lives by telling them, for they have forgotten or not finished living them, and cannot see them as wholes. So they can bring little prior order to the telling and perceive little order by hindsight. This goes back to the question of fictiveness, of course; the events in the stories do not fall into place because "objective reality" does not contain order in itself. Any "meaning" or "Pattern" we perceive in events really comes from the observer, from point of view, rather than from the events themselves.[6] Barth's narrators can't put things in order because they are not sure who they are or because they have created a self-concept that they can't sustain. And so they cannot force themselves into patterns that they believe to be immutable, inescapable, or objective.

How can this be reconciled with Barth's talk about archetypes? By his choice of material and treatment, he is certainly suggesting that there are some basic patterns, and that to seek them is not foolishly or wantonly reductive, but a return to the sources of narrative and of human experience; but at the same time he makes it clear that there is an unbridgeable gap between the pattern and the reality. The same dilemma was described by Jake Horner in *The End of the Road*:

> To turn experience into speech—that is, to classify, to categorize, to conceptualize, to grammarize, to syntactify it—is always a betrayal of experience, a falsification of it; but only so betrayed can it be dealt with at all, and only in so dealing with it did I ever feel a man, alive and kicking. (Bantam edition, p. 119)

To reduce reality only to pattern is a "falsification"; and yet our need for order is a real one and the patterns we choose or find do have meaning in general terms. Barth's use of archetypes shows the attempt at balance; the patterns themselves are never confused with "daily reality"—that would be reductive—but the use of archetypal or legendary figures "points" to concrete reality by fleshing out the basic pattern without obscuring it. To choose Scheherazade or Perseus as protagonist is not only to show an awareness that literary possibilities are "exhausted" and so add a new twist to the old forms, but also to show that the symbolic value of those figures is not lost in the unique circumstances of their "real" existence. And the fact that the meaning we perceive in such figures and situations is ultimately subjective does not eliminate the possibility of common patterns in our "psychic experience"; we create our own order, but in doing so we ally ourselves with the mythmaking tendency of all humans. The universality of that human need and activity explains why, even though meaning cannot be fixed in objective reality, it can be felt and somehow located in familiar human struggles. The struggle to articulate a reality that is ultimately beyond any articulation is one that we recognize, and so our isolation is not entire; we can communicate, however imperfectly, and we can take account of other perspectives than our own. This recognition of the similarity of human experiences is indicated by archetypal patterns.

Jake Horner follows his statement about articulation with a quiet disclaimer: "In other senses, of course, I don't believe this at all." *Chimera's* treatment of mythic material is a similarly self-mocking attempt at balance, produced by both the uncertain narrative voices and the progressive exaggeration of techniques in the novellas. How can we take seriously such extreme technical complication, narrative self-consciousness, obvious parody, and explicit authorial lecturing? Those effects tend to make us wonder whether the myth involved is really a discovery of meaning or a distortion of experience prompted by a need for a non-existent order. That kind of doubt, of course, is Barth's "point," and he misses few opportunities to demonstrate that myth and art, however necessary and "truthful," are abstractions, "distillations," common denominators extracted from experience and so can neither contain nor fully describe it. Instead of working harder to make fiction "realistic," Barth says, "A different way to come to terms with the discrepancy between art and the Real Thing is to *affirm* the artificial element in art (you can't get rid of it anyhow), and make the artifice part of your point . . . That would be my way. Scheherazade's my *avant-gardiste*."[7] Thus we get the best of both extremes: the affirmation of artifice as a human need and activity and yet the recognition that it is not "the Real Thing." The tension becomes a balance. And this fits with the solution to the earlier problem of the relationship between artist and tradition. Instead of trying to find newer and newer ways of achieving the effect of realism, the artist can make art itself his subject and explore the problems of "literary exhaustion" both by return to well-worn figures and by the kind of progressive structure *Chimera* has, at the same time that he uses that self-consciousness to explore the interaction between the need for order and the need for novelty. In the process he proves what Scheherazade and the Genie discovered, that "The Key to the Treasure is the Treasure." Just as the lover's reward is not in achieving ideal love but in the struggle for it, the behaving "as if it were" possible, so now Barth's heroes find their "apotheosis" and fulfillment in the quest and its articulation rather than in living "happily ever after." (And that parallel offers another explanation of the repeated pattern for narration in all three novellas: the lover telling his story to his beloved.) Similarly, Barth finds new form in the assertion and process of "exhaustion," and we get the meat of *Chimera* not in the end but in working through it. *Chimera* does not celebrate achievement, it celebrates struggle. And all of its other themes (for it does manage to be "passionately *about* some things" other than the artist, as the Genie says) are rooted in the emphasis on process that the narrative techniques establish.

When Melanippe accuses Bellerophon of confusing his "private uncategorizable self" with the "mythical persona" of the same name, Bellerophon replies, ". . . my identification with 'Bellerophon' is clear and systematic policy, not confusion—even as is, was, or imaginably could be the apparent chaos of this tale" (p. 247). There is a "systematic policy" to *Chimera*, and all the self-deprecation, tentative attitudes, progressive exaggerations of pattern, and narrative tensions are part of the deliberate choice of the attempt to articulate the unarticulable nature of human consciousness and existence.

Notes

1. John Barth, *Chimera*, Fawcett-Crest, p. 32. All quotations from *Chimera*, copyright 1972 by John Barth, are by permission of Random House, Inc. Parenthetic citations are to the Fawcett-Crest edition.

2. This technique may well have been influenced by Nabokov's *Ada*, in which Van's narration is repeatedly interrupted by both spoken and written comments from Ada. However, the double narration, like many of the other techniques and themes in *Chimera*, already appears in the earlier Barth collection, *Lost in the Funhouse*.

3. John Barth, "The Literature of Exhaustion," *The Atlantic*, 220, 2 (August 1967), 33.

4. Ibid.

5. Ibid., p. 32.

6. Campbell Tatham gives an excellent discussion of some of these questions of reality

and meaning in relation to Barth's earlier works in "John Barth and the Aesthetics of Artifice," *Contemporary Literature*, 12,1 (Winter 1971), 60–73.

7. "John Barth: An Interview," *Contemporary Literature*, 6, 1 (Winter-Spring, 1965), 6.

John Barth's *Chimera:*
A Creative Response to
the Literature of Exhaustion

Jerry Powell*

In three years, 1966 to 1968, John Barth published an astounding amount: *Giles Goat-Boy*, in 1966, revised editions of his first three novels—*The Floating Opera, The End of the Road*, and *The Sot-Weed Factor*—in 1967, and a collection of some previously published and some unpublished stories—*Lost in the Funhouse*—in 1968. In the middle of an extremely prolific period, Barth also published an article, "The Literature of Exhaustion," setting forth his feeling that all stories have been told—the feeling of exhausted possibilities in the narrative art form.[1] The theoretical considerations of his article are naturally related to his work at the time, for he was publishing furiously at the same time that he was talking about "exhausted possibilities." In his article Barth provides a clue to the apparent discrepancy: in speaking of the artist's ability to comment on his own themes within the art work itself, thereby turning "the artist's mode or form into a metaphor for his concerns," Barth finds that "an artist may paradoxically turn the felt ultimacies of our time into material and means for his work—*paradoxically* because by doing so he transcends what had appeared to be his refutation."[2] Citing Nabokov's *Pale Fire* and Borges' *Labyrinths* as examples, Barth adds, "if you were the author of this paper, you'd have written something like *The Sot-Weed Factor* or *Giles Goat-Boy*: novels which imitate the form of the Novel, by an author who imitates the role of Author."[3]

The problem with linking Barth's theory to his earlier works, such as *The Sot-Weed Factor* and *Giles Goat-Boy*, is that the theory follows the works chronologically. While *Giles Goat-Boy* foreshadows some of Barth's later self-conscious authorial traits—an author imitating the role of Author—as in the framing prefaces and postscripts, the novel is much more of a response to themes that evolved from *The Sot-Weed Factor* and its public reception, such as hero-hood and the quest. *Lost in the Funhouse*, which appeared the year after the article, is more clearly a

*Reprinted by permission of *Critique*, xviii, No. 2 (Winter 1976), 59–72.

228

product of the self-conscious artist who is aware of "exhausted possibilities" in his field, but it is an experiment in format as much as form, for Barth meant the stories to be recorded and played back as well as read, as the complete title suggests: *Fiction for Print, Tape, Live Voice.* One alternative to exhausted possibilities in a printed format is to change the format.[4]

Chimera, unfortunately, has received very little critical attention, mostly focused on Barth's form and technique, as though Barth had discarded "content" in favor of technique, if that is even possible. *Chimera* is far from a mere exercise in technique but an artistic product of the ideas presented in "The Literature of Exhaustion." While some of the narrative techniques were developed in *Lost in the Funhouse*, Barth has returned in *Chimera* to the printed page and to the narrative technique he is best at—"story-telling"—and his achievement is the successful integration into the novel of his ideas concerning the "literature of exhaustion."

In *Chimera* the situation facing an author—the situation of exhausted possibilities in the narrative art form—is represented by the more general problem of writer's block, which becomes a metaphor for many of the daily problems people face throughout life, such as the difficulties encountered in transitions from one stage of life to another. The idea of exhausted possibilities becomes a central theme of the novel, and the process of writing about writer's block transcends the problem—the paradox is complete. As the Genie and Scheherazade tell us over and over, "the key to the treasure is the treasure."

The problem of writer's block importantly connects the three parts of the novel, for each of the protagonists has to deal with some form of the malady. In the "Dunyazadiad" Scheherazade epitomizes the problem: she either tells a convincing story or loses her life. Ironically her "source" for the stories is the Genie, a thinly-disguised version of Barth, who has taken the stories from the treasure-house of literature—specifically, the *Arabian Nights.* The time warp should not be distracting nor should the apparent lapse in logic concerning "authorship" of the stories; the point is that all authors have drawn from the same stories for centuries.

Stories change by shifts in viewpoint. As the Genie says, "*Alf Laylah Wa Laylah,* The Book of the Thousand Nights and a Night, is not the story of Scheherazade, but the story of the story of her stories."[5] In the "Dunyazadiad" Scheherazade uses her own stories, in effect, to create her stories, but the story we read—the "Dunyazadiad"—belongs to Dunyazade. She tells the story to Shah Zaman in order to make it through "the night that all good mornings come to"—the night being a metaphor for writer's block in the first part. In the second and third parts, "Perseid" and "Bellerophoniad," the noon of one's life is compared to writer's block and night becomes more generally a metaphor for death. The shift in emphasis on night as a metaphor is appropriate because the "metaphor" is literal for Scheherazade and Dunyazade: a failure to produce stories *is* death—not a metaphoric one. This distinction is important for it helps clarify the relationship between Part One and Parts Two and Three. The "Dunyazadiad" is Barth's source for the solution to *his* writer's block. He learns from Scheherazade that the key to his problem is to write about his problem—that is, to tell Scheherazade's story. Thus Scheherazade's story is both Dunyazade's, in her time, the record of which has not come down to us, and Barth's, in our time: "There (with a kiss, little sister) is the sense of our story, Dunyazade: The key to the treasure is the treasure" (64).

What Barth learns from his writing the "Dunyazadiad" is used in writing the "Perseid" and "Bellerophoniad."[6] The two protagonists— "true and false" mythic heroes, as the Genie respectively calls them (36)—are both afflicted with writer's block, except that writer's block has become a metaphor for middle age, just as writing is so often a metaphor for life in Barth's works. Merely to write about writer's block is not the key; if that were true Barth would have stopped after Part One. Instead, by treating the act of writing as a life-or-death matter in Part One, Barth has gained a new perspective on his own writer's block. As he learned from Dunyazade, a new perspective is all that is needed to create "new" stories out of old ones. With a new awareness or consciousness, then, Barth creates Parts Two and Three. In Part Two, Perseus, the "true" mythic hero, demonstrates the right way to use that gained awareness. Bellerophon, the "false" mythic hero, demonstrates the wrong way to use that knowledge.

The central question involving these two protagonists seems to be whether a hero is defined by his actions or whether a hero's actions are heroic because a hero has performed them. Barth deals with the problem at length in his other novels, particularly in *The Sot-Weed Factor* and *Giles Goat-Boy*. The solution he comes to is that the question is misleading, or from a different perspective Barth concludes that the solution can only be a relative one.[7] Barth resolves the question into what he calls "rich paradox": a hero acts according to his conception of heroics, based on past actions, yet his present actions redefine what heroics are for the future. A hero is a hero if he acts heroically.

The formulation is part of Barth's solution to the problem of writer's block. One must understand the past in order to comprehend the present, and thus be directed in future actions. Perseus and Bellerophon differ in that Perseus recapitulates his own history in order to progress while Bellerophon tries to conform to the larger historical pattern. Instead of being himself and acting on his awareness of history, Bellerophon tries to relive the pattern of history without changing it and becomes the comic counterpart of Perseus, for he acts with Perseus's consciousness of the past but without an individual consciousness. In the "lecture scroll," Polyeidus/Barth can ironically comment on the origin of the "Bellerophoniad": "I envisioned a comic novella based on the myth [of

Pegasus and the Chimera]; a companion-piece to 'Perseid,' perhaps"
(210).

The difference between Perseus and Bellerophon is illustrated by
their actions at the various turning points in their lives. Perseus's actions
set an example of "true" heroics to which a reader can compare
Bellerophon's actions. Before Perseus's major turning point, at the end of
his First Flood (to use Bellerophon's categories),[8] Perseus is bored with
life. He admits his marriage is "on the rocks," he is "twenty kilos over-
weight," and he "became convinced [he] was petrifying" (79). Prompted
by some introspective letters concerning his past (written by Calyxa, it
turns out), Perseus decides to recapitulate his "good young days": "but it
wasn't *just* vanity; no more were my nightly narratives: . . . it seemed to
me that if I kept going over it carefully enough I might see the pattern,
find the key" (80). His recapitulation is a false lead, however, for Perseus's
attempt to follow "the pattern" eventually leads to his "drowning" in
Lake Triton (105).

The pattern Perseus follows is the one set by himself in his youth,
from which he infers that he should "be himself." What he fails to understand is that "being himself" as a middle-aged man is not the same thing
as "being himself" as a young man. Athene, representing wisdom, tries to
tell Perseus so in the temple: "in general, she concluded, my mode of
operation in this second enterprise must be contrary to my first's: on the
one hand, direct instead of indirect . . . on the other, rather passive than
active" (102). Perseus protests "that direct passivity was not [his] style"
(102), yet his actions with the "Gray Ladies" result in an illuminating dip
in the lake. As he sinks he spots "not mere folly" but the missing eye in the
lake: "Dropped from the high point of my hubris, it winked now from the
depths" (105).

Now everything comes together for Perseus. He is saved by Medusa,
discovers she is in love with him, and listens to Medusa's story of her life.
If one can imagine the various levels of narration as a series of Chinese
boxes, to use Barth's simile, then the various narratives converge in the
story as follows, starting with the outermost box: Barth writing the
"Perseid": Perseus as constellation telling to Medusa as constellation the
story of his narration to Calyxa; Perseus telling to Calyxa the story of
Medusa's narration to himself by the shore of Lake Triton. Medusa's narration of her own life is interrupted by Calyxa's birthday and Calyxa's
story of her life to Perseus, which ends coincidentally with the beginning
of Perseus's story to Calyxa and the end of Perseus's First Ebb (the failure
at Lake Triton). Such convergences, where all the Chinese boxes are
finally collapsed, have different significances in Barth's work. In *Lost in
the Funhouse* the boxes collapse around the word "love" or they collapse
into silence as with Beckett. In the "Perseid" the convergence of narratives indicates the major turning-point in Perseus's life, for he has

stopped to analyze and recapitulate his past through the use of Calyxa's murals. The last mural of the spiral gives out onto the desert, art blends into "reality," past turns into present, and Perseus sets out on the second half of his life—which should be, as for Shah Zaman, sweeter than the first half because of the awareness gained in recapitulation.

At the vertex of the turning point in Perseus's life is the unusual set of conditions surrounding Medusa's eyes—her ability to grant either immortality or petrification depending on the circumstances. Calyxa, the student of mythology, remarks on the lack of "any analogues for that motif" (116). Perseus, then, finds himself on the shore of Lake Triton in a set of circumstances outside the pattern of mythic history, and he acts on his own impulses, avoiding Medusa's eyes, though he will "face" her eventually. Perseus's instinctive action leads to the above convergences.

Perseus succeeds finally in establishing himself as a hero, for he shows that he is capable of changing a pattern and not merely imitating it. Ultimately, Bellerophon fails as a hero because he lacks individuality—he never acts independently of his consciousness of how a hero should act, reinforced in the "Bellerophoniad" by the numerous imitations and repetitions of what has gone before. Bellerophon is both the central imitator and imitation in Part Three. He is constantly looking for the Pattern, but to imitate a pattern is to leave it unchanged. As Zeus reminds Polyeidus, another shapeshifting version of Barth, "By imitating perfectly the Pattern of Mythic Heroism, your man Bellerophon has become a perfect imitation of a mythic hero" (308). The emphasis in the statement is on the ironic perfection of his imitation.

Bellerophon is always a quarter-step behind Perseus, his actions seeming to Parody those of Perseus. Bellerophon's life begins in the middle of Perseus's life (108); his *story* begins at the turning point of his life, but the transformation is a parody of the equivalent turning point in Perseus's life.[9] Both men are middle-aged at their respective turning points, but in terms of the Pattern. Perseus is between his First Ebb and Second Flow (with Calyxa), whereas Bellerophon is still between his First Flow and First Ebb—which is to say, a quarter-step behind. Ironically, the recapitulation in Bellerophon's life is not of his own life, but a reading of the "Perseid"—a review of Perseus's life. In further contrast to Perseus, Bellerophon is still married to his first wife, and she suggests the sea journey instead of Bellerophon. The final irony is revealed at the end, when we learn that Bellerophon himself is only an imitation of Bellerophon; he is actually Deliades imitating his dead brother, Bellerus (318).

The theme, then, of the "Bellerophoniad" might be called Recapitulation as Imitation or Parody. Most of the unusual paraphernalia in Part Three illustrate the theme. The actual quotation from Robert Graves' *The Greek Myths*, for example, which tells the story of Bellerophon (208–10), gives the reader some useful background information, but its primary function is ironical. Graves' account of Bellerophon is clearly part of the Pattern, an established addition to the corpus of literature, which has formed and ossified the mythological patterns, just as historians order history in their own patterns. Bellerophon, in contrast to Barth's own inclinations, attempts to fulfill the Pattern. All of Polyeidus's shapeshifting, while supposedly helping to direct Bellerophon, is ironically leading him on to that ultimate imitation in which Bellerophon turns into his own story. He becomes literally the printed words of his story, just as he literally "kills" the Chimera by ending the book—or turning into the book, as the last sentence of the novel suggests.

Another form of recapitulation in part Three is that of Barth's own allusions to his previous works, virtually all of which are incorporated into the text in one way or another. The Polyeidus/Barth lecture scroll contains direct references to *The Sot-Weed Factor* and *Giles Goat-Boy* and indirect references to *Lost in the Funhouse* and *Chimera* (207). Slightly more concealed allusions to earlier works are the two variant stories of Bellerophon's "rape" of Anteia; the first version comes out of *The Floating Opera*, the second out of *The End of the Road* (201-3). At least two stories from *Lost in the Funhouse* are alluded to in a similar fashion: the jug Bellerophon finds with a message inside is taken from "Water-Message" (Polyeidus accidentally turns into Pete), and Bellerophon's visit to his childhood haunts recalls a scene taken from "Lost in the Funhouse" (268-9, 274).

The allusions to *The Sot-Weed Factor* and *Giles Goat-Boy* are less explicit, yet these novels are thematically closest to the "Bellerophoniad." Bellerophon calls to mind Ebenezer Cooke, and Polyeidus recalls Burlingame in several passages (186-7, 198). Bellerophon has many of the same problems that Ebenezer encounters, such as the problem of self-definition—does essence precede existence or vice versa? Burlingame struggles with the same question, as does Polyeidus; one suspects Barth himself, the ultimate shapeshifter, has been plagued with similar self-doubts. An encounter between Bellerophon and Proteus raises the question in a slightly different manner (195). The passage calls to mind Giles, for one of his concerns was whether he was in fact a born hero or whether herowork was just a result of a "passionate lack of alternatives" (195). Other characters in the "Bellerophoniad" suggest *Giles Goat-Boy*, such as the ubiquitous Jerome B. Bray, who resembles Harold Bray in many ways.

As these examples show, Barth has recapitulated Barth in the "Bellerophoniad," even to the point of including himself in various degrees of disguise. The purpose of these self-conscious integrations is to reinforce the theme of imitation and artifact in Part Three. Yet the process of viewing oneself from a distance, as Barth does when he includes himself in the story, has a further purpose, for it exemplifies the process of creating new material out of old material discussed in relation to the

Genie and Scheherazade in the "Dunyazadiad." Jac Tharpe has described Barth's position this way:

> If he writes of the whole universe, he can think of himself as a powerful linguistic magician in that universe, who is a part of the comedy. If he creates universes, he may as well be a creator, a deity. He can possibly then write fictions about created universes in which the creator appears, as he does in no other universe we know. In this self-enclosed situation, finite but unbounded, the creator of the paradox is the incarnation of the paradox. Barth as-ifs Barth.[10]

The same principle is at work in the "Dunyazadiad," where Barth "as-ifs" Dunyazade within the "finite but unbounded" world of Scheherazade.

Chimera, too, is structured on a similar principle. The solution to writer's block is the paradox that both creates *Chimera* and is itself incarnated in the structure of the three parts. In the "Dunyazadiad" the "writer" is faced with the age-old problem of having only a limited number of stories to tell—of having exhausted possibilities—and yet he creates new possibilities by telling old stories with a modern consciousness. In the "Perseid" the "writer" is at his height. He tells a good story; he is a hero and lives a hero's life; and he becomes immortal, at least as immortal as language and literature or stars and constellations can be said to be. In the "Bellerophoniad" the "writer" finds that he may not be a hero; he may not be a storyteller. He suspects his life and stories are mere imitations, and that he himself is only an imitation. He believes the end is in sight, yet it is a chimera, an illusion, for one need only begin again at the beginning as Dunyazade and Barth have done.

Chimera is both a novel about the problem of exhausted possibilities in narrative art and a solution to that problem. The prominent role mythology plays in the novel is as significant as Barth's use of writer's block as a central theme, for the myths also have a double function. On one hand, the mythological tales serve as sources for the stories in *Chimera*, just as writer's block serves as a theme or motif to connect the stories; on the other, in the same way that writing about the problem of writer's block transcends the problem, the process of converting old stories—the myths—into new ones transcends the problem of "exhausted" possibilities.

In order to see exactly how mythology functions in the book, one must understand Barth's interest in myths. From his earlier works, at least as far back as *The Sot-Weed Factor* (1960), Barth has been fascinated with the idea that ontogeny (the development of an individual organism) recapitulates phylogeny (the evolution or development of a species). From this concept Barth's fundamental interest in mythology seems to spring. The concept implies that a man's development repeats the development or history of mankind, a concept which is analogous to Barth's solution to writer's block: to review the past in order to understand the present, which allows one to proceed. What especially interested Barth, however, was the relationship between the life of an individual and the historical life of mankind; the convergence of the two is myth.

In the spurious lecture scroll of Part Three, Barth summarizes some of his personal comments on mythology made in actual interviews: "Since myths themselves are among other things poetic distillations of our ordinary psychic experience and therefore point always to daily reality, to write realistic fictions which point always to mythic archetypes is in my opinion to take the wrong end of the mythopoeic stick, however meritorious such fiction may be in other respects" (207–8). If one wants to comment on daily reality through the use of fictions, why write realistic fictions that suggest mythical archetypes that point back to reality, when one could write about myths directly as they relate to daily reality? While Jungians regard myths as "original revelations of the preconscious psyche, involuntary statements about unconscious psychic happenings,"[11] Robert Graves defines true myth "as reduction to narrative shorthand of ritual mime performed on public festivals, and in many cases recorded pictorially on temple walls, vases, seals, bowls, mirrors, chests, shields, tapestries, and the like."[12] He further states that "a true science of myth should begin with a study of archaeology, history, and comparative religion."[13] Barth, obviously familiar with Graves, is not interested in "a true science of myth," but he seems to have been intrigued by Graves' conception of true myths. What Graves calls "a reduction to narrative shorthand of ritual mime" becomes for Barth "poetic distillations of our ordinary psychic experience," pointing always towards daily reality. The rituals of mankind, then, which form the common denominators of man's acquired knowledge (epistemology), become our myths. Yet myths are also distillations of ordinary experience, reflecting the individual's confrontations with daily reality—the confrontations that comprise his learning experience. If ontogeny did *not* recapitulate phylogeny, the Greek myths would presumably be of no interest to us.

Barth claims that a certain amount of knowledge is beneficial to a writer, but that too much knowledge is dangerous. Barth apparently follows his own advice, for without delving into too much mythology, he has taken ideas from Graves and rendered them fictionally. Mythology, then, becomes a means to an end instead of the end itself—it is treated symbolically. Graves cites the myth of Chimera as an example of a true myth and explains why the Chimera myth must have originated from various social, political, and religious conditions. What Barth has done by grabbing the "other end" of the mythopoeic stick is to treat myths realistically, instead of treating "reality" in accord with archetypal patterns.

Barth, in his concern with the "reality" of the Chimera myth, uses the elements of the myth that comment on daily experiences of an individual: Perseus awakens one day in a desert, "sea-leveled, forty, parched and plucked . . . and beleaguered by the serpents of [his] past"(67); Bellerophon, on the eve of his fortieth birthday, finds the "Perseid" floating on an ebbing tide and he stops to read it: "By the time he got to its last words he was forty and too tired" (145). Barth has reduced the mythical hero to middle-aged man, so that one recognizes oneself in Scheherazade, Perseus, and Bellerophon.

Apart from the obvious use of myths for his "sources," Barth has integrated a number of aspects of the Chimera myth into his novel—again, apparently using Graves as a source. Graves writes that the Chimera was most likely a common emblem four thousand years ago in the form of a composite beast with a lion's head, goat's body, and serpent's tail. Each component would have represented—among other things—a season of the Queen of Heaven's sacred year—the Queen of Heaven being one of the many titles for the Mother-goddess or Great Goddess. The three parts of the Chimera, then, would be related to a number of calendar divisions: the moon's three phases—new, full, and old; the matriarch's three phases—maiden, nymph (nubile woman), and crone; spring, summer, and winter; and even the upper air, earth, and underworld.

Similarly, each of the three parts of *Chimera* emphasizes the appropriate aspect of the triad, on various levels. Dunyazade is the maiden-figure—her virginity and inexperience are stressed throughout the "Dunyazadiad." The stories in Part One take place at night with their conclusions coinciding with the break of day; the final exchange is always "Good morning." In accord with the learning stage of the triad, Dunyazade's experience at the foot of the King's bed is emphasized; just as the Genie and Scheherazade are continually discussing the similarities between storytelling and love-making, Dunyazade's learning experience has encompassed the best of both techniques—though only at a distance until her night with Shah Zaman.

Calyxa, the nymph of the "Perseid," is a woman in the prime of life; she is twenty-five, adept at love-making, and "liberated" in a sense that Scheherazade could only hope for. Medusa is also nymph-like when she meets Perseus and "rescues" him from middle-age. Stories are begun in the evening in Part Two, opening typically with "Good evening" and ending with "Good night." Perseus sets out on his sea-voyage with Andromeda "when spring gave way to summer" (85). Once the reader is conscious of the allusions to time of day, season, or stage in life, their abundance becomes obvious.

Within the "Bellerophoniad," the third part of the triad is emphasized. Philonoe is the principal crone-figure, but Zeus's wife, Hera, the classic crone of Greek mythology, also makes a brief appearance at the end. The ebbing tide and waning moon are prevalent, just as Bellerophon is past forty and tired. After obtaining an extra-strong shot of Hippomanes from Sibyl the whore—a not unfamiliar character-type in Part Three—Bellerophon is dumped by Pegasus, only to wake up "bruised, headachy, and sore" (281).[14] Instead of being attended by nymph-like

Calyxa, as Perseus was, Bellerophon ends up in jail under the rule of crone-like Anteia, who has reasserted the matriarchal system. Finally, Bellerophon seems to have "bad nights" all too often, and his story *begins* with the greeting "Good night."

As these examples show, Barth used different aspects of mythology—especially drawing on Graves, and to a large extent the mythical elements reinforce the central theme of writer's block and middle-aged inertia and despair. The result of Barth's use of mythology is an array of details which symbolize the conversion of myth to fictional reality, ritual to daily reality. At the same time, the details enforce the overall structure and unity of the three parts, adding depth to the superstructure of the main theme.

A third way in which Barth integrates the idea of exhausted possibilities into his work is through the analogy of love-making to writing. The analogy sets the tone of the novel in that Barth's attitude towards writing is revealed in *Chimera* through the extended comparison between the two activities. Barth's attitude towards writing and life in general infuses the novel with its tone of half-irony, half-seriousness.

Barth has talent for appropriating material or ideas for his fiction and then both exalting and reducing that material within the context of the work. In *Chimera* mythology is reverenced as the treasure-house of urfictions, yet Barth seems to treat myths almost profanely in his modifications of their traditional characterizations and plots. Love, similarly, is both the final sacred mystery of mankind and the most natural, profane act. The tension between these opposing tendencies establishes the tone in Barth's works; the reader is constantly drawn to the optimism and vitality of the characters, but the attraction is countered by Barth's assumption that life is painful and meaningless. One senses Barth's frustration at having to settle for relative values and partial answers; that he feels he does have to is clearly indicated in all of his earlier novels. When Barth speaks of the "felt ultimacies of our time," he includes his sense of the lack of any absolute value system in our society. Such an attitude on Barth's part informs his approach to literature; literature becomes less a means to an end, containing some message or instruction, and more of an autonomous or self-supporting art form, with references to itself. A few examples of how Barth treats the relationship between art and love will help to illuminate his attitude towards literature.

The most immediate connection between art and love is the correlation between sexual potency and one's ability to overcome the various stumbling blocks in life—writer's block, middle-age, or whatever. Scheherazade, then, is the most prolific and apparently successful storyteller, and her sexual prowess is at least comparable. Calyxa is adept at lovemaking, but Perseus is impotent so long as he feels himself a failure. As his story and recapitulation progress, as his vanity and expectation for the future increase, his sexual potency does likewise. Bellerophon, in his various attempts to follow the Pattern, either rejects sex altogether, as with Anteia, or forces it, as in his rape of Melanippe, for the sake of the Pattern. The relatively little sex in Part Three correlates with Bellerophon's failure as a mythic hero.

The relationship between art and love, then, is most explicit in Part One, in the discussions between the Genie and Scheherazade, who both assume that life is going to be painful. Literature, like love, is one of the more pleasant aspects of life, that helps people overcome their difficulties. The Genie calls these "civilized delights," available to anyone capable of "goodwill, attention, and a moderately cultivated sensibility" (25). In particular, the Genie refers to the "treasure of art, which if it could not redeem the barbarities of history or spare us the horrors of living and dying, at least sustained, refreshed, expanded, ennobled, and enriched our spirits along the painful way"(25). The Genie and Shah Zaman both come to a similar conclusion regarding love: although love is a risky enterprise and fraught with the same dangers as life—the pain of disappointment, rejection, and despair—it is still worth the risk. The key to this attitude is the magic phrase "as if," which Barth worked through for himself in his first four novels. One must approach love *as if* it would last forever; one must approach life *as if* it had intrinsic value or *as if* it were not going to be a disappointment.

Finally, the relationship between art and love is based on technique. The success of both is dependent on a polished and varied technique or style, according to Barth. As the Genie points out, however, both activities—storytelling and love-making—are by their very nature erotic. He cites the circumstances framing the tales in the *Decameron* as one example where storytelling is a "kind of *substitute* for making love—an artifice in keeping with the artificial nature of their little society"(33). The Genie remarks in reference to Scheherazade's situation that "narrative . . . was a love-relation, not a rape: its success depended upon the reader's consent and cooperation, which she could withhold or at any moment withdraw; also upon her own combination of experience and talent for enterprise, and the author's ability to arouse, sustain, and satisfy her interest"(34).

Barth's position, then, is quite similar to that of his contemporary, Nabokov, for whom a novel is a chess game that has the author's moves already programmed into it, and that the reader plays by reading. The better the reader, the more demands he places on the author, but the process of reading is the point of the game. Similarly, Barth's main metaphor for writing is the act of love. The metaphor emphasizes the process or act of doing something, as opposed to any specific goal at the end. For both metaphors, chess-playing and love-making, *what* one says or does is not so important as *how* one says or does it. Now, however, Barth and Nabokov may part company, for Barth seems to take a more pessimistic view of the value of the game itself. They both believe in the playing of the game, but Nabokov seems to believe that the act has some kind of absolute value, while Barth appears to believe he is accepting a relative value for lack of any absolute values in life.

As Barth demonstrates in his earlier novels, any attempt he makes to discover meaning or value in life is going to resolve itself in rich paradox at best, and despairing contradiction, at worst. Ironically, literature and writing become more important to Barth than they might be if he believed in some kind of absolute value-system in life. Literature may not have any ultimate value, but Barth writes "as if" it were of life-or-death importance in his world. Barth's "as if" attitude prevails throughout his work, whether he is dealing with writer's block or life, love or mythology. A tone of deadly seriousness lies underneath the playful prose associated with Barth's "style." In the process and through the process of working out his own writer's block, the chimeric Genie has certainly "sustained, refreshed, expanded, ennobled, and enriched our spirits along the painful way."

Notes

1. John Barth, "The Literature of Exhaustion," *Atlantic*, 220 (August 1967), 29–34; rpt. in *The American Novel Since World War II*, ed. Marcus Klein (Greenwich, Conn.: Fawcett, 1969), pp. 267–79. Subsequent references are to the *Atlantic* text.

2. Barth, p. 32.

3. Barth, p. 33.

4. The only item Barth published between *Lost in the Funhouse* (1968) and *Chimera* (1972) is significantly called "Help! A Stereophonic Narrative for Authorial Voice," *Esquire*, 72 (September 1969), 108–9.

5. John Barth, *Chimera* (Greenwich, Conn.: Fawcett, 1972), p. 63. Subsequent references are to this edition.

6. The three stories were apparently written in sequence: "Dunyazadiad" was published in *Esquire* in June 1972, "Perseid" followed in *Harper's Magazine* in October 1972; "Bellerophoniad" first appeared in *Chimera*.

7. Jac Tharpe, *John Barth: The Comic Sublimity of Paradox* (Carbondale: Southern Illinois Univ. Press, 1974), pp. 84–90. As Tharpe points out, Giles carries out his assignments three times, in accordance with three different interpretations of the riddle "Pass All Fail All." The first interpretation is that passage is failure; the second is that failure is passage; and the final conclusion is that all interpretations are to some extent valid, the final paradox. The first interpretation assumes distinctions can be made (between good and evil, passage and failure); the second denies the ultimate existence of distinctions; and the final conclusion is compromise: man must make certain distinctions for personal guidelines but recognize the ultimate inadequacy of man-made distinctions in an absurd world.

8. Bellerophon divides his life, as well as Perseus's, into four "tides"—First Flood, First Ebb, Second Flood, Second Ebb—which roughly correspond to the biological changes of a woman: birth to puberty, puberty to sexual maturity, sexual maturity to menopause, and menopause to death. Cf. pp. 150–2, in particular.

9. Notice that Bellerophon's period with the Amazonian Melanippe, while in many ways parallel to Perseus's stay with Calyxa, is in no way the emotional or psychological

equivalent. Throughout the "Perseid" and "Bellerophoniad" the analogous situations are with Perseus/Calyxa and Bellerophon/Philonoe, Perseus/Medusa and Bellerophon/Amazonian Melanippe.

10. Tharpe, p. 113.

11. Robert Graves, *The Greek Myths*, 2nd ed. (Harmondsworth: Penguin, 1960), pp. 21-2.

12. Graves, p. 12.

13. Graves, p. 21.

14. An interesting addition to the story of Bellerophon and Pegasus is the use of "Hippomanes" in helping to get Pegasus "off the ground." In his Foreword to *The Greek Myths* Graves speaks of the likelihood that many of the peculiar events in Greek mythology traditionally attributed to the use of ambrosia are in fact due to a hallucinogenic mushroom apparently in wide use in that period. Barth is no doubt playing with this idea in the "Bellerophoniad."

INDEX